An Empire Far and Wide

An Empire Far and Wide

The Achaemenid Dynastic Myth and Jewish Scribes in the Late Persian Period

MARK LEUCHTER

Oxford University Press is a department of the University of Oxford. It furthers
the University's objective of excellence in research, scholarship, and education
by publishing worldwide. Oxford is a registered trade mark of Oxford University
Press in the UK and certain other countries.

Published in the United States of America by Oxford University Press
198 Madison Avenue, New York, NY 10016, United States of America.

© Oxford University Press 2024

All rights reserved. No part of this publication may be reproduced, stored in
a retrieval system, or transmitted, in any form or by any means, without the
prior permission in writing of Oxford University Press, or as expressly permitted
by law, by license, or under terms agreed with the appropriate reproduction
rights organization. Inquiries concerning reproduction outside the scope of the
above should be sent to the Rights Department, Oxford University Press, at the
address above.

You must not circulate this work in any other form
and you must impose this same condition on any acquirer.

Library of Congress Cataloging-in-Publication Data
Names: Leuchter, Mark, author.
Title: An empire far and wide : the Achaemenid dynastic myth and Jewish
scribes in the late Persian period / Mark Leuchter.
Description: New York, NY, United States of America : Oxford University Press, [2024] |
Includes bibliographical references and index.
Identifiers: LCCN 2024021443 (print) | LCCN 2024021444 (ebook) |
ISBN 9780197772744 (cp) | ISBN 9780197772768 (epub)
Subjects: LCSH: Bible. Old Testament—Criticism, interpretation, etc. |
Rabbinical literature—Yehud (Persian province)—History and criticism. |
Jews—History—586 B.C.–70 A.D. | Jews—Identity. | Achaemenid
dynasty, 559 B.C.–330 B.C. | Mythology, Middle Eastern.
Classification: LCC BS1171.3 .L475 2024 (print) | LCC BS1171.3 (ebook) |
DDC 221.60933/09014—dc23/eng/20240805
LC record available at https://lccn.loc.gov/2024021443
LC ebook record available at https://lccn.loc.gov/2024021444

DOI: 10.1093/oso/9780197772744.001.0001

Printed by Bridgeport National Bindery, Inc., United States of America

For Sari, who saved my life.

Contents

Foreword	ix
Introduction	1
1. The Achaemenid Dynastic Myth	16
2. The Priestly Scribes of Elephantine and Jerusalem in the Fifth Century BCE	36
3. Accommodating Empire: The Mythologizing of Ezra's Mission	55
4. Negotiating Empire: The Levites and the Book of the Twelve	71
5. Repudiating Empire: The Shemihazah/Asael Narrative (1 Enoch 6–11)	89
Conclusion	106
Notes	117
Bibliography	141
Author Index	163
Scripture Index	167

Foreword

Much of what I have written herein emerged from a fellowship I held in Fall 2021 at the Frankel Center for Advanced Judaic Studies at the University of Michigan. I was surrounded there by brilliant people who challenged me to think differently about sources, narrative, rhetoric, the sociology of power, and the transmission of knowledge. My hosts at the Frankel Center provided an ideal environment in which to explore the diversity of ideas in Second Temple Judaism, and the experience overall enriched my understanding of the eras and materials I was studying. Large parts of Chapters 4 and 5 in this book were written during my time in Ann Arbor, which I could not have done without the resources and company of the people there. I am especially indebted to Gabriele Boccaccini, Joshua Scott, Deborah Forger, M Adryael Tong, Shayna Sheinfeld, Cate Bonesho, Liane Feldman, Oren Ableman, Joseph Angel, Rodney Caruthers, Kelley Bautch Coblentz, and Gregg Gardner for their collegiality, creativity, and kindness during (and after) my stay.

I was fortunate to do some research for this project at the University of Sydney in August 2022. The curators of the Chau Chak Museum provided me with the opportunity to examine objects from the Achaemenid and Hellenistic period related to my topic, and made every effort to ensure that I had the time I needed to go through them. I am grateful to them for their support. At the Uni, Stephen Cook organized a lecture for me where I presented an early form of the material that appears in Chapter 3 of this book, and I thank him and the attendees for their thoughtful engagement. I must also thank William Schniedewind, Anselm Hagedorn, Jason Silverman, Adrianne Spunaugle, Ken Ristau, Seth Sanders, and Christine Mitchell for their insights and intellectual generosity during the course of this project. I also benefited greatly from discussions on matters related to this project (and scholarly life in general) with Anna Cwikla, Shaily Patel, Jacqueline Vayntrub, Robyn Walsh, Stephanie Cobb, Ben Wright and Francesca Stavrakopoulou. Sustained conversations with all of these scholars, both in person and via email, brought important ideas to the fore that had long been hiding in the background. Finally, I am very grateful to

X FOREWORD

Rebecca Scharbach Wollenberg and Tom Bolin, both of whom read earlier drafts of material in this book and provided extremely valuable feedback, and Carla Sulzbach for discussion on the material herein and help with the indexing.

I began to research the topic of this book around the middle of 2019, during the presidential administration of Donald Trump. The subject of political mythology and the colonization of communal identity became important to me because the last several years have revealed how tenuous and fragile democracy is. My friend and colleague Brian Rainey commented once that we were literally living through an apocalypse, as the veil was lifted and we could see what was lurking underneath all along. As I write these words, the rising tide of violence, bigotry, disinformation, nationalism, performative cruelty, and oppressive theology continues to expand across the landscape in the name of God and American "greatness." The sacrificial lambs in this enterprise are facts, reason, honesty, and the capacity for empathy. And despite the efforts of so many people to resist on behalf of those ideas and ideals, resistance becomes increasingly more difficult as the chaos monsters keep coming.

Shortly after submitting the manuscript of this book the editorial team at Oxford University Press, the massacre of Israeli civilians by the terrorist group Hamas took place on October 7, 2023. The barbaric cruelty visited upon the victims of this evil assault is indescribable. Not long thereafter, the Israeli military began counterstrikes against Hamas in Gaza, and the devastation experienced by Palestinian civilians as a result is, also, indescribable. Subsequent responses to this conflict have fallen along rather polarized lines. Many have attempted to characterize the bloodshed as a matter of necessity— either as a justified pathway toward Palestinian liberation against colonization, or as part of a defense of Jewish communities living in the land of their own ancestors. Mythic narratives abound in public discourse, reinforcing the most extreme rhetoric and licensing the dehumanization of the Other, steeped in narratives of ideological orthodoxies. These orthodoxies sidestep facts and reduce real human experiences into untenable theoretical categories. And all of this has been aided by a landscape of digital media overwhelmed with unverified details, unreliable sources, a rejection of fairness and nuance, a thirst for grievance and outrage, and a hunger for cultural triumphalism.

What I have written in this book is not a comment on the domestic or international conditions I've just described. Jewish scribal worldviews under ancient Persian hegemony cannot be mapped onto contemporary life in a modern society. But it is difficult for me to ignore the points of contact when it comes to demagoguery, sloganeering, propaganda, tribal polemics, and cosmogonic thinking that have characterized public discourse over the last few years, and which have even begun to worm their way (back) into the Academy, especially on matters of Jewish history, identity, and positionality in larger sociological contexts. At the very least, a study of political mythology and its effects on the formation of ancient Jewish texts provides some heuristic perspective on the way the manipulation of language and media, coercion, anxiety, and the demands of group identity affect how we perceive and react to our world—whether we want to admit it or not.

Mark Leuchter
December 24, 2023

Introduction

The Study of Jewishness and Jewish Texts in the Persian Period

The Persian period (539–332 BCE) sits somewhat awkwardly within the study of Second Temple Judaism.[1] It is at once fully a part of this area since it is during the early Persian period that the aforementioned "second" temple was constructed in Jerusalem (515 BCE), yet it commences before the construction of that sanctuary under the aegis of foreign rulers. It is also an era that saw Jewish sacred spaces (of one sort or another) which existed both before and then alongside the rebuilt Jerusalem temple—which raises the issue of whether the term "Second Temple" is an accurate way to describe this era.[2] The approach to the Persian period is also complicated by debates regarding whether the communities in the province of Yehud, in Egypt, or in the eastern Diaspora can even be called "Jewish," a label denoting a type of ethnic and religious symbiosis that some scholars are hesitant to identify any time before the mid-second century BCE.[3]

The uncertain position of the Persian period in the study of ancient Judaism is not anything new. The redactors of the Mishnah (ca. 220 CE) responsible for tractate Avot present a periodized view of history where intellectual and sacral institutions from the Persian period occupy a different category than those traced to the early Hellenistic period and beyond, as evident in Avot 1.1:

> Moses received Torah at Sinai and transmitted it to Joshua, Joshua to the elders, and the elders to the prophets, and the prophets to the Men of the Great Assembly. They said three things: Be patient in [the administration of] justice, raise many disciples and make a fence round the Torah.

In this passage, the "Great Assembly" is a metonym for the scribal groups (and specifically, temple-based scribal groups) of the late Persian period based on earlier interpretations of biblical texts like Nehemiah 8 and the

An Empire Far and Wide. Mark Leuchter, Oxford University Press. © Oxford University Press 2024.
DOI: 10.1093/oso/9780197772744.003.0001

2 AN EMPIRE FAR AND WIDE

Book of the Twelve.[4] It is significant that these groups are part of the same legendary, antiquated era that saw the revelation at Sinai, the activity of Moses, the conquests of Joshua, and the activity of the prophets. Even the phrase "they said three things" emphasizes the ambiguity, since "they" might include all the antecedent groups mentioned in the passage, as well as Joshua and Moses. A new historical period begins with Avot 1.2, with the mention of Simon the Righteous as among the last surviving members of this ancient group but also the first of many named figures in the rest of the chapter who formed a chain of intellectual authority for the work's redactors.[5] While the passage presupposes the view that the "Great Assembly" stood behind the scribal crafting of various biblical texts connected to prophecy and revelation, it also shows that the Rabbis who redacted Avot had more confidence about their perception of life under the Hellenistic empires than life under Persia. The sages in Avot 1.2ff. are remembered by name whereas the "Great Assembly" is mentioned in only generic terms.

The "Great Assembly" collapses different groups into a single symbolic lemma. They are an acknowledged and assigned authority, but the redactors of Avot see them at a distance from their own era and are hesitant to say much about them. This is especially significant because, as Amram Tropper has discussed, Avot formed against the background of the Second Sophistic, a time when literati across the Roman world (including the Roman Near East) were especially concerned with reviving rhetoric and ideas from the fifth century BCE.[6] The fifth century saw the height of the Persian empire's power, and yet the redactors of Avot engage in no detailed discussion of the era despite their periodization of history. The implication is that these redactors regarded centuries-old Hellenistic figures and traditions as accessible in a way that Persian figures and traditions were not.

Contemporary scholars who are reluctant to use various biblical texts to recover some of the social and cultural forces characterizing Persian period life thus stand within a very old tradition of hesitance and caution. And indeed, caution is warranted; no biblical text or other literary source should be read from the perspective of historical positivism or as an unencumbered/transparent rendition of historical events. At the same time, scholars who opt to continue to present the Persian period as a "dark age" in the study of Second Temple Judaism (including the insistence that the period predates a time when we can even use the term "Judaism") tread upon terrain that is nearly as problematic.[7] Such a characterization arises not only from questionable assumptions regarding the dating of biblical texts but also regarding the cultural priorities and abilities of Jews in antiquity, both before and then during the Persian period.

This has led too often to models that flatten the possible purposes of literary production, scribal function and status, and the role of material texts that were produced in less than cosmopolitan contexts. Such models unduly restrict what can be said about the sources, and do not consider a sufficient range of criteria for evaluating their contents as deriving from the era of Persian imperial hegemony.[8] If the prevailing ideology governing the rhetoric of a text reflects conditions of Persian imperialism and not that of the Hellenistic kingdoms—conditions I address in Chapter 1 of this study—the primary composition ought to be assigned to the Persian period. Caution is warranted in following this approach, and I accept that the sources I will examine passed through scribal hands working in later contexts which left traceable impressions. But the study of scribal methods over the last few decades provides us with tools to recognize when an earlier context yielded a literary tradition that received secondary and tertiary adjustments in the course of its transmission. Moreover, various theoretical and methodological approaches discussed in this study provide much-needed illumination into these processes and their intellectual and cultural ramifications that strongly indicate Persian period origination and Persian imperialism influence.

It is not my purpose here to examine the history and culture of Persian period Jewish life or the full range of YHWH worship in Yehud or elsewhere during this time.[9] Rather, this book focuses on a careful selection of literary test cases to better understand how Jewish scribes in Persian Yehud interacted with a feature of Persian imperialism that has not received adequate attention: the dynastic mythology of the Achaemenid rulers.[10] Such a study operates on certain working assumptions related to the aforementioned issues, the first of which is that we can indeed apply the terms "Jewish" and "Judaism" to some Persian period communities with certain caveats. The second is that the Persian period is hardly a "dark age" in terms of our ability to recover important dimensions of the Jewish intellectual culture of the time. Seth Sanders has shown that the literati of Yehud (and especially Jerusalem) were shareholders in the intellectual and sacral cultures in which they participated. The textual materials they produced are valuable windows into a range of social, sacral, political, and economic factors characterizing Yehudite Jewish society, especially those of the learned caste.[11] The third is that while the response of this learned caste to Persian imperialism is not an index of wider demographic responses, the textual record provides us

4 AN EMPIRE FAR AND WIDE

sufficient insight into how their response factors into a larger intellectual history shaped by centuries of imperialism both extending back, and forward, in time.

Identifying Judaism/Jewishness in the Persian Period

We must first address the contentious matter of applying the terms "Jewish" or "Judaism" to the Persian period. For some scholars, the term "Jewish" or "Judaism" applies to postmonarchic communities tracing their cultural ancestry back to monarchic-era Judah, making the fall of Jerusalem and the Babylonian exile the pivot-point for using this label and thus periodizing history according to a convenient historical criterion.[12] But Yonatan Adler has shown that there is no evidence for major features of Judaism as a religious system governed by Torah observance before the second century BCE.[13] Moreover, it is only in the Hellenistic period that we encounter Greek language texts that use the term "Judaism" (*Ioudaïsmos*) to describe the system of behavior and belief characterizing specific communities in Hellenistic antiquity that had long been identified as Jewish by later thinkers. This has led some to argue that Jewishness or Judaism cannot be identified in earlier periods, and that "Judean" is a better option for describing these groups.

But the term "Judean" causes more problems than it solves when applied as a substitute for "Jewish." The term can be used productively with respect to groups residing in the geographical territory called Judea in the Hellenistic and Roman periods, but plenty of groups beyond that territory are still referred to in ancient sources under the category of *Ioudaios*—the strictly geographic qualification cannot apply. At the same time, the term "Jewish" cannot be applied solely as a religious hallmark either, not only because religion was not a distinct category of social identity in antiquity but because, as Karel van der Toorn notes, Jewishness is not contingent upon participation in religious practices.[14] Rather, it rests on ethnographic factors such as cultural history, language, diet, concepts of ancestry and homelands, constructs of time, and shared memory—religious practice is only a part of this matrix of ethnic identity markers. Van der Toorn persuasively argues that we may apply the term "Jewish" to the variety of communities in antiquity that were characterized by these markers, all of which were in operation during the Persian period.[15] Joachim Schaper has also identified sociological features regularly associated with Hellenistic-era Judaism that are operative already under Persian rule.[16]

In his analysis of Ezra-Nehemiah, Roland Boer observes that the classification of "Jew" in the text occurs primarily when an insider group encounters the phenomenon of foreignness or a confrontation with outsider status.[17] The argument of Lawrence M. Wills is thus on point that the outlines of Jewish identity (rather than "Judean," "Judahite," or even "Israelite") take shape when members of the in-group experience a hegemonic imperial society.[18] It is the liminal space, the threshold, where important legacy concepts from pre-Persian times find redefinition as those who preserve those concepts strive to fit them into a new political, economic, linguistic, and sacral mold. Below this threshold previous and more limited terms for identity formation could be prioritized and dominate inner-group discourse or even intergroup discourse (between Jews in Yehud and the diaspora). But the retrofitting of earlier traditions into contemporary politics, economics, language, and ritual systems occurred at the juncture between the in-group and the empire that dictated the terms for performances of identity.[19] It is thus through interaction in the social dimensions of Persian imperialism that Judaism becomes manifest, a product of the inescapability of imperial dominance and its cultural demands.

Postcolonial and Cognitive Approaches to Persian Imperialism

The last few decades of research have yielded productive insights into how imperialism was experienced in Jewish antiquity. Postcolonial theory provides models for the sociology of power across the imperial terrain as experienced by subject populations; the work of Homi K. Bhabha, especially, remains a compelling resource for delineating the dynamics of imperially imposed hierarchies.[20] Bhabha's concept of hybridity—the phenomenon of a conceptual and existential "Third Space" where a subject population's identity is redefined to sit somewhere between what it once was and the imposed norms emanating from the imperial power[21]—looms large in studies on Persian period Judaism. From this point of reference, Jews under Persia might strenuously burrow into legacy ancestral traditions but always within the cultural matrix of the empire surrounding them. The self-conscious

6   AN EMPIRE FAR AND WIDE

engagement with older tradition could not be conducted without following imperially imposed scripts, a phenomenon called "colonial mimicry."[22]

R. S. Sugirtharajah states that such responses often constitute enterprises of resistance to the hegemonic culture,[23] but it is essential to recognize the variegated forms of such resistance. Violent revolt occupies one end of the spectrum; resigned submission occupies the other, and shades of grey exist in between (repudiation, ridicule, lament, negotiation, accommodation, etc.). As I will discuss in this study, it is easy to see resistance in some texts while in others the tones of resistance are oblique; writers may not even have had "resistance" in mind when setting about their work. The redactors of Ezra-Nehemiah, for example, may have produced a text that embraces in earnest the structures of Persian administration and cultural authority,[24] but nonetheless frames "official" Aramaic materials in a Hebrew narrative full of struggles and obstacles.

The phenomenon of hybridity emerging in Jewish groups under Persian imperialism also shifted the way liminality functioned as a ballast for ethical and mythic concepts. Victor Turner stressed the importance of liminal spaces and states for the definition of status and legitimation within a society, and scholars of ancient Israel have used this model to illuminate much within the biblical record.[25] This is bound to a mythology of space drawn from longstanding northwest Semitic discourse about the sanctity of the homestead and the realm of Death/Mot beyond the horizon of the familiar; to go beyond that horizon and to return intact was to herald the power of the patron deity and his triumph over cosmic adversity.[26] This model of liminality was well-entrenched within ancient Israelite society and reinforced a variety of social hierarchies: the authority of priests and scribes, the power of monarchs, the role of chieftains over segmentary lineage groups, and even group boundaries that formed during the era of the Babylonian exile.[27]

But the Persian period introduced changes and challenges. Persia was both distant and proximate: the geographic terrain of Persia-proper was beyond the Zagros mountains, but the satrapal system it imposed created a "Greater Persia" that included Semitic lands, even homelands to which exiled communities eventually returned. It was both foreign and domestic: Persians were ethnographically distinct from Semites, but the empire enabled Semites to be "Persian" through participation in the politics and economy of imperial statecraft. It was both alien and familiar: the Iranian religious and mythological system was distinct from those of Mesopotamia, but the Persian empire adopted and promulgated Mesopotamian theologies and cults from the outset, and their rulers were the *de facto* kings of Babylon. It was both opaque and transparent: Old Persian inscriptions were commissioned and made into official declarations of a ruler's authority, but they were also translated into Aramaic, a familiar Semitic language that the empire adopted as the official medium of administration, diplomacy, and scholarship.[28] The liminal *was* the proximate. This meant that the Jewish annexation of pre-Persian legacy traditions could not be done beyond the terms set by the imperial hegemon under whose auspices Jewish groups were empowered—or simply permitted—to survive.

Advances in cognitive science can help us understand the degree to which the responses to Persian imperialism were inevitable given the political, spatial, and linguistic circumstances. Cognitive researchers stress that cognition is not limited to the neuro-dynamics of the human brain but must be understood within the context of an entire human body and its interaction with its environment.[29] A human being is capable of assigning meaning to the world only insofar as their physical body within a spatial plane enables them to do so. Moreover, cognition takes shape through social interaction, both in terms of observing a neighboring human's physical motion and through exposure to the repetition of phonemes through systems of language that form within a group (and, eventually, participation in that language system). An individual's perception of self is understood through the combination of their mental, somatic and ambulatory interaction with the environment, and that interaction consistently redefines perception. As Ronald Langacker observes, patterns of meaning are reinforced through the relational functions—their position in a *domain*—of these interactions.[30]

A second relevant point relates to the concept of frames, that is, fixed mental circuits of organized knowledge that anchor and regulate cognitive processes. Frames are also predicated upon embodied experience; bodily orientation in space and time is the basis upon which the human mind constructs a linguistic or visual framework. George Lakoff and Marc Johnson described this through the example of phrases bound to physical/temporal bodily experience like "heated argument" or "stagnant relationship." The temperature of a typical person's skin is raised during the experience of anger, and this becomes the frame by which "argument" is conceived. Human beings orient themselves spatially through bodily motion, which becomes the frame through which "relationship" is understood. Accessing this framework to describe unrelated frames involves the formulation of metaphors to establishing sequences of meaning.[31]

8 AN EMPIRE FAR AND WIDE

Cognitive theory explains the why to the how of postcolonial observations on imperialism. The phenomenon of embodied cognition is not limited to an individual but manifests on the cultural level as well. An entire community functions in a corporeal manner where the products of spatial and social organization and interaction constitute the collective body that mediates cognitive experience.[32] A community's capacity to construct knowledge and assign meaning is governed by the way its communal institutions—speech and language, worship, economy, architecture, and literature—interact with and navigate the surrounding environment. The end result is that individuals within the community adopt a specific set of concepts for their own individual frames that are determined by the shared communal experience.

This becomes important in understanding why an undisturbed two centuries of Persian imperialism becomes an unshakable basis upon which Yehudite perceptions were conceived. It is through the repetition of imperial rites, linguistic tropes, administrative hierarchies, spatial organization, and so on that meaning is determined. Daniel McClellan has recently discussed how information is processed in the mind through the accumulation of experience: "meaning is generated in, and is confined to, the mind of the hearer, reader, or viewer, and based on the interpretive lenses their cumulative embodied experiences afford."[33] The longer a community remains under the hegemony of an imperial power, the more the imperial frames become the ground upon which schemas of meaning are built. Moreover, following a study by Barbara Tversky and Elizabeth J. Marsh on narrative and individual memory,[34] the longer imperial social and historiographic scripts are rehearsed within a community, the more those scripts affect what people in that community can remember about earlier, preimperial events.

Bhabha's model of hybridity is a result of shared cognitive criteria that affect everyone within a subject population under imperial hegemony. The varieties of responses ranging from embrace to tacit acceptance to outright rejection all operate within the same frames and metaphors for formulating such responses. Insofar as Persian imperialism and ancient Judaism are concerned, "Jewishness" is oriented through the frame of "Persia" and the associated metaphors connected to it. Pre-Persian ritual praxes, architectural structures, concepts of time and geography, and so forth are reframed by the experience of Persian space, Persian language, Persian economy, and Persian literature. In cognitive terms, this realignment of meaning is expressed through the relationship between schemas and instances. The schema is the basic category that creates a conceptual grounding out of which various related instances might emerge; the relationship is asymmetrical, as instances are always determined by the schema.[35] But because cognitive categories evolve through changes in social and cultural contexts, the introduction of imperial hegemony can alter or replace the schemas that ground enduring instances. Social memory (itself an important factor in both individual and communal cognition) ensured that residents of Yehud bore in mind previous sets of conditions, preserved on the levels of folklore, ritual and literature.[36] Persian period schematic sequences did not obliterate these older sequences, resulting in a cognitive quandary that dovetails with Bhabha's Third Space.

The literary output of Yehudite scribes in the fifth through fourth centuries BCE provides evidence of the attempt to navigate this Third Space. As I will discuss in Chapter 1, the Achaemenid dynastic myth affected and subsumed the various memories and other cultural myths retained by the subject populations under their control. As such, Achaemenid mythology functioned as a metaphor to bridge different frames—central versus peripheral, foreign versus native, divine versus mundane, and so forth—that governed communal cognition and perception. The literature produced by Yehudite scribes may be a matter of colonial mimicry and cultural resistance, but it is also a cognitive response to the way Achaemenid mythology suffused daily life in the province.

Myth, Mythology and Mythopoesis
in Sociological Context

At this point it is necessary to define what I mean by the term "myth" and the related terms "mythology" and "mythopoesis." Debra Scoggins Ballentine has discussed how the dominant paradigm for most of the nineteenth and twentieth centuries involved the notion that mythic worldviews demanded polytheism, and that these worldviews were deemed intellectually and theologically inferior to monotheistic theologies centering biblical texts.[37] Ballentine also addressed the shortcomings of such a theologically inflected approach to the issue, joining other scholars who point to the prominence of myth not only within the biblical material but also within the religious traditions that view those materials as foundational scripture. In so doing, Ballentine draws attention to an important aspect of myth, namely, that it presents culture as nature.[38] Mythic discourses project human-constructed taxonomies onto the natural world, licensing those constructs as fundamental, essential, and primordial. Writing such taxonomies into the realm of the gods reinforces social agendas and aligns them with timeless, eternal, preternatural models.[39]

As such, a myth can manifest as a narrative, a statement or mantra, a slogan, or other forms of communication that establish taxonomic structures that need not revolve around a deity, and a contemporary phenomenon provides a suitable example. As journalists, sociologists, and scholars of religion have noted, the rise of Donald Trump and Trumpism in the contemporary American political landscape beginning ca. 2015 was catalyzed by a populist mythology rooted in white supremacy, Christian nationalism, and patriarchy. Trump's handlers engineered a campaign slogan that recycled language used by Ronald Reagan in the early to mid 1980s, "Make America Great Again" (MAGA). Reagan had used this language to support several policy proposals in his 1980 presidential campaign;[40] by contrast, Trump used MAGA alongside language and images coded to appeal to various bigotries rooted in the legacy of the Ku Klux Klan, the Nazi party, the Jim Crow South, and nineteenth-century traditions of Manifest Destiny.[41]

MAGA collapsed historical experiences and reassigned them to a conceptual paradigm that operates outside of those experiences. It became a guiding myth of political identity for those whose ideological preferences were served by it; the terminology associated with it became performances of that identity, ultimately leading to reframing—cast as a reclaiming or rededication—of other American mythemes ("patriotism," "freedom," "liberty," etc.) and cresting in the violent insurrection at the US Capitol Building on January 6, 2021. MAGA mythology itself centers a protological American "greatness" as the ultimate guiding principle; to "restore" this greatness is to align a fallen culture with its metaphysical, cosmological, natural origins, and pristine status. In this schema, "God" is subordinate to American "greatness," and concepts of the deity's power within American society are fundamentally dependent upon it.[42]

We may define myth as an idea that connects culture to nature, but one that does so by establishing a protological, transhistorical paradigm governing social identity, ethics, memory, and action. This may well involve concepts of the divine, but it is not restricted to the realm of the divine. With this understanding in mind, I will use the term "mythology" in this study as a reference to the interactive processes (texts, rituals, architecture, economy, and correspondence) where these cognitive formulations occur. Achaemenid mythology will be understood as the system of images, language, administrative structures and cultural values that served to express, reinforce, and define it across the imperial landscape as it ebbed and flowed over time. Finally, I will use the term "mythopoesis" to describe the cognitive process by which mythology was constructed not only by the Achaemenids but by the Yehudite thinkers and writers during the Persian period, combining historical and embodied experience with ideological models that reacted, in different ways, to the durable presence of Persian imperialism.

The Late Persian Period in Perspective

While I will address a variety of sources and events taking place during and consequent to the rise of Persian imperialism in the late sixth century BCE, the formation of the texts we will examine should be viewed against the background of the last few decades of Achaemenid rule in the mid to late fourth century for two reasons. The first is that despite the overlapping cognitive frames shared between these sources I will analyze, they also exhibit radical differences. The scribes who wrote these works exhibit a diversity of reactions to Achaemenid mythology, which points to a sufficient span of time for diverse Jewish traditions to be annexed for literary development in our sources. It is one thing to either support or challenge the value of an imperial culture and its attendant mythology; it is another to have at one's disposal a *tradition* of supporting or challenging such a culture and mythology. Most of the texts considered in this study are the result not simply of reading earlier texts but of what Ehud Ben Zvi terms "re-reading;"[43] the sources comprising these works have been redacted not only with an eye to creating a new message but to the existing traditions of reading which had long been associated with them. A late Persian period setting is the most likely context for this phenomenon, and as we will see, additional literary features within these texts (some rather explicit) support this as well.

The second reason is the historical context. By its final few decades, the Persian empire was economically and militarily strong but weak in terms of political culture and diplomacy.[44] The Tennes Revolt in Phoenicia in 351 BCE undermined confidence in Persian administrative viability in the region, leading many local regents to diminish their allegiance to the throne.[45] With the earlier loss of Egypt in 401, Yehud was at the western frontier of the empire and there is evidence of administrative reinforcement in the region during this time.[46] The successes of Artaxerxes III in the 340s saw

12 AN EMPIRE FAR AND WIDE

the reincorporation of Egypt into the empire, and it is also at this time that Artaxerxes III engaged in a push to reclaim the prestige of earlier dynasts (and possibly his namesake, Artaxerxes I, in particular).[47] But even these efforts did not stave off the empire's rapid decline immediately following the ruler's death and the short-lived reigns of his successors.[48]

And still, the Achaemenid dynastic myth continued to be promulgated on the official level during this time, and religious/political leadership in Yehud (mostly under the Aaronide priesthood at that point) was dependent upon imperial patronage. The temple in Jerusalem had taken on an economic and administrative position that had led its priestly faculty to invest heavily in Persian imperial structures and institutions,[49] especially following the departure of an Aaronide faction to take up residence in the flourishing Gerizim temple in Samaria during the latter half of the fifth century BCE. This is precisely the sort of politically ambivalent situation that would lead to a variety of responses in literature produced within a small community of scribes caught between various rocks and hard places.[50]

The Contents of the Present Study

The foregoing discussion raises a number of pressing questions. How does a community recovering from exile/forced migration define its identity when memory of the past is forced through the sieve of foreign imperialism? How does the pervasiveness of competing mythologies manifest in the textual products of the literati within such a community? To what degree does such a literate elite—primarily scribal and priestly in orientation—reflect or represent larger communal values and social scripts in the texts they generate? Do we witness intergroup polemics in these different texts produced under these conditions or a different type of intertextual phenomenon—that is, what purpose do these texts serve? Finally, if the texts under examination are recognized to be foundational works of early Jewish literary identity, what are the implications of this deep impact of Achaemenid mythology for the developing role of sacred texts within consequent Judaism?

Chapter 1 will explore the historical context for the emergence of the Achaemenid line after the death of Cambyses (522 BCE), with a focus on Darius' rise to power and his creation of the Behistun inscription (constructed between 521–518 BCE) as the charter myth of the Achaemenid empire. The inscription also became a schema for scribal products throughout the empire, positioning scribes themselves as gatekeepers of the imperial myth and its reconception of time and space. This will involve a new understanding of the "Babylonian" curriculum funneled into priestly/temple settings throughout the empire via Aramaic scribal training and how the tropes of this curriculum was superimposed over earlier native/ancestral text traditions. All of this will be considered as the basis for an Achaemenid dynastic mythology involving a nested framework of royal inscriptions, imperial iconography and rituals, and social hierarchies redefined through imperial mythopoesis.

Chapter 2 will examine how Achaemenid mythology affected Jewish priestly scribes, with a discussion of pre-Persian scribal and textual traditions in Israel and Judah over against changes instituted through Persian hegemony. The chapter will address the features of Aramaic scribal culture and its sociological and sacral dimensions. It will also address the implications of cognitive categorization, by which we may better understand how and why literature produced by Yehudite scribes conformed to Achaemenid prototypes in varying degrees. Two "test cases" will be analyzed: the Elephantine scribal community and the Aaronide priestly scribes who redacted the Pentateuch. Given the significance of the Pentateuch both in biblical scholarship and the study of ancient Judaism in later periods, the majority of attention will be devoted to examining the semiotics of its redaction and the philological impact of its closing strophe within the Aaronide temple cult. The chapter will also consider the date and scope of the Pentateuch's Priestly stratum (P), which carries implications for the way priestly self-concept evolved from previous settings to that of subordination to Persia.

Chapter 3 will turn to the traditions about Ezra's mission to Yehud found in Ezra-Nehemiah, the date of which is the subject of scholarly disagreement. The chapter will argue that the shapers of Ezra-Nehemiah are deliberately vague about this. A renewed analysis of Ezra 7—in concert with evidence from elsewhere in the Ezra-Nehemiah corpus—suggests that a pretextual tradition about Ezra dates (or remembers) his activity in a much earlier era than that of the Artaxerxes implied in the chapter. But the terms of Achaemenid mythology created difficulties for the redactors of Ezra-Nehemiah whose work, at every turn, seems to venerate and support those terms. The redactors thereby skillfully abstracted Ezra from his earlier, remembered context, altering the cognitive frame by which Ezra and his activity could be constructed. The chapter concludes with some comments on the implications of this redactional goal yielding a text that presents Jewish

14   AN EMPIRE FAR AND WIDE

identity and the rebuilding of the Yehudite community as an instance of the imperial schema dominating them.

Chapter 4 considers the redaction of the Book of the Twelve, a product of Levite scribes. In contrast to the redactors of Ezra-Nehemiah, these Levites harbored a less enthusiastic view of Achaemenid mythology and attempted to negotiate its features with the legacy Jewish institution of prophecy. The first part of the chapter looks at the role that Moses plays within the Book of the Twelve; he is presented not as a patron-saint of its contents but, rather, as a typology framing how all of the other prophets within the work are patterned. The chapter then goes on to examine the role of the term *torah* in relation to late Persian concepts of royal decrees and inscriptions. The chapter points to the methods used by Levite scribes that are derived from Achaemenid mythology but which do not present themselves as dependent upon it, thereby creating a new framework for perceiving Jewishness within the empire.

Chapter 5 directs attention to a very different textual tradition, that of the Book of Watchers (1 Enoch 1–36). The chapter examines the antiquity of Enoch in pre-exilic Israelite tradition as part of a tradition of knowledge and revelation obscured by later writers. But this forms the crucial background for why the authors/redactors of the Book of Watchers turned to Enoch overall: these authors sought alternatives to the "standard" curriculum that had accrued within the Jerusalem priestly establishment under the aegis of Persia. The Shemihazah/Asael Narrative in 1 Enoch 6–11—a product of scribes living at the very end of Achaemenid rule—fully repudiated the Persian imperial enterprise and the Jewish intellectual and sacral traditions that emerged from it. This paved the way for the later Hellenistic re-engagement of the figure of Enoch among those who inherited this narrative and built upon it, identifying alternative methods and sources for celestial knowledge that were not sullied by an imperial imprimatur.

The conclusion to this study will return to some of the questions posed above in light of how these early Jewish texts respond to Achaemenid my-thology in different ways. First and foremost, the social topography and self-perception of Jewish scribes in the late Persian period will receive a reevaluation, challenging certain common assumptions about scribal factions as well as assumptions about scribal unity. In conversations with later Jewish traditions, Persia's uniqueness in Jewish memory will be discussed as both a liminal and centrifugal *topos* in the development of Jewish identity over time. The remnants of Achaemenid mythology in

Second Temple Jewish writings will shed light on how and why the rise of demonology formed in the wake of Persian imperialism, and why the power associated with these supernatural forces figures was grounded not only in the process of text production but in the materiality of texts themselves. This carries implications for rabbinic discourses on why sacred texts "defile the hands," and why other systems of textual formation in later Jewish antiquity were conceived against the inherent danger of sacred texts occupying a central place in Jewish ritual and communal formation.

Note: Old Persian translations are primarily taken from Roland G. Kent, *Old Persian: Grammar, Text, Lexicon* (New Haven, CT: AOS, 1953), and Rüdiger Schmitt, *The Bisitun Inscriptions of Darius The Great: Old Persian Text* (London: SOAS, 1991) and *The Old Persian Inscriptions of Naqsh-i-Rustam and Persepolis* (London: SOAS, 2000) with some minor adjustments and variations as needed depending on context.

1

The Achaemenid Dynastic Myth

The architects of Persian imperialism were concerned from the outset with projecting a sense of qualified continuity with the past. It is this sense of continuity that resonates through the decrees and apparent actions of Cyrus the Great, who is reported to have entered Babylon to the acclaim of its traditional priesthood followed by his declaration of devotion to Marduk, the chief deity of the Babylonian pantheon.[1] In this he presented himself as a restorer of Babylonian greatness following the fraught reign of Nabonidus, the last of the Neo-Babylonian emperors who was a devotee of the Syrian deity Sin and who had elevated the city of Haran over Babylon itself.[2] As his own propaganda would have it, Cyrus's taking of Babylon was presented as a matter of heavenly will. In actuality it was a carefully managed exploitation of Babylon's vulnerability, when internal leadership was divided and administrative hierarchies for maintaining economic and social stability were weakened and strained.[3]

Cyrus's arrival made the restoration of Babylonian greatness entirely a matter of Persian facilitation, which in turn forced a rereading of Babylonian culture overall, one where the great founding myths of Mesopotamian civilization implicitly pointed to their fulfillment, on an international level, with Cyrus. It is with Cyrus and through Persian imperialism that Babylonian hegemony could reach its full destined potential, extending well beyond the boundaries of Semitic societies and cultures. In this way, Cyrus managed to position himself and Persian imperialism as the key to realizing the will of the gods, Babylonian or otherwise. This was evident to authors such as Deutero-Isaiah, who read the Cyrus's rise not as a disruption of inner-Semitic society but, in fact, as the key to restoring compromised theological and social institutions with heavenly approval (Isa 44:28–45:3).

Thus began the Persian period, an era where claims of maintaining longstanding local praxes and institutions were made alongside challenges, disruptions, and innovations emanating from a foreign royal court and their dutiful agents and fixers in outposts across the empire. It is easy to see how the rise of Cyrus was welcomed by Jewish writers and their communities.

An Empire Far and Wide. Mark Leuchter, Oxford University Press. © Oxford University Press 2024.
DOI: 10.1093/oso/9780197772744.003.0002

Here was an Indo-Aryan conqueror emerging from beyond a distant mountain range who managed to dismantle an inner-Semitic cultural struggle that had decimated countless smaller states. This other-conqueror declared a Babylonian deity to be his own divine sovereign and restored traditional modalities of cultic hierarchy in the great and ancient city, or at least was perceived as doing this.[4] The entire turn of events heralded the possibility of something very new.

Nevertheless, there is a strong current on both literary and iconographic levels that likens Persian imperialism to that of the neo-Assyrians; the imagery in Achaemenid reliefs take up visual motifs from neo-Assyrian reliefs, and as Amélie Kuhrt has argued, the self-presentation of Cyrus recalls tropes from the legend of Sargon forged during the neo-Assyrian era.[5] The biblical record also contains evidence of the intertwining of Persian imperialism with neo-Assyrian tradition (e.g., Ezra 4:2, 10; 6:22), supporting the view that Cyrus was perceived as standing in the tradition of Mesopotamian imperialism.[6] But breaking the centuries-long cycle of zero-sum Mesopotamian domination, Jewish writers saw him as ushering in an historical epoch where the painful forced rifts between past and present could be mended.

The empire that Cambyses inherited upon Cyrus's death in 530 BCE was still in its relative infancy and unstable; a shift away from the policies that had obtained under his predecessor would be ill-advised.[7] The records regarding Cambyses's conquest of Egypt shows how the ethos of renewal and restoration through imperial hegemony was maintained during his reign.[8] This is especially the situation with his recruitment of the Egyptian priest and military officer Udjahorresnet (ca. 525), who served as a facilitator of Persian interests while presenting those interests as consonant with Egyptian culture and religious tradition.[9] But the difficulties that accrued during Cambyses's reign led Herodotus and other Greek historians to regard him as a compromised leader, no doubt because the circumstances surrounding his death and the immediate fallout nearly spelled the end of Persian imperialism after it had only just begun. Records from the era are contradictory; both Persian propaganda and later Greek historiographies claim that Cambyses murdered his own brother Bardiya before his own death, while other less ideologically charged records affirm that Bardiya was briefly recognized as ruler after Cambyses' death in 522.[10]

What all sources affirm is that shortly after Cambyses' death, contestations regarding power and succession arose with bloody consequences. By the end of the day, one person emerged as victor: Darius I, who claimed the throne

18 AN EMPIRE FAR AND WIDE

in late 522 BCE and thereby inaugurated the beginning of the Achaemenid dynasty that lasted nearly 200 years.[11] In order to justify his claims to the throne, Darius began a propaganda campaign wherein his predecessor was painted as a fraud named Gaumata who was simply impersonating Bardiya. By contrast, Darius presented himself as a close relative of Cyrus, claiming that both were descendants of a patriarch named Achaemenes, and positioned himself as a restorer of dynastic integrity. The amount of resistance that Darius encountered in seizing the throne strongly suggests that he, in fact, was regarded as a usurper of Bardiya's otherwise fair claim to succession and probably was the culprit behind his death.[12] So widespread was this resistance that Darius himself acknowledged it in a document he quickly commissioned to serve as an apology for his rise to power.

This document is the famous Behistun inscription (DB), carved into a cliffside in western Iran that served as an imperial boundary marker. DB defended Darius's rise, but it was more than just a royal apology. It was crafted to function as a deeper meditation on the relationship between the cosmic and the political in Darius's time. That it was constructed at a place whose named meant "Residence of the Gods" ("Behistun," Old Persian *Bagastana*) already positions it as a record of divine agency in human affairs. Much scholarly ink has been spilled on the composition history of DB, the historical reality standing behind it versus the rhetoric it contains, and the propagandistic function it served as evident in other Achaemenid texts.[13] But an insufficient amount of attention has been devoted to its function as a foundation for a dynastic mythology that extended far beyond its material boundaries and its temporal setting. The following discussion will survey the contents of the inscription and their function as building blocks of a myth of Persian imperialism that extended into all avenues of life during the reign of the Achaemenids.

The Behistun Inscription as the Achaemenid Charter Myth

Before continuing, it is important to clarify how the term "charter myth" applies to DB. A charter myth, as formulated by Branislaw Malinowski, is a concept that defines the relationship between the functional, operational features of a society and the timeless, transhistorical ideas that generate them, reflecting the the agenda and priorities of the myth's framers.[14] A major dimension of this and other charter myths was the persistent concept that the era antedating the events conveyed within the myth constituted a chaotic "before-time."[15] The myth delineated the terms by which this chaotic, dangerous state of affairs was set at a distance from the society that upheld the myth. This in turn was built from earlier mythologies involving power hierarchies, spatiality, the organization of time, and the ever-present threat of death.

The Achaemenid dynastic myth initiated in DB (henceforth, "the Myth") functions similarly when we look to its centrifugal place in the expanse of royal inscriptions, propaganda, decrees, and expressions of power throughout the Achaemenid era. Previous studies of DB have noted that it draws extensively from old Iranian ideologies of creation, kingship and governance, but the inscription rebuilds them into a discourse that frames itself as the international *telos* of earlier mythologies leading up to Darius's reign.[16] An instructive example is found in Lydian coinage minted early in Darius's reign, featuring images from Lydian preAchaemenid mythology (Fig. 1.1).[17] That they appear on Achaemenid coinage points to the imperial absorption

Figure 1.1 Details of the Behistun Relief

Credit/caption: Korosh.091 on Wikimedia Commons. File licensed under the Creative Commons Attribution-Share Alike 4.0 International license.

of this mythology and the positioning of its administrative and economic apparatus as a mediator of its terms.[18] If coins like these were struck consequent to the establishment of DB as a charter myth, the resulting impression is that earlier mythologies are to be reread as always pointing in the direction of the Achaemenids and the establishment of their rule over the broadest of international horizons.

A closer look at the operative mythopoeic strategy of DB is thus in order, the first of which is the stigmatizing of Cambyses. In DB, Darius explicitly blames Cambyses for Bardiya's murder, conducted in secret (DB 10). The historical veracity of this claim is doubtful, but more important is the rhetorical implication that it is only through the inscription's disclosure that a secret act of violent betrayal is brough out into the light. The compositional act itself taps into the ancient Iranian concept of *aša* (cosmic order/justice),[19] set against the secrecy and duplicity of Cambyses. Moreover, because the inscription characterizes Cambyses's conquest of Egypt as subsequent to his slaying of Bardiya, it further suggests that Cambyses's imperial enterprises were conceived under illicit, corrosive contexts.

If DB functions as a charter myth, then these enterprises were extensions of things from the chaotic "before-time," and could not be retained without obtaining a new, sanctified royal imprimatur. It is no wonder, then, that Darius would himself reenlist the aid of Udjahoressnet and deploy him once again to restore religious institutions in Egypt, "resetting" conditions that emerged from Cambyses's earlier recruitment of this figure.[20] In this way, whatever benefits persisted from the initiatives of Udjahoressnet dating from the time of Cambyses could be retained and utilized for administrative and economic capital without bearing the stain of Cambyses himself. It would not be enough to cast Cambyses in such condemnatory tones; DB goes a step further and introduces a crucial—indeed fundamental—motif, that of *Drauga* ("The Lie"). *Drauga* is presented throughout DB as the corrosive force that had permeated imperial society in the wake of Cambyses' death, and which threatened to tear apart the very fabric of creation.

The concept of *Drauga* was not novel in Iranian thought, which had long pitted it against *aša* as an elemental force.[21] These earlier Iranian discourses periodically presented *aša* as a sentient being.[22] So too could *Drauga* be personified, and this is what takes place within DB. As Darius tells it, *Drauga* took control of the empire and worked through human agents like the alleged-imposter Gaumata but also those who supported him (DB 5, 8–10). Yet because *Drauga*'s entry is intimately connected to Cambyses's death, the

THE ACHAEMENID DYNASTIC MYTH   21

implication is that it was also intimately connected to Cambyses's life and regnal activity. It is therefore Cambyses's reign that is rendered the chaotic "before-time" of the charter myth, while Darius and his subsequent actions fortify against the destructive danger of this antecedent period. DB presents itself not only as a commemoration of Darius's deeds but as perpetual edification of them; to know, accept, promulgate or recite the terms of DB is to affirm the dangers of the interim period characterized by Cambyses's reign and that of Gaumata and to actualize Darius's accomplishments anew. And considering the self-presentation of Darius in both DB and in his subsequent inscriptions, to do so was to experience, to actualize, Ahuramazda's acts of creation.[23]

The terms of this mythology were not mere invention but drawn from ideas circulating on the ground in relation to Darius. If Darius was widely perceived to be a usurper, then the likelihood is that he stood directly behind Bardiya's death. In this case, Darius is the one whose actions may have been viewed as the entry point for *Drauga*, with many viewing Darius himself as a *dregvant*, that is, an agent of this destructive cosmic force.[24] We know that Darius was suitably concerned with questions of his ascent by his highlighting of his familial ties to Cyrus (DB 4, 8) and the emphasis on his marriage to Cyrus's daughter Atossa. These concerns clearly extended well into the latter days of his reign, since it was his son with Atossa (that is, Xerxes), and not his firstborn son from an earlier marriage, who was named heir (Herodotus, *Hist.* 7.2). The prominence of these family dynamics in DB suggests that the inscription takes up real matters surrounding Darius's social and political position. Likewise, the prominence of *Drauga* as a recurring trope must be a response to actual sentiments or charges that hounded Darius at the outset of his reign.[25]

DB's mythologizing of events relies on strategic confusion. The inscription's narrative categorizes figures and events in a stark manner, aligning Darius and his supporters with Ahuramazda and all those who stand against him with *Drauga* (DB 52, 54), drawing from longstanding Iranian myths of kingship. But Darius's rhetoric is effective because it annexes perceptions just familiar enough to the audience that the language possesses a measure of authenticity. The reader or listener is confronted with a dizzying array of things that were historically genuine alongside spins or takes that question the way they took place. The narrative contains a stream of assassinations, claims to power, pretenders, usurpers, rebels, loyalists, and so forth, that capitalizes on the disorienting trauma of warfare and bloodshed

22 AN EMPIRE FAR AND WIDE

that erupted during 522–521 BCE. The narrative of DB situates the audience within these traumas, but then present a set of factors that offers some way of making sense of what must indeed have felt like a period suffused with *Drauga's* presence.

The rhetoric of DB floods the discourse with contradictions that make the audience question what they know, yet it loosely draws from the semblance of recognizable events or facts without committing to demands of factual context. This is followed by the projection of a stable mythic narrative that projects the possibility of order into which the audience will invest themselves. Here, the relationship between the textual content of the narrative and its material representation becomes important. The narrative—inscribed in three languages (Elamite, Akkadian, and Old Persian)—appears beneath a detailed relief carved into the cliffside. From the cognitive angle, the use of two longstanding written languages alongside Old Persian (the script for which Darius claims to have invented) grounds his account in the semblance of fixed, trustworthy modes of imparting information.[26] By purporting to express the true sequence of events, DB *itself* is the force that dispels *Drauga*; its materiality as a written text carries metaphysical effects.

But the relief above the trilingual inscription is even more significant. It depicts Darius standing victorious over his vanquished enemies, chief among them Gaumata, whose body is crushed under Darius' foot (Fig. 1.2). Hovering above the scene is a winged figure often identified as a representation of Ahuramazda; the image may also by a symbolic representation of the Achaemenid ruler assimilated into or cojoined with Ahuramazda or a more general allusion to *farnah*—identifying the ruler as blessed by the decree of heaven.[27] In any case, Darius is victorious with heavenly approval, and his enemies have been trampled into the dust of the Earth. The image ossifies this idea, extending the moment it depicts in perpetuity and thus transferring the event into mythic time beyond the scope of Darius's tumultuous early years. The image shows no conflict or struggle, only triumph and the crushing of enemies. Viewers of the inscription would encounter the image first and foremost; although the text of the inscription was composed before the image was struck, the inscription seems to issue forth *from* the image, explicating its visual impact in lexical and lemmatic terms.

The spatial dimensions of the image establish the basic tropes of the Myth. Darius stands between Heaven and Earth, and his towering height and resemblance to the humanoid in the winged figure is suggestive of a supernatural status. The trampling of Gaumata into the ground is the foil for the

Figure 1.2 Persian Man Image from Coin
Credit/caption: Daric with king. Gold coin from Achaemenid dynasty, ca. 4th century BCE, Iran. Courtesy the Metropolitan Museum of Art, New York. Gift of Edmund Kerper, 1952.

winged figure floating freely in the heavens, indicating that Darius' enemies are the enemies of heaven, and his victory over them is nothing less than an establishment of heavenly order over the Earth. The inscription qualifies these visual tropes in various ways: it equates "Earth" and "Empire" as a composite "Earth-Empire" (*bumi*); imperial statecraft is thus made synonymous with the landscape over which heavenly order has been imposed.[28] This also renders statecraft an extension of Darius' victorious combat over his enemies, infusing ordinary administrative mechanisms with a mythological dimension.[29] The metamessage is that the chaotic interim during and following the reign of Cambyses stands not only against the superstructures of Darius's realm but against the "proper place" (DB 17–18, 53, 55) of all lineages within it. By contrast, the standards of imperial business under Darius's rule sustain heavenly will across the imperial landscape for the common good.

24   AN EMPIRE FAR AND WIDE

This last point constitutes the most important part of the Myth, enabling discrete military victories to take on protological significance and self-perpetuate through the ongoing mechanisms of imperial administration.[30] The victory depicted at Behistun is made the fundamental substance of ordinary power structures on the local level which had, by 521 BCE, already bought into and benefitted from the Persian administrative system. The rhetoric of the inscription creates a vision of ongoing stability and power for local leaders with a divine seal of approval from both local deities and Ahuramazda, encouraging a submersion of local theologies and identities within that promoted by Darius. The closing strophe of the inscription ensures that this becomes a curricular matter, and warrants a closer reading:

> King Darius says: By the grace of Ahuramazda this is the inscription which I have made. Besides, it was in Aryan [i.e. Old Persian] script, and it was composed on clay tablets and on parchment. Besides, a sculptured figure of myself I made. Besides, I made my lineage. And it was inscribed and was read off before me. Afterwards this inscription I sent off everywhere among the provinces. The people unitedly worked upon it. (DB 70)

The import of these lines (which appear only in the Elamite and Old Persian sections of the inscription) is too often missed by commentators. The copying and circulation of propagandistic inscriptions is no novelty in ancient near eastern imperialism. But DB represents the first time that the inscription in question narrates its *own* copying and even notes the medium—parchment, the conventional material used in circulating Aramaic texts. This is significant for a few reasons, the first of which is that by the latter half of the first millennium BCE, Aramaic literature had been firmly intertwined with Akkadian political and scholarly texts, especially Babylonian literature.[31] A symbiosis of sorts developed between the study of this material as a hallmark of prestige and numinous power on the one hand and positionality within an imperial hierarchy on the other. Local elites were intimately involved with the administrative hierarchy of the Achaemenid empire,[32] and scribal groups held a special role in this matrix. Literate elites who supported imperial hegemony did so in part by engaging in the Aramaic-Babylonian scholarship that funneled the high-learning of Mesopotamian culture into their hands.[33] For scribal guilds across the empire, the Aramaic-Babylonian curriculum became a symbol of the power entrusted to them not only by the Achaemenid rulers but indeed by the various gods who patronized them.

From a cognitive perspective, the practice Aramaic-Babylonian scribal scholarship itself became an instance of this imperial myth—a fitting feature of a dynasty that had become the *de facto* kings of Babylon.

Second, the claim that DB was spread throughout the empire through Aramaic copies implies that it is one of the various languages now "belonging" to Darius in the inscription (alongside Elamite, Akkadian and Old Persian). The implication is that Aramaic text traditions from the Babylonian period or earlier must now be understood through Persian imperialism. The inscription not only positions Persia as the culmination of all cultures and histories, but of the written records of those cultures and histories that were transmitted in Aramaic. By the Seleucid period, Babylonian scribal scholarship was primarily transmitted through Aramaic language and script conventions.[34] The central position of the Achaemenid administration in claiming Aramaic as the principal language of the empire's intellectual discourse—administrative and sacral-scholarly—catalyzed this process.

Lastly, if DB is a charter myth, then the inclusion of its own copying and circulation throughout the empire in DB 70 is made *part of that myth*. The scribal act reproducing the inscription is, in some metaliterary way, an actualization of its terms. Darius took measures to make it impossible for close inspection/reading of the actual graphemes of the inscription. In Donald Polaski's words, it was made "visible but not legible," ensuring that official copies wrought by scribes were the only way its contents could be consulted or studied.[35] This strategy shifted a tremendous amount of imperial power to scribes as the scribal craft became a major vehicle for the dissemination of the Myth. Scribes were thus motivated to create written materials that served Achaemenid interests, for such materials served their own in the process.[36] This draws from a lengthy Babylonian tradition of elite scribes viewing their material texts as iterations of divine language, but it is here channeled into a paradigm where the words of an Achaemenid ruler carry divine potency as well.

Empowering local scribes as agents of Achaemenid ideology could serve as a cudgel against the possibility of rebellious local elites seeking to recover pre-Persian autonomy. Such rebellious elites would have a more difficult time producing their own propaganda if local scribal elites were committed to the Achaemenid imperial project.[37] Even more importantly, though, the elevation of scribes as gatekeepers of the Myth granted them the power for their *interpretations and adaptations* of official texts to function with imperial authority.[38] The essential nature of interpretation/adaptation is attested

26 AN EMPIRE FAR AND WIDE

already within DB: Paul Alain Beaulieu notes that the Akkadian version of the inscription truncates and alters what is found in the Elamite and Old Persian versions.[39] The inscription thereby models adaptation *as part* of its own rhetoric of disclosure.

The surviving copies of DB point to such adaptations in every case as well. The Aramaic copy discovered at Elephantine contains a major departure from the Behistun prototype through its interpolation of verses deriving from Darius' tomb inscription (DNb), and the Babylonian copy contains other notable departures showing influence of local culture. Herodotus's account of Darius's rise closely matches DB in many respects but also contains significant departures that may have originated, in part, with a copy to which he was privy in some way (directly or indirectly).[40] Not only does this confirm that copies did indeed circulate throughout the empire, it confirms that scribal craftwork was an integral part of the dissemination of Achaemenid mythology. A later textual phenomenon provides some perspective. Sanders observes that Seleucid era scribal reproductions of Cuneiform documents done in Aramaic carried as much, if not more, prestige and power than the Cuneiform documents themselves. They were understood not simply as copies but as "exemplars" (*gabarû*) or sources of discourse that functioned as prototypes with the force of an original.[41]

The exemplars/*gabarû* texts were independent products of scribal circles who worked under Greek and Parthian rulers. Nevertheless, some antecedent for what we find in this Hellenistic-era material may be traced to the Achaemenid period and its ideology of scribal phenomenology. The material products wrought by scribes who derived authority from the Aramaic scribal culture of the empire functioned as material extensions harnessing the power of royal inscriptions. We should not view them quite as the exemplar/*gabarû* materials but, rather, as textual avatars of royal inscriptions. By working the act of scribal reproduction into the Myth in DB 70, the avatar texts created by scribes became more than propaganda, they became extensions of the cosmic language originating at Behistun. In this way even texts preserving local traditions could carry the imprimatur of the Myth, weaving once-independent ideas into the imperial project.[42] As time went on, other royal inscriptions that echoed and rehearsed terms of DB's charter mythology were incorporated into this mythological discourse.[43]

Achaemenid royal texts also persistently appeal to the concept of the "Persian Man"—a brand of imperial masculinity representing each emperor or, perhaps better, a cosmic pattern for supernatural masculinity that each emperor embodied in their reign (Figs. 3–4).[44] The latter interpretation is more likely in light of the crucial observation made many years ago by Margaret Cool Root that the iconography accompanying each of these monumental inscriptions presents the emperor in question in exactly the same way as their predecessors; no one Achaemenid emperor is ever depicted in an individual or distinct manner.[45] Instead, Root's study of Achaemenid iconography shows that these images fold each emperor into a common recurring image connected to the motif of the "Persian Man" in the text of royal inscriptions, creating a visual reinforcement of DB's mythology. Each emperor thereby fulfills the same role as trustee of Ahuramazda's will and overseer of the sacred landscape. Official documentation, dispatches, and records refer to these larger motifs with regularity, weaving basic administrative processes into the dynastic mythology.[46]

The Protological Rhetoric of DB in Subsequent Achaemenid Inscriptions

Several researchers have observed that the vast majority of royal inscriptions from the Achaemenid emperors following Darius draw from the language and rhetorical imagery of DB. A brief consideration of these inscriptions demonstrates that this is not simply a matter of imperial stereotyping but carries a type of ritual dimension, invoking speech, action and positionality that renders each inscription an extension of Darius's own foundational composition. This in turn transforms each emperor a manifestation of Darius's "Persian Man." This much aligns with the stereotyped iconography in the reliefs identified by Root, but in light of the scribal charge in DB 70, the written-ness of these inscriptions demands increased attention. In particular, the language given repeated written form in these inscriptions functions in the manner of a cosmic invocation, binding the terms of creation of the structure of the heavens to the reign of the emperor in question. The "Daiva Inscription" from the reign of Xerxes provides a salient example:

> A great god is Ahuramazda, who created this earth (*imam bum*), who created yonder sky, who created man, who created happiness (*siyatim*) for man, who made Xerxes king, one king of many, one lord of many . . . I am Xerxes, the great king, king of kings, king of countries containing many kinds of men, king in this great earth-empire (*bumiya*) far and wide . . . And

28 AN EMPIRE FAR AND WIDE

among these countries there was a place where previously demons (*daiva*) were worshipped. Afterwards, by the grace of Ahuramazda I destroyed that sanctuary of demons . . . And there was other business that had been done ill. That I made good. That which I did, all I did by the grace of Ahuramazda. Ahuramazda bore me aid until I completed the work . . . The man who has respect for that law (*data*) that Ahuramazda has established and worships Ahuramazda at the proper time and in the proper manner, he both becomes happy (*siyata*) while alive and becomes blessed when dead.

The tropes of this inscription replay many of the motifs present in DB: the scope of the empire, the "proper" time and manner of structuring society, the "good" (*siyatim/siyata*) in carrying out his initiatives, and the equation of rebellion with demonic forces (*daiva*), and the prominence of the "Persian man" concept. But the mythic resonance of this last concept is implied by its juxtaposition with other "kinds" of men who are explicitly subordinate within the hierarchy of lands and peoples that Ahuramazda has willed into being through his creation of the Earth-Empire (*imam bum*). In this way, the inscription invokes the international *telos* that characterizes DB, extending the eternal moment of that inscription into Xerxes's own reign and, just as significantly, the writing of his account. Unlike DB, the inscription does not narrate its own textualization in explicit terms, but its textual quality is suggested by function of "law" (*data*) in the closing instruction, as well as the happiness (*siyata*) that this will secure. The *data/siyati* language connects back to DB, which also presented its written-ness as a matter of Ahuramazda's *data* as much as that of Darius, and which presents peaceful statecraft as a matter of popular agreement and effort.

As a written document, then, the Daiva inscription presents itself as the *data* that subsequent audiences should study and uphold for their own blessed benefit in life and even in death. The text is thus something that transcends the ordinary business of imperial administration and become a cosmic declaration, positioning the Achaemenids, their empire, and the imperial curriculum as the factors mediating life and death, the heavens and the netherworld, the past and the present. All of this is predicated by the declaration at the start of the inscription that the empire forged by the Achaemenids was in fact forged by Ahuramazda, equating the two and establishing the Achaemenid line as protological in origin.[47] Consequently, the written decree of the emperor is no less than the decree of heaven.

Achaemenid Geomythology

Achaemenid inscriptions repeatedly describe the realm as "an empire far and wide" for good reason. Persian boundaries stretched beyond those of previous Mesopotamian empires, and the concept of both space and time was reformulated. As Robert Rollinger has observed, the immense size of Persia enabled Darius to claim that his empire crossed beyond the "great sea," the symbolic boundary between ordinary space and cosmic space and thus ordinary time and cosmic time, uniting both.[48] This motif, the Achaemenid mastery of "the sea," recurs in various royal inscriptions, each relating some aspect of reality once bounded by the sea but now unimpeded by it.[49] Imperial texts, then, were not ordinary texts but gateways to the esoteric knowledge that earlier understandings of geomythology had sequestered from ordinary matters of statecraft. In a sense, as Rollinger notes, the empire brought history to an end by uniting historical time with mythic time and political space with mythic space. The geographic organization of the empire is an extension of heaven; the decrees of the emperor and the textual mechanisms that preserve and promulgate those decrees are cosmic, transforming a terrestrial landscape into an extension of the celestial realm.[50]

It is worth reconsidering the tropes of the Daiva Inscription which replays many of the motifs present in DB: the scope of the empire, the "proper" time and manner of structuring society, the "good" in carrying out royal initiatives, and the equation of rebellion with demonic forces, and the prominence of the "Persian man" concept Darius inaugurated for himself. The text transcends the ordinary business of imperial administration and become a cosmic declaration, positioning the Achaemenids, their empire, and the imperial curriculum as the factors mediating life and death, the heavens and the underworld, the past and the present. All of this is predicated by the declaration at the start of the inscription that equates Achaemenid statecraft with creation, establishing the Achaemenid line as protological in origin. Consequently, the written decree of the emperor is no less than the decree of heaven. The archetypal "Persian Man" embodied in the emperor becomes the *Axis Mundi*, an idea reinforced through royal relief imagery.[51]

The inscriptions of Xerxes's successor, Artaxerxes I, carry forward the identical ideologies found in Darius' inscriptions even when applied in a different direction. In the case of the "Inscription from Persepolis" (A1Pa) the text commemorates the expansion of a royal palace:

30 AN EMPIRE FAR AND WIDE

> A great god is Ahuramazda, who created this earth, who created that heaven, who created man, who created happines for man, who made Artaxerxes king, one king for many, one leader for all . . . I am Artaxerxes, the great king, the king of kings, the king of countries with all kinds of men, the king in this (earth-)empire far and wide, the son of king Xerxes, the grandson of Darius, the Achaemenid . . . Artaxerxes the great king says: by the grace of Ahuramazda, my father, king Xerxes, built this palace. After that, I built [it]. May Ahuramazda and the gods preserve me, my kingdom, and what I have built.

A related inscription, composed in Akkadian in the "Hall of Hundred Columns" (A1Pb) reinforces the connection between structure, design, space, lineage and cosmos:

> King Artaxerxes says: My father, king Xerxes, laid the foundations of this palace . . . with the protection of Ahuramazda, I, king Artaxerxes, have finished it.

It is notable that Artaxerxes here specifies that he continues what his father Xerxes had done, and that the statement is made in Akkadian. The use of the language reaffirms the Achaemenid hegemony over Babylon. The palace is not simply a residence or a testament to royal wealth or privilege, but a monument to the structure of surrounding geopolitical hierarchies. Using Akkadian to express or narrate Achaemenid initiatives was a longstanding practice by the reign of Artaxerxes, but we should note its function here serves a larger purpose than propaganda. To build the palace (and to commemorate it through invoking Ahuramazda in Akkadian) was to construct the empire in miniature, an act that embodied Ahuramazda's own creation of the cosmos and the place of cultures (like Babylon in Transeuphrates) within it. Both the heavens and the landscape *en masse* are imagined, and indexed, by the ruler's specific construction enterprise.[52] The design of Persepolis, the principal capital of the Achaemenids, reinforces this ideology through its structures and its own monumentality, making the ruler's mythological hegemony the keystone of international cultures and purposes.[53]

What has often gone unnoticed in this mythology is the specificity of lineage/genealogy in the rhetoric of monumental inscriptions. At least as far as the Achaemenids themselves were concerned, the venerated ancestors are not just remembered in these inscriptions but, in a real sense, embodied within them. After all, if Ahuramazda created these rulers alongside the Earth-Empire (as the royal inscriptions repeatedly stress), then these rulers embody the Earth-Empire and are cojoined to it in both life and death. This is demonstrated by the placement of inscriptions at Darius's tomb at Naqsh-i Rustam, cojoining an inscription full of royal *data*, the physical body of the ruler, and a postmortem space carved into the landscape itself.[54] Darius's delineation of dynasties under the Achaemenid rubric projects the ancestors and their place in the living religion of the empire into the Behistun inscription itself. His victory is theirs, his rule is theirs, his connection to Mazdean conceptions of heaven is theirs, and all of it is represented by the structure of the imperial landscape. The subsequent inscriptions discussed here do the same with both geopolitical organization and royal palatial structures, as do the tomb designs of Darius's successors that largely emulate his own and cojoin ruler and landscape in death.

In brief, the postmortem existence of the ancestors persists *as* his empire, far and wide, especially with regard to the Achaemenids themselves—their inscriptions present the dynasty as cosmogonic.[55] The expanse of Earth-Empire and the orchestration of peoples and power within it is where the royal ancestors now reside; so long as Earth-Empire stands, the ancestors are still vital and powerful. They endure within its institutions and speak through the texts inscribed upon them or housed within them. Moreover, the nature of these royal inscriptions breaks with more familiar conventions of propagandistic literature to take on sacral-numinous dimensions on the scholarly level. Royal inscriptions highlighting this aspect of the empire and the structures emerging from it were thus issuances from heaven, containing divine disclosures that could claim to define the realms of both the living and the dead. The "Xerxes at Persepolis" inscription (XPh) puts the matter bluntly:

If you who come hereafter should think, "May I be blessed/happy while alive and *one with Order when dead!*" then behave according to the law which Ahuramazda set down.

You should sacrifice to Ahuramazda according to the Order up on high. The man who behaves according to the law which Ahuramazda set down and sacrifices to Ahuramazda according to the Order up on high, he will both be blessed while alive and *one with Order when dead.*

32 AN EMPIRE FAR AND WIDE

The inscription is unsubtle in making the point that it is the imperial project that embodied the fullness of divine will and cosmic order. Following imperial *data* ("the law which Ahuramazda set down") is the vehicle through which blessed postmortem existence could be secured. Root has noted that Achaemenid imagery identifies the person of the king with the entirety of the landscape;[56] this would hold in death as well as in life, and the incorporation of the dead into the Earth-Empire rendered death a part of Ahuramazda's act of creation. The force of such rhetoric must have strongly affected how native praxes and ideologies regarding mortality and death were framed under Achaemenid hegemony.

The Impact of The Myth on Jewish Communities

Darius's seizure of the empire and the institution of DB's mythology imposed new standards over Jewish life that took firm root as Jewish society continued to develop from the late sixth century BCE onward in different loci.[57] In the hands of priestly scribes across the empire (by virtue of DB 70), the Myth's strategic flexibility enabled the hybridization of native traditions and imperial doctrine. The extent of this hybridity is evident across Jewish communities in this general era; a recent examination by Gad Barnea surveys the manner in which Jewish concepts of YHWH across various communities were submerged with other deities to form both pairs and triads of divinities, showing a greater capacity of adaptation and adoption of non-Yahwistic traditions into their own than previously thought.[58] Jews living under Persian hegemony were thus inclined to form bonds with external concepts that held pragmatic social, economic, political and mythological appeal.

This transformation is coeval with the increased influence of Jews returning from the eastern Diaspora to Yehud. We have only scant direct evidence for how this operated among Jews residing in Babylon throughout the neo-Babylonian and Achaemenid periods from the various archives found in Mesopotamia (i.e., TAYN and Nippur).[59] The evidence is important, though, because what it reveals is that in less than a single generation, Jews (Judahites) had fully integrated into Babylonian life. There is nothing extraordinary in these documents regarding unique religious, social, military, or economic organization among communities that endured forced migration from Judah to Babylon. Names identify their ethnicity and heritage, but behavior does not, at least in terms of how the archive documents depict the daily business of ordinary Jews.[60] The integration of these early Jewish communities into Mesopotamian life explains why the majority appear uninterested in returning to their ancestral homeland in the early years of the Persian period; their identities were intertwined with their generation, linguistic, and geographic setting.

Whatever group of exiles did return in the late sixth century was fairly meager; the rebuilding of Yehud and Jerusalem took several generations and remained modest. Archaeological surveys of Jerusalem for the entirety of the Persian period reveals a small city with no more than 1500 inhabitants.[61] Given the small size of Jerusalem, its scribal population must have been quite limited in number; William Schniedewind suggests no more than "a dozen or so."[62] Schniedewind is probably correct in terms of a group strictly stationed in the temple, although Mitchell's work on Zechariah suggests that literary activity at Ramat Rahel—the imperial administrative center for Yehud—flowed into Jerusalem as well.[63] It is difficult to say how many literate figures would have been active between these two sites (and others as well such as Mizpah).[64] Administrators with advanced literary training would have straddled both locations, and lists from the fifth century BCE that include Levites point to a number that goes beyond the small group of scribes exclusively working at the Jerusalem temple.[65]

It is not only Levites who held land interests and residence beyond Jerusalem; the fact that Aaronide priests in the second half of the fifth century BCE departed the Jerusalem temple to found the Samaritan priesthood at Gerizim suggests that some Aaronide clans already had interests beyond the Jerusalem temple even before this time and could envision other regions where their lineage groups could flourish. This finds support in texts depicting the inner-Aaronide priestly hierarchy and passages like Joshua 24 that assign towns to various Aaronide families well beyond Jerusalem's boundaries.[66] This does not mean that the Yehudite literati constituted a vast class of people, but there are reasons to view the circles of scribes in Yehud as not quite as meager as the priestly demographics of Jerusalem in the 6th-fourth centuries would imply. It is more accurate to envision a limited caste of literati in various Yehudite loci that revolved around the sphere of the Jerusalem temple. These small groups would operate mostly—but not exclusively—under the aegis of the Aaronide priestly establishment therein, participating in a common provincial literary culture.

34 AN EMPIRE FAR AND WIDE

What most of these different types of priest-scribes had in common, though, was a strong influence from the exilic (*golah*) experience with foreign imperialism. Texts reflecting the interests of the *golah* group repeatedly center history and power not in ancestral territory but in the eastern Diaspora close to the source of Achaemenid power.[67] Avenues to the restoration of ancestral tradition radiated outward from the eastern Diaspora in Mesopotamia and was facilitated through imperial statecraft. It is understandable how Achaemenid ideology regarding the empire as postmortem residence of the ancestors would hold appeal to the *golah* group, who for a generation had been separated from the preexilic chthonic traditions. The *golah* positioning much of the literature of the Persian period suggests that Jews living in the eastern Diaspora accepted the benefits of Persian imperialism, and that their representatives in Yehud held a similar attitude.[68]

A relatively obscure notice in Ezra 8 provides us with hints regarding the incorporation of the Myth among Jews in the eastern Diaspora. In Ezra 8, Ezra recruits to his delegation to Jerusalem a group of Levites residing in the city of Casiphia (Ezra 8:15–19). The narrative is probably a stylized account, but a real historical event likely stand behind its composition. Caroline Waerzeggers has shown that the consequences of the failed Babylonian rebellion of 484 BCE involved the loss of power among the elite priests of prominent Babylonian temples.[69] Priest-scribes steeped in Aramaic-Babylonian discourse—a caste already enjoying increased imperial positionality—filled the void left behind, amplifying their own power and sacerdotal prestige.[70] As Sanders has discussed, the growing predominance of Aramaic scribalism throughout the ensuing Achaemenid era is closely bound to the events of 484 and their repercussions for the mechanism of knowledge production among priest-scribes in Persian antiquity and beyond.[71]

The literary characterization of the Levites of Casiphia should be understood against the background of these developments: a "second tier" priestly group characterized by scholarly skill is brought into a central temple establishment, off-setting the dominance of the primary group.[72] Still, the episode contains an important presupposition, namely, that the Levites of Casiphia are not only suitable for advancing the interests of Persian imperialism but are *essential* to this goal. The text specifies that the basis for this suitability rests in their scholarly scribal training (Ezra 8:16, 18); in context, this assumes fluency with Aramaic-Babylonian learning and other dimensions of Aramaic scribal culture.[73] The episode overall suggests that priestly groups among the Jews of the eastern Diaspora cultivated a sacral tradition where devotion to YHWH involved Aramaic scribal curricula. This would have been worked into the imperial curriculum among the literati within the group that returned to Yehud and rebuilt Jerusalem and its temple.[74]

In Sum

The rise of the Achaemenids entailed the persistent propagation of their dynastic myth, which became a schema for all forms of imperial conduct. Concepts of space, time, the afterlife, and the realm of heaven were grounded completely in the production of imperial ideology, which eclipsed and absorbed earlier local destinies, histories, and traditions of sacred knowledge. In this way, the Achaemenids positioned themselves as the fulfillment of all previous epochs and realms, creating an empire that was once current and protological. This was expressed repeatedly in royal inscriptions that became curricular for the empire's classes of scribal literati, who were enculturated in the language and imagery of these compositions. But this occurred alongside their enculturation in the Aramaic-Babylonian scholarship that served as a cultural capital within the empire, reinforcing the idea that the near-timeless networks of Mesopotamian knowledge production were entrusted to the Achaemenids. Participation in this system of knowledge transmission was an affirmation of the empire and its mythology as much as it was a vehicle for establishing prestige and power within the traditional social structures of local communities. But this also meant that local traditions could only now be subsets of the Achaemenid mythology. In the next chapter, we will identify how the activity of Jewish scribes living under Persian hegemony participated in this phenomenon, and how the governing force of the Myth affected their annexation of legacy Jewish memories and institutions.

2

The Priestly Scribes of Elephantine and Jerusalem in the Fifth Century BCE

As we saw in the previous chapter, Achaemenid mythology was in full floruit by the mid-fifth century BCE. The reign of multiple emperors emulating the same discursive prototypes in their inscriptions and reliefs, coupled with the adoption of those inscriptions alongside Aramaic-Babylonian scholarship by scribes throughout the empire, ensured that an intellectual hegemony rooted in and supported by the Myth would remain in place. We also saw that even before the rise of the Achaemenid dynasty, Jewish scribes began taking up imperial ideas and weaving them into their own transmission of earlier traditions and tropes that had been a regular part of the legacy Jewish scribal lexicon. Before looking more closely at how the Myth was factored into the ideologies of Jewish scribal communities in the fifth century, a brief overview of the precursors to Jewish scribal culture in the pre-Persian period is in order.

Scribes in Pre-Persian Israel and Judah

It was common in the mid-twentieth century for scholars to envision a vibrant literary culture in Israel from an early period, ushered in by what Gerhard von Rad called "the Solomonic Enlightenment" in the tenth century BCE.[1] Research in more recent decades has demonstrated that the picture is much more complicated than what von Rad assumed. There is sufficient evidence pointing to loci of literary activity in the early monarchic period, although the outlets for literature were limited. We may posit scribal activity in both the north and in Judah by the tenth century, but conventional scribal methods (such as a standard alphabetic script) do not surface in a measurable way until a century later, and many scholars see a tiered scribal infrastructure in Judah congealing only in the eighth century.[2] In any case, by the late monarchic period, a number of different scribal groups seem to have

An Empire Far and Wide. Mark Leuchter, Oxford University Press. © Oxford University Press 2024.
DOI: 10.1093/oso/9780197772744.003.0003

emerged: scribes connected to the royal court and the monarchic administration,[3] priestly scribes situated in the Jerusalem temple and Levite scribes scattered between rural and urban settings, and as Schniedewind has recently argued, scribes among the "landed gentry" (the elusive *'am ha-'aretz*).[4] Literacy itself was still relatively scarce among the general Judahite public, but by the seventh to early sixth centuries, the idea of writing and presence of texts and textuality were familiar fixtures of the culture.

The book of Jeremiah is particularly illuminating in its depiction of scribal status during this time and into the early years of the postmonarchic era. Scribes are not simply record keepers or transcriptionists; the book presents them as partners of prophets and as influential figures in regional politics. The book even subtly hints that Jeremiah himself was a scribe or had scribal training/credentials, and incorporates the scribal craft and even its material implements into prophetic phenomenology in different ways.[5] This picks up concepts developed within the (slightly earlier) book of Deuteronomy, where Levite priests are positioned as scribes whose written *torah* transmits the authoritative prophetic teachings of Moses.[6] The book of Jeremiah ramps this up, especially in episodes like Jeremiah 36 where the scribe Baruch becomes a stand-in for the prophet. And throughout the book, scribal methodology shows a deep knowledge of broader ancient literary genres, methods of composition, and hermeneutics; Israelite and Judahite scribes were full participants in the trends characterizing ancient scribal discourse, especially regarding the textualization of prophecy.[7] But the book also demonstrates that scribes were not united. Different scribal factions appear to have existed side by side and in disagreement with each other (even within the same corners of society), sometimes with notable hostility.[8]

The rise of Persia and the restoration to Yehud created major realignments in scribal identity. As commentators generally agree, the major divides during this time were no longer between Deuteronomists and Priestly thinkers but between homeland groups and *golah* groups repatriated to their ancestral lands. The ideological divisions between scribal communities once in exile dissolved in this new environment, especially since the economic and sociological structure of restoration-era Yehud positioned the Jerusalem temple and its priestly faculty as the principal symbol of community organization and power.[9] Early responses to Persian imperialism involved the production of prophetic oracles in a learned, scribal manner among Jewish populations both in the eastern Diaspora and in Yehud (Deutero-Isaiah; Zechariah 1–8).[10] With the institution of Achaemenid mythology and the central role of scribes within it, Jewish scribal groups found renewed opportunity to affirm their identities and their craft as part of a new social and political environment.

The incorporation of scribes into Achaemenid mythology and the increase in local power it granted to them catalyzed the colonization of scribal identity. Training was contingent upon imperial social hierarchies and relationships, materials were derived from an imperial economy, and the promulgation of royal or high-ranking administrative inscriptions, decrees and edicts became curricular alongside legacy traditions.[11] To be a Jewish scribe was to be an imperial scribe in all practical respects. The cognitive angle sheds additional light on how this overtook concepts of scribal identity, since researchers on cognition stress that repetition and the formation of language systems affect perception, values, ethics, and memory. Given the centrality of repetition both in the copying/reproduction of text and their memorization in the training of ancient scribes, the cultural and cognitive impositions of the empire saturated the self-perception of scribes and their function.[12]

The invariability of this process of cognitive categorization is explained by George Lakoff in his "elephant" paradigm: upon saying to a listener "don't think about an elephant", the listener's thoughts can *only* be formed with the elephant in mind, whether the listener wants to think of it or not.[13] Jewish scribes were not capable of engaging in their craft beyond the horizon of Achaemenid mythology. In what follows we will consider the work of two Jewish scribal groups—the priest-scribes at Elephantine and Jerusalem—to gauge how the texts they produced served as instances of Achaemenid literary schemas, heralding the mythology that those imperial decrees and inscriptions imparted. Chief among them stands DB, which we will see left a palpable impression on the compositional choices of both scribal communities, though other royal inscriptions will factor into the discussion as well.

The Myth at Elephantine

The examination of the Elephantine documents must begin with the copy of DB itself found at the site (DB Aram). True to the closing notice in the Old Persian and Elamite prototype, DB Aram appears in Aramaic translation, largely faithful to the original with the exception of the section that interpolates DNb (a point to which we will return below). Christine Mitchell notes that the copy must have been made from an *earlier* copy already well-entrenched in the scribal curriculum at Elephantine.[14] The original was likely transmitted on a parchment scroll as the local avatar edition for the community; the papyrus copy we now encounter is the end result of successive study and material reproduction of the original within the tradition maintained at the site. Whenever its contents first reached the colony, DB Aram serves as an affirmation of the Myth's ongoing applicability. The production of DB Aram is therefore not only a nod to Achaemenid authority but to that of the priestly scribes at Elephantine who had to power to produce it.

The Function of DNb within DB Aram

It is this power that is on display with the interpolation of verses from DNb into DB Aram, an obvious departure from the prototype at Behistun. Mitchell notes that DB 70 from the prototype does not appear in DB Aram; in its place is the material interpolated from DNb (the final lines of the inscription), which accomplishes three important things. First is a matter of intellectual practicality: the notice in DB 70 that Aramaic copies were produced would appear redundant in an actual Aramaic copy. By contrast, the replacement of DB 70 with the words of another Darius inscription maintains the spirit of the original's rhetorical power, serving as just the sort of scribal performance that DB 70 licenses. The interpolation demonstrates the essence of the Myth in action, shuttling the vitality of a prototypical royal inscription—a different one—into the culture of a provincial population through their priestly-scribal elite.

Second, the specific lines from DNb included in this interpolation (lines 50–60) reveal the perceived relationship between the priestly scribes behind them and the imperial hierarchy. These lines contain instructions from Darius to his successor regarding the ethics of ruling the realm. These very same lines make up the closure not only of DNb but of an inscription (known as XPl) dating from the reign of his son and successor Xerxes. In keeping with the ethos of submerging the identity of emperors into a common typology, Xerxes impels his own successor with the exact terminology that his predecessor directed to him. The content of the lines are telling:

40 AN EMPIRE FAR AND WIDE

> O man, vigorously make you known of what sort I am, and of what sort my skillfulnesses, and of what sort my superiority. Let not that seem false to you, which has been heard by your ears. Listen to what is said to you.
>
> O man, let that not be made to seem false to you, which has been done by me. That do you behold, which has been inscribed. Let not the laws be disobeyed by you. Let not anyone be untrained in obedience.

The relationship between the literary contents of the document and the scribal culture that wrought it revolves around a typology of succession and continuity, a type of "Once and Future King".[15] That this discourse is interpolated into DB Aram characterizes these royal inscriptions as typologically equivalent despite their observable differences (commissioning emperor, spatial or geographical placement, material media). It is the scribal *reproduction* of these inscriptions that reveals this, demonstrating the agency of the scribes themselves in unearthing the deeper curricular resonance of the sources.

Third, the motif of succession/continuity carries meaning for the positionality of the priest-scribes themselves within the Elephantine community. The texts they created transmitted imperial tropes just as the post-Darius emperors themselves did; these priest-scribes also explicate the meaning of the imperial texts through the variations we encounter in DB Aram, where interpolations and substitutions reflect the priest-scribes' own prerogatives. Yet the reproduction of imperial texts in the Aramaic documents wrought by these scribes (variations included) is what reveals their cosmic potency, facilitating their interchangeability, ergo the interpolation of text from one inscription (DNb [or XPl]) into another (DB).

The form of DB Aram reveals that the priest-scribes of the Yahu temple viewed themselves as the pivotal agents in infusing the Myth's cosmic force into their own documents.[16] And just as the Achaemenid successors carried forward the essence of regnal dynamics that began under Darius, the succession of the priestly scribal office from one generation to the next in Elephantine preserved the sacral power of the office itself. The Yahu temple housed a unique brand of theology and ritual practiced and preserved by its priesthood, with roots long pre-dating the Persian period.[17] But Mitchell's study of the materiality of DB Aram shows that it became a central part of the temple's curriculum, its papyrus document carrying various written memoranda from generations of scribes who consulted it, and who did so alongside their recording of other affairs related to the temple's communal function.[18] The entire document presents a picture of ordinary life suffused

THE PRIESTLY SCRIBES   41

with imperial mythology, with the priest-scribes standing at the nexus of both.

Jedanaiah's Letter to Bagohi

Another well-studied document sheds important light on the place of the Myth at Elephantine, namely, Jedaniah's famous letter to Bagohi seeking permission to rebuild the destroyed Yahu temple (A4.7–4.8). The letter conveys a wealth of historically valuable information: a Yahu temple stood at the heart of the community for a long time and was destroyed in 410 BCE following tensions with the nearby temple to the Egyptian deity Khnum. The letter also relates that the community had earlier attempted to obtain permission to rebuild their temple from the Jerusalem priesthood, and that the current letter was composed after receiving no earlier reply. Finally, the letter promises that the community would repay Bagohi for his intercession in the matter by incorporating his name into the community's regular liturgy, presenting such an offer as a valuable and practical prospect for a busy, high-ranking administrator.[19]

Within the letter, we see that the community required permission for the rebuilding of their own cult site and was thus beholden to a structured administrative system. The reported appeal to the Jerusalem priesthood and to Bagohi indicates a recognition of the political and social authority of priests alongside an administrative hierarchy. And despite the declaration that its temple was an ancient institution, the liturgical *quid pro quo* further suggests that by the time of its demolition, its liturgy had already made accommodations to imperial figures or ideas. Granerod's work on Elephantine Yahwism reinforces this by showing how the site amalgamated aspects of Ahuramazda into their depictions and expressions of YHWH. According to Granerod, the deities were indeed mutually assimilated which attests to the inextricability of the cult at Elephantine from the imperial matrix.[20] The evidence both from official response to Jedaniah's letter and from the letter of Hannaniah (the so-called Passover Letter from 419 BCE, which depicts a royal appointee provide regulation for observing a Jewish festival) further attest to this relationship.

The letter's language reveals that Jedaniah and his community conceived of imperial power, operative both within and outside of their community, according to the terms of the Myth. The letter is sure to note, for example,

42   AN EMPIRE FAR AND WIDE

that the temple structure they sought to rebuild originated *before* the reign of Cambyses. The letter does not say how far back before Cambyses's reign this was. Far more important is that this language invokes a major trope from the Myth evident as early as the DB prototype, namely, that Cambyses is the figure associated with the introduction of *Drauga* into an otherwise ordered world governed by *aša*. The notice in the letter regarding Cambyses is not simply a statement on the antiquity of the Yahu temple but associates it with this idyllic period brought about by Cyrus before the era of Cambyses, and reestablished in the reign of Darius.

The letter thus implies that the temple, when it stood, was one of the items Darius fixed into its "proper place" within Earth-Empire. By implication, the destruction of the temple violated the order set in place by Darius; the longer it remained unrestored, the greater the risk of *Drauga*'s reappearance. It is perhaps for this reason that Vidranga, the Persian official who oversaw the destruction of the temple, is cursed in such violent terms:

> After this had been done to us, we with our wives and our children put on sackcloth and fasted and prayed to YHW the lord of heaven: "Show us our revenge on that Vidranga: May the dogs tear his guts out from between his legs! May all the property he got perish! May all the men who plotted evil against that temple—all of them—be killed! And may we watch them!" (TAD A4.7)

Granerod's proposal that the letter's promise of Bagohi's inclusion into the rebuilt temple's liturgy is compelling,[21] so the language about Vidranga may constitute a liturgical curse similarly to be included in the reconstituted temple liturgy. But an additional possibility is that the letter *itself* functions as a type of liturgical document. In the temporary absence of a temple, a text about its past and its prospective future might function as a forum for the performance and even actualization of ritual statements or incantations. One might object that the letter is clearly a utilitarian document meant for administrative/bureaucratic processes, but we will recall that Achaemenid statecraft itself was perceived as an enactment of the Myth. It is not that the letter could only serve a practical purpose. Rather, as implied already in DB 70 concerning the administrative order for scribal copying, the practical dimensions of the letter *were* mythopoeic.

Jedaniah's letter to Bagohi combines the historical experience of the community with DB's own motifs. It is uncertain if Jedaniah was himself a priest, but his level of literacy, obvious training in the conventions of diplomatic language, fluency in the sacral traditions at the Yahu temple and apparent power to promise expansions and changes to the temple's future liturgy suggest that he was.[22] In addition, Jedaniah refers to the priests at the site as his "colleagues" in the same way that he refers to the Jerusalem temple priests as the "colleagues" of the high priest Johanan; the shared language is indicative of his own priestly status.[23] At the very least, he possessed a scribal training steeped in priestly thought, or worked alongside and with the support of priests as the letter was crafted.

With this in mind, we may view the letter as both a bureaucratic initiative and an invocation of Achaemenid mythology. The letter falls into the category of instance in relation to the schema created in DB and repeated in later royal texts like the Daiva inscription: a sacred order is corrupted by agents of evil who abuse the mechanisms of imperial power established by a legitimate ruler from the past. The letter folds these agents of evil—Vidranga and his supporters—into DB's taxonomies through the brief but potent invocation of the name of Cambyses. The act of textualizing the letter with these mythic tropes embeds those tropes in the very identity of the community moving forward. If DB Aram is any indication, Jedaniah's letter would also have become curricular among the priest-scribes of Elephantine and would thus contribute to the cultic praxes and ideology of the restored site. In becoming such a foundational-liturgical document, the letter (and the response to it) would provide evidence that the restored Yahu-temple was cosmogonic in nature.

The Myth and the Aaronides in Jerusalem:
The Redaction of the Pentateuch

An enormous amount of scholarly effort has been devoted to the study of the Pentateuch's redaction in the context of Persian period Judaism, and scholars remain divided on how best to account for imperial influence. Still, all scholars agree that the cultural and social effects of Persian imperialism affected the formation of the Pentateuch in a substantial form, and very likely in relation to (though not identical with) local legal praxes that operated under the principle of imperial *data*.[24] I would suggest that the Babylonian revolt of 484 BCE functioned as a catalyst for the eventual redaction of the Pentateuch in the decades that followed. The long influence of Babylonian

44 AN EMPIRE FAR AND WIDE

scholarship was dramatically changed as a result of that event, and created a ripple effect in the production/transmission of sacral knowledge across the Achaemenid empire.[25]

We may see the growth of the Pentateuch as a bid for the Aaronide priests to retain their own position of influence within this ripple effect. It is instructive to reconsider the presentation of Ezra in light of the post–484 BCE events to obtain some context for why the Aaronides redacted this document. Within the text of Ezra-Nehemiah, Ezra is featured as a scribe in the imperial sense of the term and thus schooled in Aramaic learning. Yet this learning is presented as his skill in the "*torah* of Moses" (Ezra 7:6; 10); David Lambert adeptly identifies this as a method of textual mediation rather than a document.[26] It is Ezra's skill in this method that facilitates his authority over the reading and teaching of the Pentateuch in Nehemiah 8, with no (other) Aaronide priests in view—Ezra is thus presented as replacing them, taking over ceremonial readings and interpretations of sacral *torah* traditions.

None of this should be taken as a transparent window into historical events regarding Ezra. But the parallels with Aramaic scholars taking up influential positions in Mesopotamian temples are difficult to ignore, and suggest that the Pentateuch's redaction emerged from this seismic shift. Both Nehemiah 8 and the *torah* notices in Ezra 7 presuppose an existing document that is subjected to Ezra's expertise, that is, a Pentateuch, and it is significant that Neh 8:2 refers explicitly to Ezra's priestly status in his ability to fetch the scroll from the temple. The implications is that its regular place of residence was within the temple in an area restricted to priests. Though a work of sophisticated scribal skill, Nehemiah 8 understands the document as one that the Aaronides created to reinforce their ritual power. But their ritual power stands within the miasma of Achaemenid events unfurling across the first half of the fifth century BCE, leading to the Pentateuch's emergence by the mid-point of that century.[27]

The Rhetoric of the Pentateuch's Concluding Notice

Very telling in this regard are the closing verses of the Pentateuch in Deuteronomy 34, which offer a summation of Moses and his legacy:

> And there has not arisen a prophet since in Israel like Moses, whom YHWH knew face to face, in all the signs and the wonders, which YHWH sent him

THE PRIESTLY SCRIBES   45

> to do in the land of Egypt, to Pharaoh, and to all his servants, and to all his
> land, and in all the mighty hand, and in all the great terror, which Moses
> wrought in the sight of all Israel. (vv. 10–12)

These verses form a closing "seal" to the Pentateuch, making clear that no other prophetic tradition or text could rival it.[28] The verses are retrospective; the implied narrator looks back on Moses's time at a distance and thus evaluates the history of Israelite prophecy as subordinate and supportive.[29] At the same time, the rhetorical structure of the Pentateuch prioritizes the book of Leviticus, a self-contained work presenting priestly ritual as the substance of revelation situated in the center of the scroll. Even the book of Deuteronomy, which originated in the monarchic era as a Levite-wrought *torah* of its own,[30] becomes subordinate to Leviticus within the Pentateuch. It functions as a model of how the teachings of sages might mediate the overwhelming power of priestly ritual texts, the latter forever fixed at the mythic Sinai while the former is imparted on the plains of Moab (Deut. 5:1). The closing seal of the Pentateuch implies that the entirety of this tradition—both the priestly ritual texts and the way they could and should be taught—rests in the hands of the (Aaronide) priest-scribes who textualized this material.

The retrospective dimensions of Deuteronomy 34:10–12 convey the sense that the material in the scroll redacted by the Aaronides contains written material from long ago and far away, a motif found in Mesopotamian texts purporting to harness numinous revelation.[31] The closing verses highlight the special dimensions of Aaronide scribal status in connection to these written, textual revelatory discourses. This concept of scribalism is found in monarchic and exilic era biblical texts with non-Aaronide origins (most notably Deuteronomy), but the texts in the Pentateuch that scholars view as stemming from earlier Aaronide circles do *not* make these claims. Throughout the Priestly (P) strata of the Pentateuch, writing and textuality are seldom mentioned; when they are, they are set in ritual contexts and support ritual authority rather than declare scribal prestige.[32] The Aaronide writers from the late monarchic and exilic eras who composed these texts were skilled scribes, but scribal skill was not commodified at that time in making priestly power claims rooted in textual materiality.

By contrast, the closing verses of the Pentateuch show the Aaronide scribes placing their scribal status front and center, utilizing the convention of the "scribal report" that had earlier marked Deuteronomy as the *torah* of a Levite scribe bearing Moses's legacy.[33] Here we may find an explanation for why

46 AN EMPIRE FAR AND WIDE

the Pentateuch outweighed the value of a Hexateuch.[34] The latter may have emerged alongside the Pentateuch or possibly even before it, but it could not yield the same rhetorical or mythic effect in terms of positioning the Persian period as symbolically consequent to the death of Moses and the end of the wilderness period.[35] The creation of a Pentateuch on a single self-contained scroll separates it from the eras of Joshua, the Judges, the monarchy and the exile. The closing notice in the Pentateuch positions the Aaronides as the priestly scribal mediators of sacred testimonies entrusted to Moses, and their usage of the Pentateuch within the Jerusalem cult makes the society it regulated a direct actualization of the Pentateuch's terms. This matches very closely with the closing discourse in DB 70 that not only gave scribes license to serve as mediators of imperial power but set up a scenario where their own local text traditions could be reimagined as subsets of the empire's mythology.[36]

The Significance of Aramaic Script

Scholars remain divided on whether the Pentateuch's sources can best be understood according to a documentary theory (assigning its contents to four once-independent literary sources), or if it grew from a Priestly source and many other non-Priestly sources. Both approaches have their merits and invite caveats. At least in the broad strokes, the documentarian approach aligns better with our discussion of Achaemenid imperial myth when we consider one crucial aspect of it, namely, the symbolic force of retexualizing older complete sources containing legacy traditions onto new scrolls in Aramaic script.[37] First are practical matters: the resources for scribal activity, both material and intellectual, were now regulated through Achaemenid economic and political hierarchies. Menahem Haran noted several decades ago that Jewish scribes living under these conditions would first and foremost be trained in Aramaic convention They would develop facility in the tools, materials, and forms of Aramaic language, writing and scroll production, and Hebrew traditions would consequently be transmitted within this new paradigm of literary practice.[38]

The use of Aramaic script is even more important when considering how the redactional process operated. Though the Aaronide scribes of Jerusalem inherited and preserved Hebrew language texts, by the fifth century BCE these texts were recopied using Aramaic script instead of the Paleo-Hebrew script of earlier eras. The adoption of Aramaic script to transmit Hebrew language texts signaled a new phase of Jewish scribal identity and how they preserved vestiges of older tradition.[39] Within the Aramaic framework, the transformation of long-existing written sources would yield a stronger statement regarding the role that Persian imperialism now played in refracting earlier ideologies; in cognitive terms, this grounded the Pentateuch within an Achaemenid textual domain.[40] By adopting an imperial technology, these texts became instances of imperially dictated textual schemas.

But the adoption of Aramaic script carried another purpose. The Pentateuch's sources call attention to themselves: two creation stories, intertwined flood accounts, inconsistent lists and genealogies, legal collections with different social foci and language, colophons, literary interruptions, repetitive resumptions (*Wiederaufnahme*), and so forth. In brief, the redacted work prompts the ancient reader or listener to be aware that it was a composite of material—its literary face is "bumpy", not smooth, and each bump points to the compositional prehistory of the source in question, as Brian Peckham suggested many years ago.[41] Peckham's observation should be extended to the function of Aramaic script in textualizing these sources. Variations in style, syntax, linguistics and literary theme are discernible, but the sources, irrespective of origin, were bound together through their retextualization in Aramaic script. Consequently, the Pentateuch's contents were factored into a stream of dynamic tradition shared across the empire that was rooted in Aramaic-Babylonian sacral curricula. The legacy Jewish traditions it contained suddenly became symbols of a more timeless, international system of sacral thought.[42]

The Special Category of Scribal Power

Some further comment is required on the special role of scribes such as those surveyed above. With the end of native kingship in ancient west Asia, the centers of scribal learning and literary production were no longer subordinate to royal dynasties that had long dominated from region to region.[43] Cyrus recognized the utility of this shift early on and sponsored propaganda that would further separate Babylonian royalty from claims of sacral knowledge; this encouraged scribal independence from native kings, heralding the bigger change with the sidelining of Babylonian elite priestly families after 484 BCE.[44] After 484, the rise of Aramaic priest-scribes in temple compounds was accompanied by their working their own scribal lineages into lists with supernatural figures on the one hand and restricting their knowledge to their own ranks on the other.[45]

At Elephantine and Jerusalem, these priest-scribes served as mediators of an imperial ideology by connecting their local traditions (steeped, to be sure, in old communal values and ideas) to the larger network of Aramaic-Babylonian learning throughout the empire. This bestowed upon them a unique category of power different from top-down authority of an administrator like a satrap or provincial governor. The Jewish priest-scribes at Elephantine and Jerusalem represented a more grass-roots type of power, intermingling on multiple levels the legacy of their ancestors with the terms of Achaemenid mythology that conceived of administration as a safeguard and fulfillment of native cultural destinies. Embodying Bhabha's Third Space, the unique position of these scribes as translators of the Myth on the local level suggests that top-down administrators relied on them to reinforce their own initiatives as royal appointees.

Postcolonial theorist have noted that this is an essential tool of imperialism, constituting a colonization not only of space and population but of language and media.[46] It is the reason why DB was first created as an effort to reframe what it meant not only to be an Achaemenid but to be a participant in Persian culture and heritage. This sheds some light on why Darius emphasizes that his inscription is the first time the Old Persian language manifested in written form alongside the Elamite and Akkadian versions of the account at DB (DB 70). Material and script provided the key for redefining language and culture, be it stone or parchment, Cuneiform or Aramaic. In the case of Jerusalem, the Aaronide Pentateuch serves as a parade example (as an "Aramaic" document), and the fact that it endured as a basis for Aaronide ritual authority suggests that its significance as an icon of both ancestral tradition and imperial power was recognized more generally by nonpriestly communities in Yehud.[47] Like the scribes empowered to adapt DB as gatekeepers of that text, the Aaronide priestly scribes did the same with the Pentateuch, positioning themselves as the exclusive mediators of its numinous meaning to the larger nonpriestly population.[48] In Elsie Stern's terms, they became "text brokers" in Yehud, akin to those found elsewhere in the Achaemenid empire.[49]

The question arising from this is why alignment with the Myth required a redaction of the Pentateuch's sources into a new, more comprehensive document. Why not simply reproduce the discrete sources themselves in Aramaic script, that is, why not simply reproduce the earlier version of Deuteronomy, the P document, the putative J source, etc., as "Aramaic" documents? The sources were obviously available to the Aaronide scribes; retextualizing them in Aramaic script and on parchment would serve as a performance of scribal power and instances of Achaemenid textual schemas. Why, then, undertake so gargantuan a project as a Pentateuchal redaction? How does this reflect the special power of the Aaronide's scribal status?

One possibility is that the redaction of distinct, discrete sources into a single document served as a metaphor for the diversity of lineages and traditions within Yehud that now functioned as a singular Achaemenid province. More to the point, it related to *the diversity of scribal groups* that had long characterized Jewish tradition in contradistinction to the Aaronides. I noted above that already in the late monarchic period, we find a variety of literate/scribal groups: royal scribes, landed hinterland elites, former northern urban elites, Levites and Aaronide priests. Within some of these groups, we find further subvarieties: Levites who participated in Deuteronomistic ideology and those who did not, priests who stood behind the "Holiness school" of thought and those who abided by earlier priestly discourse, and probably others as well.[50] Even if the scribal class in Yehud was smaller than in the late monarchic period, the echoes of earlier affiliations and biases no doubt persisted in some fashion.

By the mid-fifth century BCE, the originators of these sources had long passed from the scene, but memory of earlier discrete autonomous scribal groups was no doubt sustained by the durability of these self-contained sources. This is especially the case if scribal communities in Yehud are better understood as existing in different groups orbiting the Jerusalem temple where the Aaronides dominated. The redaction of such well-known, well-established Hebrew scrolls into a single "Aramaic" document thereby constituted a powerful rhetorical statement on the role of priest-scribes in the context of imperial Yehud. It declared that the concept of once-discrete scribal identities must be submerged within the larger literary culture supported by the Achaemenid hierarchy and its mythology. To paraphrase a later Jewish thinker, there is no Yahwist or Deuteronomist—all are one in the Pentateuch under Persia and the Aaronides, at least from the perspective of the Pentateuchal redactors.

The Date and Scope of P within the Redacted Pentateuch

For the last several decades, debates about the dating and division of the Pentateuchal sources have returned to question of the Priestly source as a barometer for evaluating the redaction history of the entire Pentateuch. There is broad consensus on what passages should be assigned to P (and the "H" substratum), but this is accompanied by different proposal on whether this material is monarchic, exilic, or Persian period in origin. What does not seem to be up for debate, though, is the fact that P seems to undergird the macrostructure of the entire Pentateuch, most likely due to the priorities, values, and worldview of its Aaronide redactors. All other sources and accretions rest on the broader P narrative and the theology it promulgates.

In recent years, scholars such as Christophe Nihan and Konrad Schmid have produced nuanced analyses of P that shed important light on its literary and theological subtleties, and they join others who argue that P is itself a product of the Persian period.[51] Because P envisions a mobile sanctuary, Schmid argues for a composition before the rebuilding of the fixed temple structure ca. 515; more specifically, he follows the position of Albert de Pury that P's hostility toward Egypt reflects the latter's place beyond the reach of Persia, and thus proposes P's composition before Cambyses's conquest of Egypt in 525.[52] By this time, P's authors would know the contents of Deuteronomy, which Schmid argues is presupposed by P's and its knowledge of the earlier "the cult centralization of Deuteronomy."[53]

But the position of Schmid and de Pury regarding P's attitude toward Egypt is problematic. It imagines an almost robotic type of mimesis on the part of the P writers, with cues about perceptions of Egypt entirely regulated by its position *vis á vis* Persia. This ignores one of the most important and enduring legacy ideologies in Israelite and Judahite thought, namely, the hostility toward Egypt as a military force. The very earliest attestations of Israelite ethnogenesis focus on Egypt's military threat in the clearest of terms; this is evident explicitly in the premonarchic Song of the Sea (Exod. 15:1–18, especially vv. 1–12) and is encoded in passages in early traditions in Joshua and Judges as well.[54] It surfaces in the eighth century prophetic literature (Isa. 10–11, etc.; Hos. 7–9, 11:1–5; Mic. 6:4) and persists down to the late monarchic and even exilic eras in the oracles of Jeremiah and Ezekiel.[55] Schmid's (and de Pury's) proposal does not account for the weight of this anti-Egypt tradition, one that emphasized military threat because this had always been a major component of Israelite/Judahite concepts of Egypt.[56]

With respect to P's concept of the cult presupposing a Deuteronomic reform program or its literary expression in Deuteronomy, the matter is more complicated than that of linear literary dependance. Why, we must ask, should a P author need to take an earlier text regarding a society's cult as the sole stimulus for writing his own text about that society and its cult? Israelite and Judahite cultural experience did not exist in a literary vacuum where later writers could only access ideas ossified in earlier textualized documents in a temporally successive manner. Such a view does not account for cultural memory or cognitive variation based on social positionality, let alone the complex sociological forces involved in an oral-literary culture.[57] To wit, the relationship between the experience of cult centralization and the composition of Deuteronomy is indirect and theoretical in purview. Van der Toorn, for example, notes that the reforms of Josiah are connected to the rhetoric of Deuteronomy, but that the latter is likely a literary-theoretical response to Josiah's purge of the rural cult (a position I have also argued).[58] If this is the case, then there was no actual "cult centralization of Deuteronomy" per se, only the composition of a document that theorizes how Josiah's purge could be aligned with traditional hinterland values, invoking the authority of Moses to do so.

The very concept of the centralized cult in P is a world apart from that in Deuteronomy. Whereas the latter negotiates between royal initiatives and egalitarian values, P establishes a hierarchical gradation where holiness flows outward into the lives of the people who reorganize their households and society to accommodate it.[59] Moreover, P's cult originates in a cosmic otherspace—the Sinai wilderness—and serves as a myth of the priestly cult rather than a response to on-the-ground conditions.[60] The vision of a central cult is used alongside the ritual texts in P to establish conceptual models of priestly power and the centrality of their ritual authority.[61] This obviously had great significance for priests in a restored Yehudite community in Jerusalem, but the concept is not limited to such an historical or even geographic setting. The composition of an idealized, mythic discourse on sanctuary space and cultic conduct should not be reductively viewed as a reflex of Persian period social conditions or solely derived from an earlier text like Deuteronomy.

Christophe Nihan proposes that P is a fifth century BCE composition, and that the redaction of the Pentateuch represents a fourth century ideological

52 AN EMPIRE FAR AND WIDE

negotiation between the priesthoods in Jerusalem and Gerizim.[62] But anthropological factors make such a negotiation unlikely. Priesthoods at rival sanctuaries prioritize their claims to traditions (written, oral, ritual, etc.) to the exclusion of others in segmentary agrarian societies; negotiations of tradition take place only when rival groups are subsumed within an overarching sacral hierarchy, at which point the weaker/subordinate group adopts the terms of the dominant group into which they assimilate.[63] Because Samaria was far more powerful than Yehud during the Persian period,[64] the Aaronides at Gerizim would not have negotiated with those in Jerusalem; the latter would have submitted to and adopted the former's authority and theological priorities. This, of course, did not happen. The commonalities between the Samaritan and Jewish Pentateuchs should thus be viewed not as a matter of cooperative negotiation in the fourth century BCE but rather as arising from respective recensions of a precursor document, deriving from the mid-fifth century that both groups inherited. If the Pentateuch took shape in the mid-fifth century, then the composition of P must antedate such a setting.

Yet placing the composition of P before the fifth century BCE does not provide support for Schmid's dating of the work to the early Persian Period as a better alternative. In arguing this position, Schmid states that P's Table of Nations in Genesis 10 draws from the conventional language of Persian inscriptions addressing the variety of nations under Achaemenid control.[65] But Schmid does not account for similar elements already at work in earlier texts like Deuteronomy 32 and the Deuteronomistic tradition overall; as Brian Rainey writes, this tradition understands nations and ethnicities as spatially bounded in terms of ancestry, language and culture.[66] Moreover, significant differences are evident between these inscriptions and Genesis 10, the latter of which stresses the genealogical relationships between the various groups of people it lists. This is not a feature of the Persian inscriptions: peoples are listed but not as segments of lineages.[67]

The argument contains an additional problem, and that is that the inscriptions in question are Achaemenid, and thus *postdate* the reign of Cambyses.[68] This undermines Schmid's (and de Pury's) position that P dates from a time before Cambyses's conquest of Egypt. Though Schmid suggests that P could have feasibly been composed down to ca. 515 BCE (the completion of the second temple construction) conventions of Achaemenid inscriptions could not have taken root by so early a point in the dynasty's tenure, even if the first of these inscriptions (DB, completed ca. 518) had just begun to circulate throughout the empire. More time would be required for such conventions to assimilate into the ranks of priest-scribe groups to the degree proposed by Schmid, de Pury, and others who characterize P as so strongly conditioned by Achaemenid literary tropes. The failure of the argument ultimately rests on the contradictions in the evidence used to build it: if P is influenced by a well-established tradition of Achaemenid inscriptions, it must date from the latter half of Darius's reign or later, and cannot be dated to the era of Cyrus or Cambyses. If P dates from an earlier period predating Darius's reign, then it cannot be influenced by Achaemenid inscriptions.

While there are grounds for seeing the fleshing-out of P extending well into the Persian period, the entirety of its composition should not be assigned to this period; its origins are earlier.[69] This matters for the present study because if P was perceived by the fifth century BCE redactors of the Pentateuch as a (partly) pre-Persian Jewish legacy tradition, it too was reframed by the redactional process, its earlier function and significance transformed and yet also fulfilled by its new textual iteration. P and its particular worldview was subordinated to the new cultural setting responsible for its new literary setting.[70] The social structures delineated in P were now only accessible in a text taught by a priesthood that had accommodated new hierarchies introduced by the Achaemenids. And a source that was once the exclusive province of an insular priesthood was now part of the flow of an international, intertextual exchange of knowledge into which the Jerusalem temple and its cult were networked.

In Sum

Following the Achaemenid schema of the empire as the culmination of all histories and cultures, the Pentateuch served as the culmination of all Jewish scribal identities and their attendant worldviews. The very redaction of the Pentateuch is evidence that a massive literary enterprise—displaying the full power of scribes working on behalf of the empire. But by the second half of the fourth century BCE, history had shown the empire's vulnerabilities through the twin blade of internal dissent and regular (and mounting) threats from external Greek forces. The persistence of the "Persian Man" typology and recurring formulaic phrases in imperial inscriptions show the Achaemenids' ongoing commitment to the Myth, but also suggests that such commitment was something in need of regular defending. Questions regarding the Jewish relationship to it would invariably arise among the literati in Yehud hearing of the turbulence in other parts of the empire or witnessing more local disputes that disrupted the alleged *Pax Persica*. The pervasiveness of rebellion in the Achaemenid period is somewhat lampooned in the Hellenistic Book of Esther, where Haman warns Ahasuerus of a potential rebellion of the Jews in the realm (Est 3:8). Although a practical impossibility in historical reality given the vulnerability of Jews as a minority community (especially in the eastern Diaspora), the text preserves a memory of the degree to which rebellion was a real problem for the Achaemenids.[71]

This reality challenged the impregnability of the Myth and became a source of anxiety within the Jewish scribal establishment. Jewish scribes in Jerusalem shared a common imperial-sacral curriculum, but their responses to it differed significantly according to older concepts and values, some of which were well-served by Persian imperialism. Others, by contrast, saw less alignment and continuity between Persian-inflected notions of scribal identity and those they inherited from their ancestral forebears. Works that passed through the hands of Aaronides were, unsurprisingly, supportive of the Myth and its schematics of power and authority. Other priestly scribal works produced by non-Aaronides of the era were more cautious about the durability and scope of the Myth and its applicability to Jewish life and institutions. Others still were unrestrained about their repudiation of it. What is clear, though, is that toward the latter decades of the Persian empire, Jewish scribes were immersed in creating works that navigated the past in conversation with the imperial ideology of their own day, and in ways that varied dramatically. In the following chapter, we will examine how this scribal anxiety is expressed in approaches to the redaction of Ezra-Nehemiah and the reframing of Ezra's mission according to Achaemenid schemas.

3

Accommodating Empire

The Mythologizing of Ezra's Mission

Ezra-Nehemiah is neither a work of "history" or historiography nor strictly a fictional work. Laura Carlson Hasler identifies it as a "fantasy," a narrative that encodes contradictory and unresolved desires and needs from a community reacting to the ubiquity and cumulative trauma of imperial experiences.[1] Hasler's characterization holds much appeal and dovetails with Bob Becking's argument that the narrative should be understood as a myth that constructs a retrospective rendition of Yehudite Jewish identity.[2] This is the perspective I adopt in what follows, and like all myths, it can be mined for a sense of how historical experiences and cultural agendas shaped its rhetorical, linguistic, and ideological profile, telling us something about the concerns of its redactors active in the late Persian period and why they reframed the materials they inherited.[3]

Overall, Ezra-Nehemiah bears the stamp of an Aaronide worldview. Its shape repeatedly draws attention to the importance of the Jerusalem temple and its cult, its vessels, and its priestly faculty.[4] To be sure, earlier sources with less priestly centered priorities remain discernible, but these sources have been submerged within a narrative that supports the ritual authority of Aaronides and the Pentateuch. The work's opening verses establish these priorities, and it is through the prism of temple reconstruction through imperial mandate—highlighting pilgrimage to spaces of priestly power and sources of priestly social authority—that everything else in the work is refracted.[5] In this, we may see the work of a scribal group closely related to the priest-scribes who redacted the Pentateuch, not only because the concept of *torah* is so prominent throughout, but also because multiple and once-independent older sources have been similarly preserved with relatively detectable boundaries.[6]

As most scholars agree, the vast majority of these sources were composed during the Persian period. Despite some arguments to the contrary, the book's primary redaction derives from the late Persian period, at a time

An Empire Far and Wide. Mark Leuchter, Oxford University Press. © Oxford University Press 2024.
DOI: 10.1093/oso/9780197772744.003.0004

56 AN EMPIRE FAR AND WIDE

when its redactors had cause to reaffirm commitment to the myth against the background of political uncertainty. The presentation of Moses within Ezra-Nehemiah is one potent indication of a redactional shaping during the lifespan of Achaemenid hegemony: A detailed study by Yishai Kiel shows that the Moses discourse in the book closely matches concepts of Zoroaster and Mazdean religious ideology.[7] The reframing of Moses and the Pentateuch along these lines should direct us to reconsider the characterization Ezra, a figure whose towering stature in post-Persian Jewish lore should be traced to the careful literary arrangement of biblical narratives about his activity.[8] Although these narratives can be mined for historical information, their primary value rests in what they reveal about how priest-scribes of the era understood their role in the transmission of and accommodation to the myth.

Scholarly Approaches to Ezra-Nehemiah

There was a time when the view shared by many was that the narrative material in Ezra 1–6 reflected the work of a writer who lived close to or even during the late sixth century BCE, providing testimony to the events he and his initial audience both witnessed and remembered from their own personal experience. Scholars also overwhelmingly agreed that the ensuing materials in Ezra 7–10 and the Nehemiah Memoir (Neh. 1–6*, 12–13*) similarly presented details and recollections of the historical Ezra and Nehemiah and were drawn from their own writings. In this reconstruction, both figures were active in the mid-fifth century BCE during the reign of Artaxerxes I. A notable minority of scholars took issue with one dimension of this reconstruction, namely, that Ezra's activity should not be dated to the reign of Artaxerxes I but rather to that of Artaxerxes II, placing his mission in the year 398 BCE after Nehemiah's period of activity.[9]

The discussion has shifted significantly in more recent decades, especially regarding the compositional origins of major blocks of material within Ezra-Nehemiah. Most scholars still see much in the Nehemiah Memoir as a product of Nehemiah's own compositional hand, although not as an uninflected account of events. Even among scholars who view the reports in Ezra 7–10/Nehemiah 8–10 as drawn from memoirs of events, there is recognition that these sources underwent significant redactional shaping. Most researchers still view the composition of these materials in the late Persian period, using materials culled from oral and written records spanning several centuries of Achaemenid rule.[10] For instance, the lists in Ezra 2/Nehemiah 7 and elsewhere reflect demographic conditions of periods well beyond that to which they have been assigned in Ezra-Nehemiah, and the various edicts and letters may reflect memories of actual proclamations and correspondence but are, likewise, products of later writers.

This is especially the case with the most significant letter in Ezra-Nehemiah, namely, the Artaxerxes Rescript in Ezra 7:12–26. Although it has much in common with what we know of official administrative letters, it also departs from those documents in significant ways.[11] It does not follow the structure of correspondence from the imperial court, it contains flourishes that resonate with post-Persian conditions more at home in the Ptolemaic period, and some commentators argue that its Aramaic form seems distinct from the grammar and syntax of Achaemenid-era Aramaic. Most scholars now conclude that it is a hermeneutical composition—a "midrash" as David Janzen has called it—added late in the development of Ezra-Nehemiah.[12] It may well have originated in the Persian period with Jewish scribes cultivating an Ezra tradition, but it is more a product of mythmaking than of imperial administrative interest (and its literary form likely continued to developed down into the Hellenistic period).[13]

A significant number of scholars in the last two decades have advocated for a much later historical setting for the composition of these materials, arguing that the texts must have emerged only in Hellenistic times when Jerusalem's political and demographic character matched the implications of the text's surface features. So, for example, the account of Nehemiah's wall project must reflect a much later era in the second century BCE, when there is sufficient archaeological evidence to support the existence of a substantial wall surrounding the city.[14] A similar late-dating ethos attends the view that the Aramaic linguistic forms in Ezra 4–6 and Ezra 7, along with their departures from imperial correspondence, are evidence of late composition.[15] Finally, a growing number of scholars question whether there was ever an early literary interrelation between the Ezra and Nehemiah materials.[16] Arguments along these lines propose that earlier Ezra material had not yet obtained written form because later writers like Ben Sira and the author of II Maccabees do not mention Ezra, or that if the Ezra material did exist as an independent corpus, the aforementioned writers were unaware of it.[17]

Each of these points, however, is problematic. First, the position that a text must derive from a specific historical setting because its thematic features seem at home in such a setting is faulty. Benjamin Sommer has deftly shown

58 AN EMPIRE FAR AND WIDE

how such an approach to dating is untenable, placing arbitrary limits on the date of a text that ignore additional possibilities beyond a strictly realist concept of the authors' goals or interests.[18] The narrative of Nehemiah's wall building does not demand that the author lived at a time when Jerusalem had a wall; such a one-to-one ratio between an author's quotidian reality and a text's contents is reductive and leaves little room for symbolic discourse. This narrow reading of the texts in Ezra-Nehemiah extends to the evaluation of its Aramaic units and warrants a similar criticism. Scholars who identify Aramaic linguistic forms exclusively as late do not reckon sufficiently with evidence suggesting earlier diversity of Aramaic formulation, as H. G. M. Williamson has addressed.[19] Late linguistic forms can also be introduced into the transmission of material composed much earlier; scribes from the Hellenistic era recopying older documents likely altered some forms of expression to reflects the changes in Aramaic that were fixtures of their own day.

This does not mean that a text like Ezra 7 actually derives from a royal edict. It constitutes a scribal adaptation of imperial edicts, but this constitutes its own form of authenticity. Scribal adaptation is, as we have seen, an expression of their place as cultivators of esoteric knowledge licensed through imperial support.[20] As Hasler has shown, the collection and arrangement of these materials must be viewed in conversation with the function of imperial archives as loci of administrative authority and historical memory.[21] The archival form of Ezra-Nehemiah mimics Persian institutions, and at least one of its episodes (Neh. 8) directly references features of Persian imperial ritual iconography as a source of authority.[22] Although Hellenistic-era writers did periodically invoke Achaemenid precedent,[23] it is unlikely that a Hellenistic-era author engaged Achaemenid-era ritual iconography in an authoritative manner following the catastrophic fall of the Persian empire. The books of Daniel and Esther provide much better examples of how Jewish scribes would characterize Persian rule in works composed during the Hellenistic period.[24]

The nonmention of Ezra in Ben Sira or 2 Maccabees is not evidence that Ezra texts did not exist or were not known to these authors. The existence of traditions about Ezra did not demand that a later writer use those traditions if they did not serve the writer's interests. Hellenistic texts that do not mention one or the other figure may have more to do with the reliance upon oral traditions surrounding Ezra or Nehemiah specifically, especially since there is evidence that lore regarding these and other figures beyond the biblical sources affected the later development of those sources over time.[25] Put differently, a writer like Ben Sira or the author of 2 Maccabees had traditions *in addition* to the text of Ezra-Nehemiah that informed their compositional decisions, which means it is precipitous to claim that the texts in Ezra-Nehemiah regarding Ezra either did not exist or were unknown to these writers.

Ezra-Nehemiah and the Reign of Artaxerxes I Reconsidered

We therefore have ongoing reason to look to the sources within Ezra-Nehemiah for some indication of how Persian period writers thought about the events and figures depicted therein, including Ezra's commission. Aaron Demsky attempted to resolve the problem by suggesting that the Ezra material used a different standard of dating than the Nehemiah texts, lending the impression that one came before/after the other; in Demsky's view, they were actually contemporaries.[26] In his article, Demsky proposes that the Artaxerxes of the text is indeed Artaxerxes I, and the difficulty is resolved through recognizing different ways respective scribes accounted for the complexity of time-keeping in a multiethnic imperial society. Demsky's study did not settle the debate, but it demonstrated that there were more creative ways to approach the problem of Ezra's mission. Is the model of a written Ezra "source" the best way to account for the variety of texts that recount his activity?[27] Why do ambiguities surrounding a firm dating for Ezra's mission exist within the text in the first place? And why does the received version of the text feature lacunae that makes it difficult to fix Ezra within a definite moment in history?

Ezra 7 in Redactional and Rhetorical Terms

Central to all these questions is the relationship of Ezra to the emperor "Artaxerxes" named in Ezra 7. The current form of Ezra 7 can be divided into three parts:
    Part 1: Ezra 7:1a: temporal introduction
    Part 2: Ezra 7:1b-10: Ezra's background and credentials
    Part 3: Ezra 7:[11]12-26: the Artaxerxes Rescript

60 AN EMPIRE FAR AND WIDE

Two issues require attention, the first of which is that Ezra 7 is plainly a redactional composite. The Artaxerxes Rescript is presented as a source lifted from an official setting (v. 11) distinct from the information regarding Ezra, his lineage and his credentials occupying verses 1b–10. The Rescript dominates the chapter and functions as a hermeneutical linchpin for the entirety of Ezra-Nehemiah,[28] which reinforces the connection to Artaxerxes I. Read with an eye to the larger work, the Artaxerxes of Ezra 7 seems to be the very same king who appears in the Nehemiah Memoir and who charges Nehemiah with his executive responsibilities (Neh. 2:8–9).

But the dominance of the Rescript also serves the authority of the redactors, who have not shied away from drawing attention to the composite nature of the chapter. Ezra 7 creates the impression that its redactors were elites privy to authoritative, archival documents that were the "property of empires" (in Hasler's words),[29] and were licensed to arrange them into the sequences now found in the text. This matches the elevated social and sacral position of scribes and scribalism in the Achaemenid era.[30] With respect to Ezra 7 and its arrangement of sources, the chapter's literary topography signals that the rendition of events it presents is not only to be trusted but to be viewed as sacral and even holy.[31] But this carries a particular implication, namely, that their work reconfigures a different set of circumstances standing behind the redactional orchestration of these sources. And this in turn raises the possibility that these earlier circumstances may not have had as firm a connection to Artaxerxes I as the final form of the chapter implies.

The narrative that follows in Ezra 8, which focuses attention on the scribal and sapiential authority of Levites recruited from the city of Casiphia (vv. 15–19), provides some illumination. This narrative is best viewed as a tradition developed either during or shortly after Nehemiah's tenure, providing a propagandistic precedent for his own empowerment of Levites and assumption of control over the temple.[32] The historical Ezra, whoever he was, had left a sufficient impression upon earlier Yehudite society that he could be recruited as a *topos* for such propagandistic narratives in the second half of the fifth century BCE. But Ezra 8 reflects a degree of ambiguity regarding which Persian emperor is in view. The name "Artaxerxes" is mentioned briefly in verse 1, but all other references to in the chapter simply refer to the ruler of the day as "the king" (vv. 22, 25, and 36). "Artaxerxes" in Ezra 8:1 may be a redactional gloss motivated by the prominence of that name in Ezra 7.[33] But even if this is not the case, the generic nature of the "king" that predominates the narrative over against the single brief reference to "Artaxerxes" in verse 1 suggests that the narrative was adapted from an even earlier network of discourse about Ezra that was not firmly placed within the reign of Artaxerxes I.

The ambiguities in Ezra 8 suggest that Ezra traditions existed even *before* Artaxerxes I took the throne. This would explain why Ezra was a figure of memory subjected to a grand, stylized "officializing" decree such as the Rescript, rather than one whose record of activity was marked by the same type of documentation and firm historical referents that we find in the Nehemiah section of the book. A more significant gap in time between Ezra and Nehemiah would also explain why such *different* memories of Ezra developed among groups in Yehud (in addition to those in Ezra 7, i.e., Ezra 8; 9–10; Nehemiah 8), and why they are deployed in a way that bolsters Nehemiah's policies and positionality.[34] If an Ezra tradition existed even before the reign of Artaxerxes I, under which earlier emperor was Ezra active, and how does this relate to the redaction of sources in Ezra 7?

To answer these questions it is important to draw attention to the creative approach to history that pervades Ezra-Nehemiah. This is clearly the case with the list of early "returnees" in Ezra 2 (and Neh. 7); Oded Lipshits has shown that these lists reflect residents of the fifth century BCE, whose names were projected back into the narration of events in the late sixth century.[35] Jason M. Silverman has also argued that the historical Sheshbazzar was a late neo-Babylonian period appointee retrofitted into a grand narrative of return during the subsequent Persian period (Ezra 1).[36] All of this supports Sara Japhet's salient observation that "in the matter of chronology it is clear that the book is not built on any chronological structure that can be verified in historical-political terms."[37] I propose that the memory of Ezra has been subjected to these same processes.[38] A fresh evaluation of the details in Ezra 7:1b–10 (and vv. 1b–6 in particular) will shed light on a more specific period with which he was initially associated.

Ezra 7:1b–6 as an Independent Tradition

Ezra 7 relates that Ezra was sent to a relatively well-established community in Jerusalem described in chapters 1–6. As we have already noted, the temporal distinction is conveyed through the locution of Ezra 7:1a:

62 AN EMPIRE FAR AND WIDE

> Now after these things (*ve-aḥar ha-debarim ha-'eleh*) in the reign of
> Artaxerxes king of Persia . . .

This verse fragment is widely recognized to be a redactional seam that
connects one part of Ezra-Nehemiah to another; it may be safely assigned to
the book's final redactors in the late Persian period, stitching Ezra 1–6 into
the rest of the book.[39] Yet this is not simply a mechanical device meant to
connect separate literary scenes. We are informed that we should view Ezra's
mission as taking place well "after these things,"[40] but this expression is also
connected to "the reign of Artaxerxes," a proleptic reference to the name's
reappearance in Ezra 7:7 that itself anticipates its later appearance in the
Rescript (vv. 11–12, 21).[41] The function of "Artaxerxes" within this chapter
is thus *entirely* a product of the redactors, and an indication of a careful rhetorical design. On the *peshat* level, Ezra 7:1a binds together various eras and
events in a linear fashion. But it is precisely this neat and linear literary utility
that invites a reassessment when the component parts are decoupled and
examined on their own.

Commentators have often noted that Ezra 7:1b–5 constitutes a unified
block of material regarding Ezra's lineage;[42] Lester Grabbe has argued that the
information contained in v. 6 is a "second" way to identify Ezra that connects
to the verses which follow.[43] But this is beset by two problems. First, the lineage information in vv. 1b–5 is syntactically pedestrian on its own. Even if we
expand the range of this material to include the entirety of vv. 1–5, the unit is
narratively nonfunctional, ending with a dangling genealogy that does not resolve the narrative schematic initiated with "after these things." The information contained in these verses may come from an independent source, but the
verses themselves cannot function as a self-contained syntactical unit.

Second, the "Artaxerxes" of Ezra 7:1a and 7:7 form a frame around Ezra
7:1b–6 (*Wiederaufnahme*); this frame identifies vv. 1b–6 as a distinct and cohesive unit that does possess literary functionality and can stand on its own:[44]

> Ezra the son of Seraiah . . . the son of Zadok . . . the son of Aaron the chief priest,
> this very Ezra went up from Babylon; and he was a proficient scribe in the *torah*
> of Moses which YHWH, the god of Israel, had given; and the king granted him
> all his requests, according to the hand of YHWH his god upon him.

On their own, these verses do not demand a mid-fifth century BCE context.
There are no quoted decrees or charges, no reference to a standing temple or

temple restoration, no allusions to royal inscriptions, and so forth. Instead, vv. 1b–6 emphasize exclusively inner-Judahite tropes: Ezra's priestly lineage, his scribal training in the *torah* of Moses, and a nod to the experience of exile with the note that he "went up" out of Babylon. The only connection to Persian imperialism is the brief and ambiguous notice that Ezra's intent to administer *torah* resulted from the permission of "the king," who is not explicitly named.[45] Taken on their own, vv. 1b–6 remain focused on legacy Jewish traditions that predated Persian imperialism, even if the final verse nods to the emergence of that empire. When read on their own, Ezra 7:1b–6 do not assume any connection to Nehemiah's policies or the reign of Artaxerxes. These verses may have been textualized well into the Achaemenid dynasty, but the institutions depicted therein do not carry the imprimatur of hybridity that would come with a deep-seated experience with decades of Persian imperialism.[46]

An Early Persian Period Setting for Ezra 7:1b–6

It is difficult to determine whether what we encounter in Ezra 7:1b–6 was inherited by the chapter's redactors as an oral source, a written one, or just a general perception/public recollection. Nevertheless, a closer look at the ideas referenced in these verses provides clues to the era against which an early impression of Ezra formed. The three main features of this unit—Ezra's priesthood, his enculturation in Mosaic *torah*, and his emergence from a Babylonian community—speak to issues that dominated exilic thought and which remained predominant in the early days of the postexilic era following the demise of Babylonian imperialism. Two of these factors address sociological tensions that characterized Levite and Aaronide groups in exile; comparisons between the oracles of Ezekiel and the formation of an early version of the book of Jeremiah show that each faction claimed sacral legitimacy during this turbulent period and fostered polemical attitudes toward each other.[47]

Exilic Era Ideologies

Dalit Rom-Shiloni has shown that a polemic inhabits Ezekiel's oracles regarding exclusionary boundary markers cultivated by the exiles of 597 BCE against subsequent waves of exiles.[48] It is not too far a leap to imagine the

64   AN EMPIRE FAR AND WIDE

exilic development of the Priestly/Holiness material regarding communal holiness as an attempt to reinforce the boundaries proposed by Ezekiel, affirming the insider/outsider dynamics as a matter of Sinaitic revelation.[49] But among these newer exiles were figures aligned with Jeremiah and more closely associated with Levite identity; not surprisingly, the book of Jeremiah contains material that advocates for the inclusion of these latecomers to the already-established Jewish communities in Babylon. Jeremiah 26–45 highlights the role of Levite scribalism as an authorized vehicle for revelation and applies unilaterally to all exiles irrespective of proposed sociological hierarchies; this influenced the ongoing growth of Deuteronomistic texts by the same circle of (now exiled) authors.[50]

The end of the neo-Babylonian period did not see the sudden disappearance of these concerns, but it did see new forms of emphasis and tradition-making. The return from exile is characterized already in Deutero-Isaiah as a new Exodus (40:3–11; 41:17–20; 42:14–17; 43:1–7).[51] The concept of the exile's end is distinctively cast as a reexperienced Exodus from Egypt, determining membership within the folds of the nascent Jewish community forged through the experience of forced migration from the homeland.[52] The concept of the return from exile as a new Exodus also invokes the memory of Moses, who was inextricably linked to the preexilic Exodus traditions. The invocation of Exodus motifs would also trigger some interaction with the exilic Priestly and Deuteronomistic traditions that had each incorporated both Moses and the concept of the Exodus into their textual discourses (legal or otherwise).[53]

These exilic-era concerns are woven into virtually every verse of Ezra 7:1b–6, but the rhetoric of the passage creates a paradigm where they are resolved in the person of Ezra himself. He is a priest of both Zadokite (via both Seraiah and Zadok in vv. 1b–2) and Aaronide heritage (via the reference to Aaron in v. 5) and thus a scion of the P/H ideology forged within those circles.[54] Yet—as highlighted by the deictic "this Ezra" in Ezra 7:6—this very same priest is also a scion of the *torah* of Moses, pointing to the language associated with the Deuteronomistic tradition fostered by Levite scribes and developed extensively during the exile in Babylon.[55] It is his emergence from Babylon that resolves the tensions between the two. In vv. 1b–6, Ezra is a synecdoche for the mythopoesis of the Exodus concept in its new, postexilic iteration. The entire restoration narrative in Ezra-Nehemiah is consciously patterned upon Pentateuchal Exodus traditions,[56] but the foundation for this lager literary project begins with the characterization of Ezra in these brief verses.

ACCOMMODATING EMPIRE   65

Yet behind this attempt at fusion is the notice that Ezra's initiative was facilitated by the Persian empire. Ezra 7:6b concludes with the notice of "the king" who "gave him" all that YHWH had provided to him. While the larger context of Ezra 7 implies that the king in question is Artaxerxes, Ezra 7:6b simply relates that the covenantal dimensions of Jewish history now unfold through Persian rule—an idea that is already attested in Deutero-Isaiah ca. 540 BCE (Isa. 44:28–45:1). The datum in Ezra 7:6 regarding his royal appointment makes clear that Ezra's ability to bring together rival theologies is a matter of a new empire replacing that of Babylon, where such rivalries flourished. Taken on its own, Ezra 7:1b–6 points to an early postexilic context when exilic issues continued to radiate with significant force.

A Temporal Setting for the Memory of Ezra's Activity

This leaves open the possibility, then, that vv. 1b–6 describe a Persian period setting closer to the end of the exile. Early Persian bids for power rested on the reconciling inner-cultural rifts or attending to insular concepts of identity in the lands now under Persian control. Both Persian and non-Persian sources inform us that Cyrus managed to secure power by restoring the worship of Marduk after tensions between the priests of Esagila in Babylon and Nabonidus.[57] It is also during this period that Cambyses recruited Udjahorresnet—in his capacity as both military officer and priest to Neith— to facilitate the perception of the ruler in local religio-cultural terms and to restore facets of traditional religious devotion in the region.[58] This extends into the reign of Darius, of course, but there is little in Ezra 7:1b–6 that speaks to any awareness of the Behistun ideology, and much to suggest alignment with pre-Behistun interests.

Because of the gulf in time and circumstance, many scholars have opted to see Ezra's mission along the lines of that of Hannaniah, an ambassador working on behalf of Artaxerxes II for similar goals among the Jews living at Elephantine, evidenced by his letter to the community at the site.[59] But Hannaniah identifies himself only as a "brother" of the Jews at the site (TAD A4.1); no further status is indicated in the papyrus document mentioning his name. In this he differs from Ezra, whose formal status markers more closely align with those of Udjahoressnet; both are identified as both "priest" and "scribe." If the historical Ezra was in fact active in a period more proximate to that of Udjahoressnet, the commonalities between the two become more

66 AN EMPIRE FAR AND WIDE

apparent.[60] Ezra's mission emerges as less focused on imposing extant imperial administrative standards than on introducing the empire as a stabilizing factor in resolving local religious tensions.

We may suggest a more precise time in which Ezra advocated for Persian interests among Jews in Yehud. A time predating the return of 521 BCE seems feasible, as Ezra would have surely been at least mentioned alongside Zerubbabel and Joshua in Ezra 2–3 if he was active at that time. The archival material preserved (or at least reflected) in Ezra 4–6 which mentions the prophets Haggai and Zechariah (Ezra 5:1–2) would also have made at least passing reference to Ezra if he was their contemporary who had left a notable impression.[61] We might also expect those very same prophets to have referred to Ezra in their oracles alongside Zerubbabel and Joshua, but they do not. The beginning of the reign of Darius I's therefore seems an unlikely background for Ezra's activity, but it also seems unlikely that his royal mission took place in the earlier reign of Cyrus. Both Ezra 1 and Ezra 4–6 clearly invoke the name of Cyrus and in a highly approving manner, and Darius took measures to incorporate Cyrus into the Achaemenid line (DB 4, 8). Had Ezra's goal of reconciling earlier Jewish traditions been commissioned by Cyrus, this would have been celebrated by Jewish scribes enculturated in Achaemenid ideology.[62]

This leaves us with another option for Ezra's historical activity: the reign of Cambyses or its immediate aftermath (530–522 BCE). We have seen that in the Behistun inscription and its mythology, Cambyses becomes a symbol of destabilization and chaos, whose reign ushered in the cosmic forces of *Drauga*. It is Darius who purges *Drauga* from the realm through the violent vanquishing of human/political enemies, eradicating the danger arising from the instability that Cambyses introduced into the empire (DB 27–35).[63] Consequently, the historiography in Ezra 1–6 is completely silent on the reign of Cambyses, excising his name from any consideration of events from the time of Cyrus (Ezra 1:1–4) down to the days of Artaxerxes I (Ezra 6:14). Even the very mention of this king's name would compromise the sacred history of the community delineated in these chapters.[64]

"After These Things": The Implications of Ezra 7:1a

We should therefore reevaluate the rhetorical implications of the "after these things" notice in Ezra 7:1a. While the fragment serves as a redactional

ACCOMMODATING EMPIRE 67

bridge between Ezra 1–6 and the chapters that follow, the foregoing proposal suggests that it also restructures time. Philip Yoo has addressed the way the phrase is used in the book of Genesis to compensate for gaps in temporal information or to address obscurities in temporal sequences.[65] It is telling, then, that the phrase appears here. The fragment's rhetoric builds a narrative sequence more interested in a mythology of Jewish imperial identity than in recounting a sequence of historical events in chronological order.[66] The literary framework of the material is structured in a linear manner, but the sources placed within this plotline have been abstracted from disparate contexts to construct it. The earlier tradition attending Ezra 7:1b–6 set it *before* "these things," not after them. But if the "before" in question was the reign of Cambyses, the "after these things" fragment in v. 1a dislodges Ezra from this volatile time and deposits him in an era of greater significance to the late Persian redactors of Ezra-Nehemiah.

Achaemenid mythology factors significantly into this literary-temporal reworking, and saturates Ezra-Nehemiah overall: Ezra 1–3 stress the return of the *golah* group to their "proper place," the letters in Ezra 4–6 position the decrees of the emperors as the basis for social and cosmic order, the Nehemiah Memoir takes up its *taxa* and applies it to his political enemies, and even the reading of the *torah* in Nehemiah 8 is characterized as a Persian liturgy supporting the will of the empire's chief deity.[67] With so definitive an imperial mythology in place, Ezra's enduring legacy was itself under threat, guilty by association with Cambyses and the framework of danger he symbolized. The resituating of Ezra 7:1b–6 into a setting well *after* the time of Cambyses removes any possibility that Ezra might be perceived, in any way, as a residual agent of *Drauga* that dominated the "before time" period between the death of Cyrus and the rise of Darius.

This was, to be sure, a reckoning with the *realia* of Jewish discourse and ideology regarding imperial attitudes toward Cambyses and enduring local traditions regarding Ezra. The varied narratives into which he factors within Ezra-Nehemiah reveal that different corners of the Yehudite community already regarded him as a sort of patron-saint of their respective interests. We find Ezra as the champion of the *haredim* (Ezra 9:4, 10:3), an exponent of priesthood (Ezra 7:14–17), and a leader of the Levites (Ezra 8:15–19/Neh. 8:1–12), all of which presuppose the towering status of Ezra in Jewish identity in the Persian period attested in Ezra 7:1b–6. But by abstracting Ezra 7:1b–6 from an earlier era and situating it "after these things," Ezra's connection to Cambyses is dissolved. The "king" in v. 6b thereby becomes the "Artaxerxes" of Ezra 7, a ruler whose name and prominence is already anticipated in the material in Ezra 4–6 (4:6–8, 23; 6:14).

Additional support for this is found in the rhetoric of Tattenai's letter in Ezra 5, which James D. Moore has shown to be the product of a Jewish scribe rather than an authentic administrative document.[68] The letter deliberately obscures the chain of royal authority standing behind the command to rebuild the Jerusalem temple.[69] Moore suggests that this is a matter of a Hellenistic-era crediting of the temple's restoration to a growing collection of lore regarding Cyrus.[70] But in light of the mythological profile of Ezra-Nehemiah overall and the demands of Achaemenid mythology, another possibility is that the reframing of the temple account obscures details showing some connection to Cambyses. This is consistent with the reframing of Ezra's mission as a concern of Persian period writers guided by imperial ideologies and their cognitive strictures. In both cases, the text creates a narrative that sits between the memory of history and the mythological demands of communal identity, and as a result, the connection to a figure representing the threat of *Drauga* is severed.

We encounter here a logic akin to Silverman's proposal, regarding Sheshbazzar, whose identity is purged of features from an era that came before Persian imperialism.[71] The redactors of Ezra-Nehemiah have done the same with Ezra, replacing earlier perceptions with one governed by the new literary context in which his name appears. In the case of Sheshbazzar the transfer is from one imperial context to another (Babylonian to Persian); for Ezra, the move obviously involves a Persian timeframe, but from a threatening period to one characterized by the stability of a long-entrenched Achaemenid dynasty. Just as Darius's recruitment of Udjahorresnet "resets" that Egyptian figure's record of accomplishments as consistent with Achaemenid ideology (and notably, following his temporary residence in Susa);[72] so, too, does the literary presentation of Ezra 7 "reset" the memory of Ezra through his own residency in the east (Ezra 7:7–9) under a ruler following in the typological mold of Darius, bearing the same power of heaven.[73]

Implications for the Mythic Reframing of Ezra's Mission

If the historical Ezra was active long before the reign of Artaxerxes I, the reason for the ambiguities surrounding which Artaxerxes is intended in Ezra

ACCOMMODATING EMPIRE   69

7 come into clearer focus. The loose reference to "Artaxerxes" rather than a concrete specification that it was Artaxerxes I (or II) would facilitate the literary abstracting of a well-known figure like Ezra from the sixth century BCE and into a later period while drawing attention away from more limiting details. This is not the first time that deliberate ambiguity has been used for similar literary purposes: one thinks of the Exodus narrative featuring unnamed Pharaohs, whose identities are never enumerated in order to broaden the mythological applicability of the tradition to diverse groups with disparate memories of past experiences. This helps explain why Ezra's mission is so often likened to that of Moses in the reception history of this material from late antiquity down to the era of modern critical research.[74]

This also carries implications for why the era of "Artaxerxes" is left somewhat open in Ezra 7. By the final decades of the Persian period, Artaxerxes I became the namesake of three subsequent emperors: Artaxerxes II (404–358 BCE) and Artaxerxes III (358–338 BCE) and Artaxerxes IV (338–336 BCE). The ultimate or penultimate redaction of Ezra-Nehemiah is most likely to be set in the reign of the Artaxerxes III, which saw attempts to reconnect with more auspicious conventions of earlier days, and well as one that saw royal reinforcement for local agents loyal to imperial interests.[75] This provided a fitting time for Jewish adherents to Achaemenid mythology to follow in-step and construct their own mythic narrative of the past, and one that was similarly triangulated around the name "Artaxerxes." It also turns Ezra-Nehemiah into a sort of Artaxerxes "archive" (following Hasler's work), fixing that throne-name as a centrifugal force in the mythopoesis of Jewish life under Persian imperialism.[76]

Finally, the foregoing reveals an additional support for Blenkinsopp's arguments for a connection between the *haredim* of Ezra 9–10 and Isaiah 65–66. The Isaiah oracles attest to the presence of a proto-sectarian group of that name originating in the late sixth century BCE.[77] Because Blenkinsopp took Ezra to be a mid-fifth century figure, he concluded that this group persisted into that era and Ezra was among its members at that time. But the relationship between Ezra and the *haredim* may well have been forged around the same era that the author of Isaiah 65–66 has in view if Ezra's activity is dated to the reign of Cambyses. This carries implications for further investigation of the background to the "mixed-marriage crisis" in Ezra 9–10. The text suggests the way later authors might narrate a situation arising during a liminal and dangerous time in Persian imperial history.[78]

In Sum

The textual rendition of Ezra found in Ezra-Nehemiah emerges from the efforts of scribes to reimagine him in line with Achaemenid mythology. The role of Cambyses within traditions of memory revolving around the historical Ezra tainted the latter through association. Yet whatever Ezra accomplished during his activity left a sufficiently deep impression on Yehudite Jewish society that he could not be excised or forgotten. The redactors thus created a mythic narrative of their own, abstracting Ezra traditions from their original position in Jewish social memory and setting him in the reign of "Artaxerxes," pointing to the reign of Artaxerxes I but also suggesting the typological significance of that name that had obtained by their own time. In this way, Ezra-Nehemiah rearranges the sequence of major events in Persian period Judaism to resonate at the same frequency as the myth, accommodating Achaemenid hegemony. In the next chapter, we will see how a different faction of Jewish scribes addressed the myth in a very different manner.

4

Negotiating Empire

The Levites and the Book of the Twelve

The reality of Levite origins (and their relationship to the Aaronide line) is remarkably complex. Textual, archaeological and anthropological evidence points to their origins as a social caste mediating between lay lineages and powerful priestly dynasties in premonarchic Israel, especially those that claimed Moses as a distant ancestor.[1] Scholars remain conflicted over how to identify the Levites of the Persian period, how many of them may have existed, where their allegiances or priorities resided, and whether they were affiliated with the *golah* or Homeland communities. I have argued elsewhere that in the early Persian period, Levites were numbered among both.[2] But whether Homeland or *golah* in affiliation, Ehud Ben Zvi is surely correct to note that "the evidence from the late Second Temple does not allow us to construe the Levites as a powerful, substantial group like that proposed by many scholars for late-Persian Yehud."[3] Levites were all forced to abide by the new temple-based pecking order under the Aaronides and the cultic system they helmed.

Nevertheless, Levite scribes of this period were fully conversant with the Aramaic scribal methods promulgated in Yehud. The production of Chronicles, a late Persian text that can be assigned to Levite authorship, features the full range of intellectual methods that characterizes the scribal elite of the time.[4] But Chronicles also features a very different approach to Achaemenid mythology than that witnessed in Ezra-Nehemiah. Chronicles repeatedly qualifies legacy Jewish ideas according to Achaemenid schemas, but also abstracts Achaemenid ideologies and conventions, writing them back into pre-Persian Jewish institutions and assigning them to ancestral figures from earlier Jewish history.[5] Chronicles theoretically negotiates aspects of legacy Jewish identity and the contemporaneous demands of Persian imperialism, especially with regard to the concept of Jewish political leadership and traditions of monarchy. The very same type of negotiation features

An Empire Far and Wide. Mark Leuchter, Oxford University Press. © Oxford University Press 2024.
DOI: 10.1093/oso/9780197772744.003.0005

72   AN EMPIRE FAR AND WIDE

prominently in the Book of the Twelve, redacted by the same group of Levite scribes at roughly the same point in the history of Achaemenid rule.[6]

The Book of the Twelve as a Levite Work

The redaction history of the Book of the Twelve is complex, and countless redaction-critical studies have attempted to identify layers of composition and glosses that built independent oracular units into larger corpora.[7] Debate continues regarding the stages behind the development of the Book of the Twelve, and alternative versions of the work raise questions about authoritative/fixed editions and their historical background.[8] Yet alternate versions are best understood as departures from the version that we currently possess, one whose features reflect a deliberate rhetorical shaping.[9] Although the majority of material within the Book of the Twelve originated well before the rise of Persia, the definitive form of the work is widely regarded as a product of scribes working in the mid to late fourth century BCE.[10] It was at this time that earlier, briefer oracular collections were redacted onto a single scroll; although this is periodically understood as part of an effort to merely preserve these oracles, this redactional enterprise yielded a new model for reading, teaching, and interpreting prophetic texts as literary works.

That the scribes responsible for this were Levites is evident from a variety of factors. First is the rhetorical framework of the book, which opens and closes with two prophetic works steeped in Levite thought and language, namely, Hosea and Malachi. This provides a levitical framework to the entire document, qualifying its various contents as "Levite" and indicating that prophecy was entrusted to Levite scribes.[11] Second, as James Nogalski notes, is the regular introduction of liturgical material that punctuates the book at regular intervals. While Levites active in the temple cult read prophetic texts in ritual contexts, the redactors of the Book of the Twelve flip the script, so to speak, by bringing cultic language into the textual forum.[12] Among these liturgical formulations is the "grace formula" found across the Book of the Twelve that also appears in the Levites' prayer in Nehemiah 9:17, suggesting that the formula was a well-established Levite maxim utilized in ritual performances.

But the third and most relevant factor is what concerns us here: the careful structuring of the book around the repeated references, explicit in distinct ways, to Moses. In the Pentateuchal sources, Moses is crucial in delimiting the relationship with foreign nations: he liberates Israel from Egypt, he brokers interaction with Midianite-Kenites, he negotiates Israel's passage through foreign territory en route to Canaan, and his parting words establish strict boundaries between Israel and the Canaanites themselves. Even the late-monarchic prophet Jeremiah extends the international/intercultural aspect of Moses' status, since Jeremiah's own discourses on Judah's relations to foreign nations (MT Jer. 46–51) and his repudiation of illicit practices are conditioned by his status as a "prophet like Moses" (Jer. 1:9; cf. Deut. 18:15–18).[13] The Book of the Twelve therefore sits in a well-entrenched tradition where the figure of Moses functions as a ballast for the variety of topics covered within its chapters.

Another role for Moses in the Book of the Twelve can be identified when we recall that the redactors of the Pentateuch deployed the memory of Moses in "sealing" that work (Deut. 34:10–12). By contrast, the redactors of the Book of the Twelve unlock the Moses tradition and reinfuse it into the history of prophecy covered in their work. By doing so, the Levite redactors affirm their own much earlier connection to Moses as the patron saint of their order in the pre-Persian period.[14] The reliance on Moses as a structuring device is a clear departure from the rhetorical implications of the final verses of the Pentateuch and thus a departure from the idea of the Pentateuch as the exclusive repository of Mosaic legacy. This also departs from what we encounter in Ezra-Nehemiah in terms of the role the Pentateuch was to play in the mythologization of Jewish life under Persian rule.

References to Moses within the Book of the Twelve

We will begin our examination with Hosea not only because Hosea is the first unit in the Book of the Twelve, but because Hosea is among the earliest of the prophets whose oracles are preserved in the work.[15] The placement of Hosea within the Book of the Twelve returns us to the days of Assyria, the foreign empire in power during that prophet's activity. This is significant because as we have seen, the Achaemenids sought to forge continuity between their empire and the neo-Assyrian empire of earlier times, a continuity that the biblical record acknowledges. By starting the Book of the Twelve with the first prophet to "take on" foreign empires in his oracles, the redactors situate Persia within a much longer expanse of imperialism and suggest that the

74　AN EMPIRE FAR AND WIDE

words of "former prophets" (Zech. 1:4) of earlier days like Hosea are every bit as forceful even in much later eras.

But starting the Book of the Twelve with Hosea is rhetorically significant from the Levite perspective as well. Many scholars since Hans Walter Wolff have identified dimensions of Hosea's oracles that intersect with Levitical traditions, and Stephen Cook has made a strong case for the prophet's actual Levite heritage.[16] The majority of commentators have also observed that Hosea's oracles are set in a northern-Ephraimite context,[17] and it is among Ephraimite circles that traditions about Moses initially took root. Early Levite Moses lore (adapted from even earlier Moses traditions in emergent Israel) was appropriated by agents of the royal court of Jeroboam I to form a charter myth for the northern monarchic state in the late tenth century BCE.[18] The sidelining of Levites from state religion led to a sustained response against this myth, with Levite countermyths utilizing the trope of Moses to criticize what they viewed as the aberrations of monarchic culture and religion.

It is from this wellspring of tradition that Hosea forms his protests against northern society: the kings fall prey to his invectives, as do the people, but his criticism is primarily aimed at the priests on the royal payroll who promoted the state mythology that used Moses to justify monarchic mores. Hosea's oracles allude to a number of traditions elsewhere connected to Moses— such as the Golden Calf tradition (Hos. 8:1–6)—but these build to a distinct rhetorical unit within the book, Hosea 12–14, where a final cosmic drama is played out.[19] And it is here where we find a more focused reference to Moses:

> Jacob fled to the land of Aram;
>> there Israel served for a wife,
>> and for a wife he guarded sheep.
> But by a prophet (*ube-nabi'*) YHWH brought Israel up from Egypt,
>> and by a prophet (*ube-nabi'*)he was guarded. (Hos. 12:13–14)

There is broad scholarly consensus that the "prophet" (*nabi'*) in this passage is Moses, for no other figure in Ephraimite lore was more firmly associated with the Exodus tradition. Hosea's reference to Moses is typological: he is the prophet who sustained Israel as they emerged from Egypt, but Hosea's Exodus mythology is one that sees the emergence from Egypt as a mythic concept that informs Israelite identity across diverse historical epochs.[20] For Hosea, the historical Moses is the prototype for other prophets who become the Moses of their own eras as they once again liberate Israel from whatever forces manifest the typology of Egyptian threat and oppression.[21]

The background to this is decidedly political, as the figure of Moses was used in state religious rituals to reinforce the sanctity of the northern monarchic office.[22] Hosea's rhetoric fires back against this, reclaiming Moses from a political context that benefitted monarchic hierarchies and economies. The implications for the Aaronide use of Moses within the Pentateuch to uphold the mythology of Achaemenid rule is obvious, and reveals that the late Persian period Levites remained aware of the background to Hosea's rhetorical motivation from centuries earlier. To begin the Book of the Twelve with the oracles of Hosea (especially when the superscription for Amos makes clear that Amos pre-dated Hosea) is to declare that all of the prophets within the work are prophets like Moses, whose words sustain the identity boundaries of Israel in different historical periods. This implies, consequently, that the Levite redactors follow in their footsteps: they take up the Mosaic mantle through their scribal enterprise, and their sociological priorities were thereby legitimized.

We now turn to Micah, whose book is situated directly in the center of the Book of the Twelve. In and of itself, there is little in the book of Micah that one might identify as specifically "Levitical." The superscription identifies Micah with a rural Judahite town, his language represents the worldview of Judahite agrarianism, and the most potent oracle in the book places the blame for Judah's ills squarely on the shoulders of northern refugees (which included Levites) whose influence in Jerusalem has led to corruption and social ruptures.[23] Yet many commentators have observed that the ideology informing Micah's worldview has strong points of contact with that of Deuteronomy and the Deuteronomistic History, both of which are the products of Levite scribes residing in late monarchic Judah.[24] The Deuteronomistic embrace of Micah's ideology involved the embrace of Micah's oracles themselves: the book of Jeremiah bears witness to this in its equation of Jeremiah's oracles as consistent with those of Micah (Jer. 26:17–19). By the exilic period—which saw a substantial shaping of the Jeremiah tradition—Levite groups had accepted Micah's worldview as consistent with their own and presented their literature as an expression of Micah's value system.[25]

This exilic-era engagement with Micah facilitated the Levite redactors' adoption of Micah's oracles within the Book of the Twelve. The placement of these oracles in the center of the work aligned it with the Jeremiah tradition's

76 AN EMPIRE FAR AND WIDE

citation of Micah and the Deuteronomistic recruitment of Micah's world-view. But it also established that legacy agrarian values lay at the heart of the ideology of Levites with connections to the Jerusalem temple. Cook has demonstrated that Micah's language is carefully designed to invoke pre-state (and therefore pre-Jerusalemite) agrarian institutions as essential to Israelite identity.[26] Following the raw invective in Mic. 3:9–12, the sequence of the oracles in the book build to a crescendo in the covenantal lawsuit-*rîb* found within Mic. 6:1–4:

> Hear what YHWH says: rise, plead your case before the mountains,
>> and let the hills hear your voice.
> Hear you mountains the controversy of YHWH,
>> and you enduring foundations of the earth;
>> for YHWH has a controversy with his people,
>> and he will contend with Israel.
> 'O my people, what have I done to you?
>> In what have I wearied you? Answer me!
> For I brought you up from the land of Egypt,
>> and redeemed you from the house of slavery;
>> *and I sent before you Moses, Aaron, and Miriam.* (Mic. 6:1–4)

The reference to Moses in this passage contrasts the dire straits of monar-chic Israel's social reality with the remembered and idealized premonarchic past. In so doing, Micah (or whoever stands behind these verses) appeals not only to Moses, but also to Aaron and Miriam. Commentators often view these verses as a late Deuteronomistic addition to the book of Micah, thus downplaying the reference to Moses, Aaron and Miriam in Mic 6:4 as a sec-ondary gloss.[27] But even if the passage shows signs of adjustment emerging from successive stages of scribal transmission, there is much in the *rîb* that does not require assigning it to postmonarchic hands. Mic. 6:4 is very much at home within the *rîb*—this genre of prophetic speech regularly appeals to ancient agrarian ideals in critiquing the sins of later monarchic-era culture.

The appeal to Moses alongside both Aaron and Miriam aligns with Micah's interest in prestate institutions and social values. It does not hold a view where Moses stands above either of these other figures; rather, it suggests a time before such hierarchies were constructed, when each figure was equally and perhaps independently venerated by different groups in Emergent Israel.[28] That an appeal such as Mic. 6:4 is placed in the middle of the Book of the Twelve suggests that the rhetorical implications of the Pentateuch's closing verses, which privileges the Aaronides, do not represent the original nature of Moses' place in Israelite religion, and that even a Judahite prophet of the eighth century affirmed this and positioned his own oracular pronouncements as iterations of Mosaic revelation.

We finally now turn to the reference to Moses at the end of the book of Malachi:

> Remember the teaching of my servant Moses (*torat moshe 'abdi*), the statutes and ordinances that I commanded him at Horeb for all Israel. Lo, I will send you the prophet Elijah (*'elyah hanabi'*) before the great and terrible day of the Lord comes. He will turn the hearts of parents to their children and the hearts of children to their parents, so that I will not come and strike the land with a curse. (Mal. 3:22–24)

This invocation of Moses—specifically, to *torat moshe 'abdi*—is read by some as a reference to the Pentateuch as part of a legitimizing process or even, as van der Toorn suggests, as a proto-canonizing move.[29] I am more hesitant than van der Toorn to see something resembling canonization involved in the Malachi passage, but it does seem likely that scribes behind these verses were interested not simply in completing a collection of Malachi oracles but, rather, in providing a seal of sorts to the entire Book of the Twelve that recalled the seal closing the Pentateuch in Deuteronomy 34:10–12. By the time the redactors of the Book of the Twelve set about their project, the Pentateuch predominated as the foundation text for the Jerusalemite temple cult, so a phrase like *torat moshe* nods to the Pentateuch's existence but also, following Lambert, subsumes it within a wider intellectual phenomenology.[30] But the verse goes one step further than the role Moses plays in the closing seal of the Pentateuch—here, the invocation of the Pentateuch itself "seals" the Book of the Twelve.

While Mal. 3:22 alludes to the Pentateuch in this manner, the locution of the verse dislodges Moses from the literary/textual strictures of that document. The addition of the term *'abdi* emphasizes Moses the man in social, historical and mythological context rather than the Aaronide document that claimed the encapsulate Moses' revelatory legacy. As with Hosea, Moses once again becomes a prophet in a series of other prophets; the invocation suggests that the Pentateuch is not a stand-alone charter myth that empowers the Aaronides by altogether skipping over a history of prophecy.[31]

78   AN EMPIRE FAR AND WIDE

Rather, Moses' identification as an *'ebed* of YHWH in Mal. 3:22 is immediately followed by the reference to Elijah the prophet (*'elyah hanabi'*) in the following verse . . . suggesting that what makes Moses YHWH's *'ebed* is his status as a prophet, and that this typology extended beyond his lifetime. This reemphasizes prophetic voices of a Mosaic timbre in literary works that extend down into the Persian Period, entrusted to the Levites who stood behind the Book of the Twelve.

In this paradigm, Moses is no longer an archetype of the distant past whose authority is directly transferred to the Aaronides. Instead, he appears among a group of prophets who repeatedly cite each other even as they appear to cite him.[32] These are indeed prophets like Moses—Moses predates them, but does not outrank them. What is more, the scribal authority of the Levite redactors of the book made *them* the living embodiments of the prophetic legacy they had shaped. The final verses of the Pentateuch added by the Aaronides obscure this by attempting to create an unbridgeable rift between Moses and the leadership types that followed after him. By contrast, the Book of the Twelve eliminates this rift by making Moses' *torah* not an ossified text but a still-living process that operated beyond ritual and imperial mythologies.[33]

Moses as an Alternative to the Achaemenid Emperors

In the Book of the Twelve, Moses becomes a prototype upon which prophetic identity is repeatedly fashioned. The redactors take steps in this direction by drawing, ironically, from the imagery of the Persian emperors that accompanied royal inscriptions and reliefs. We will recall the typological uniformity of these reliefs: the imagery depicting Darius is reproduced in the reliefs commissioned by his successors over the texts of their inscriptions. The rhetorical effect of this aesthetic strategy is that all the Achaemenid rulers were typologically identical, each filling the mythological and sacral role of their predecessors, irrespective of their unique actions or policies, or the particular content of each inscription. The "Persian Man" was embodied—in royal iconography—by every emperor.

The invocation of Moses within the Book of the Twelve serves the same purpose, persistently folding the message of each oracular unit from disparate prophets into a shared symbolic category. In the place of Darius we find Moses; in the place of succeeding rulers we find the variety of Mosaic prophets, in the place of formulaic royal rhetoric we find repeated lemmas across these prophetic books. This gives us a new way to understand the function of Hosea in the book's opening frame, for it is Hosea who invokes Moses according to typology rather than by name.[34] In the context of the Book of the Twelve, this Mosaic statement both looks forward to the oracles in the remainder of the book and backward to the earlier history of prophecy, starting with Moses but extending to figures such as Samuel, Nathan, Ahijah and Elijah.[35] And by preserving the words of prophets who themselves appear to read and transmit the words of prophets, the redactors position themselves within this trajectory of sacral stewardship.[36]

The Use of *Torah* and Legal Terminology in the Book of the Twelve

The Moses discourse weighs heavily upon references to *torah* as "law" or "instruction" in the Book of the Twelve. As we have seen, the construction of the Book of the Twelve must be understood in light of the Pentateuch, the laws in which served hermeneutical and rhetorical purposes rather than statutory ones. On a case by case basis, the term *torah* and related legal language (*mishpat, ḥoq,* etc.) within the Book of the Twelve may relate to a specific ritual or legal instruction, but the collective implications of these terms unfolds a tableau of authorized order and the right to reach authorized decisions as a matter of cosmic consequence. While these *torah*-related terms appear peppered throughout the oracles collected in this document, it will be more productive to survey their role as a structuring device akin to the structuring role of Moses discussed above. And like the Moses references, *torah*-related language appears strategically throughout the work.

We turn, once again, to Hosea's oracles, the contents of which are (mostly) authentically northern and Levite in orientation and construct an image of a priestly prophet qualified to take up legal concepts as the building blocks of his oracles.[37] Scholars often draw attention to Hos. 8:1, where the term *torah* is used explicitly:

Set the horn (*shofar*) to your mouth. As a vulture he comes against the house of YHWH; because they have transgressed my covenant (*beriti*) and trespassed against my law (*torati*).

80   AN EMPIRE FAR AND WIDE

The larger context of the chapter makes clear that the threat conveyed in this verse relates to Israel's interaction with Assyria (v. 9) and the way this has compromised Israel's theological fidelity. The language of this verse is saturated in the language one would expect from a Levite with priestly enculturation: the *shofar* as a ritual instrument initiating battle, the highlighting of YHWH's covenant (*berit*), and the paralleling of this covenant with the idea of *torah*. The question is whether *torah* here connotes general priestly instruction in covenant or a written text with divine traits.

The concept of priestly teaching is earlier addressed in Hosea 4, which is famously structured as a *rîb*. The chapter enumerates the transgressions not only of the nation but of its priestly caste, and the chapter's opening verses cite a litany of transgressions:

> Hear the word of YHWH, you children of Israel! For YHWH has a *rîb* with the inhabitants of the land, because there is no truth, nor mercy, nor knowledge of God in the land. Swearing and lying, and killing, and stealing, and committing adultery, they break all bounds, and blood touches blood.

Many scholars have noted that these transgressions closely match the prohibitions in the second half of the Decalogue, and have suggested that this constitutes an explicit appeal to the Decalogue as an authoritative legal collection well known already by the mid-eighth century BCE.[38] If this were the case, then the reference to *torah* in Hos. 8:1 could conceivably relate to an established body of teaching and possibly one that had obtained textual form. But such a view is difficult to sustain, as more contemporary research points to a late eighth–seventh century BCE context for the written composition of the Decalogue, and one strongly informed by a formal (Jerusalemite) scribal setting.[39] The overlaps between Hosea and the Decalogue may reflect common sources used by both rather than a linear model of literary influence. The litany of transgressions in Hosea 4:2 is less a reference to extant legal compositions than a building block en route to the creation of such works.

A subsequent oracle (Hos. 6:5) provides a much more substantial contender for just such a reference, albeit one that is encumbered by an abundance of syntactical difficulty in the MT tradition. In English translation, the text is cumbersome to say the least:

> Therefore, have I hewed them
> By the prophets I have slain them,
> By the words of My mouth
> And thy statutes (*mishpatehah*) go forth as the light.

The explicit reference to "statutes" (*mishpatehah*) places the verse within the parameters of legal discourse, but any clearer understanding of what this means is obscured by the state of the text in its current form. Virtually all commentators have observed that the verse has suffered some error in transmission; the sudden shift to a second-person address ("thy statutes") does not make sense in light of the larger passage, which speaks on behalf of the deity in the first-person voice. More significantly, the verse presents prophets as agents of destruction who have "hewed" and "slain" Israel through YHWH's word, which clashes with the mention of prophets elsewhere in Hosea's oracles either as victims and targets of public scorn (Hos. 9:7–8) or as caretakers of the people (Hos. 12:14). As with other parts of the book of Hosea, this passage demands emendation, and an old reconstruction proposed by Shalom Spiegel remains an attractive and likely way to make sense of the verse, yielding the following translation:[40]

> In rock have I hewn [them],
> Through prophets I communicated to them,
> In words of my mouth my statutes (*mishpati*) went forth
>   clearly as the light.

An attractive aspect of Spiegel's proposal is that it does not require the introduction of additional syntactical material. It restructures the textual material already present within the verse, and fits with the larger liturgical form of the material surrounding the verse. Spiegel extrapolated from this that the statutes in question were none other than the Decalogue, relying obviously on the narrative tradition regarding the Decalogue at Sinai as hewn upon stone tablets. Such a conclusion is questionable: although the Sinai motif itself is very old,[41] this does not mean that the written Sinai Decalogue was a cultural artifact with which Hosea would have been familiar.

A more likely context for understanding the reconstructed verse is the *realia* of Assyrian imperial praxis. Hosea's oracles appeal on one hand to Israel's old, prestate agrarian traditions and, on the other, to the tenuous position of the northern kingdom as a vassal of the Neo-Assyrian empire. The

82 AN EMPIRE FAR AND WIDE

superscription to Hosea's book dates his activity to roughly the same era as the Syro-Ephraimite war (734–732 BCE) or shortly thereafter, a time when both agrarian and urban populations in northern Israel were subject to Assyrian administration, taxation and, notably, propaganda. There can be little doubt that much of this propaganda circulated on the oral level within Israelite communities, but this was invariably a reaction to Assyrian textual traditions, display inscriptions and possibly propagandistic tablets that were made known to those enduring the threatening dominance of the empire.[42]

It is doubtful that many residents of the northern kingdom of Israel would have had the facility to encounter these Assyrian texts in a way that enabled them to understand their contents. But texts in the ancient world served iconic, even numinous purposes.[43] Texts in the Neo-Assyrian period were the loci of revelation; they were the voice of the gods in material form.[44] We know that the presence of such literary works in Judah throughout the late eighth–seventh centuries BCE left a tremendous impression upon Judahite scribes, affecting their stylistic, linguistic and even conceptual models for the role and function of texts in the shaping of identity. It is reasonable to propose that the northern Israelite literati were affected in a similar manner in Hosea's day.[45] The cosmic dimensions and cultural implications of Neo-Assyrian literature must have reinforced impulses to capitulate to Assyrian sovereignty among the elites of northern Israel, something against which Hosea rails at various points in his oracles (Hos. 5:13; 7:11; 11:5).

We must view the reference to divine law in Hosea 6:5 in light of this climate. A statement identifying divine law as written in stone would constitute native Israelite response to Neo-Assyrian conventions of power-projection. If Neo-Assyrian deities spoke through stone tablets and inscriptions, so too could YHWH. The later narratives regarding the composition of the Decalogue as hewn in stone are the unavoidable consequence of Hosea's rhetorical innovation. But this means that Hosea 6:5 is temporally anterior to this understanding. In our verse, we find a more general reference to law as something written: once-oral *torah* is reconceived as a written phenomenon that is subsequently taught by prophets like Hosea. The role of written law in this text, then, is not a matter of civic or ritual regulation but a trope recruited to aid in the *Kulturkampf* between Israel and foreign imperialism in the latter half of the eighth century BCE. This gives us a deeper understanding of the function of *torah* in Hos. 8:1, and it is fitting that the Book of the Twelve, redacted under the shadow of Persian rule, places such a concept at its outset.

Our next reference to *torah* occurs in Habakkuk 1:4, in the last part of the prophet's opening query (vv. 1–4):

Therefore the law is impotent (*tafug torah*) and justice (*mišpat*) never goes forth;
for the wicked besets the righteous; thus justice (*mišpat*) goes forth perverted.

At first glance, this passage seems to possess a concept of law that hovers closer to something resembling applied legislation that regulates civic society. The perversion of justice results in the proliferation of wickedness, and the situation points to a law (*torah*) that loses its potency. Scholars often connect the legal references in this verse to the Deuteronomic legislation given the common dating of the prophet to ca. 609–597 BCE,[46] a time that also saw the activity of Jeremiah and the regular appeals to Deuteronomy in that prophet's oracles. There is no *prima facie* reason to deny Habakkuk's similar interest in Deuteronomy: the pairing of *torah* and *mišpat* in Habakkuk 1:4 recalls the same pairing of these terms in Deuteronomy 33:10, and there can be little doubt that the Deuteronomistic concept of law was a going concern among the learned castes of Judah's last decades. One might also look to Habakkuk's use of the wicked/righteous language in relation to what Moshe Weinfeld termed the "wisdom substratum" of Deuteronomy.[47]

If Habakkuk's allusion in 1:4 is to the laws of Deuteronomy, however, it is unlikely that it conceives of law as a simple code of conduct. Deuteronomy itself uses the genre of law for mythopoeic purposes: the written *torah* of Deuteronomy is a cosmic boundary marker which marginalizes cosmic threats that might otherwise permeate Israelite society from without or corrode it from within.[48] Law is thus not a matter of social policy but serves cosmic and symbolic purposes, expressing YHWH's power as the divine warrior through its affirmation within the boundaries of the Israelite community. That this concept of law informs Habakkuk 1:4 is reinforced by the unit that immediately follows, namely, a vision of encroaching chaos embodied by Babylon (the Chaldeans in vv. 5–11).[49] A few select verses in this unit (Hab. 1:7–9) demand special attention:

They are terrible and dreadful; their manner (*mišpato*) and their majesty proceed from them. (v. 7)

84 AN EMPIRE FAR AND WIDE

Their horses also are swifter than leopards and are fiercer than the wolves of the desert; and their horsemen spread themselves; yea, their horsemen come from far, they fly as a vulture that hastens to devour. (v. 8)

They come all of them for violence; their faces are set eagerly as the east wind; and they gather captives as the sand. (v. 9)

In his analysis of this unit, Robert Haak argued that Habakkuk 1:7 ultimately refers to YHWH, and the term *mišpato* thus refers to the fearsome manner of the deity.[50] Such a reading is understandable given both the earlier references to mytho-cosmic figures earlier in the chapter (*šod* and *hamas* in v. 3) and in anticipation what follows in the deeply mythological hymn in Habakkuk 3. However, Haak's reading does not account for the cosmic dynamic associated with the law in Deuteronomy. In my view, it is better to read v. 7 as a reference to Babylonians or Chaldeans, with *mišpato* ("their manner") functioning as a collective singular, plus pronominal suffix. In this frightening vision of the impeding threats that Judah face, Babylon is not a political force but a natural, cosmic and elemental one: the cavalry are leopards, wolves and vultures, and collectively depicted as a blistering sandstorm emanating from the east. The order of the natural world is disrupted by their arrival—it is they who are terrible and dreadful.

Read in such a manner, the abrogation of the law in Habbakuk 1:4 is not simply a matter of offending the deity who gave it, it is a matter of opening the floodgates to cosmic chaos, and the relationship between law, nature, and the cosmos is highlighted by the strategic use of *mišpat* in 1:7. The perversion of *mišpat* rooted in the law leads to the eruption of a different, more destructive type of *mišpat*. A similar idea informs Jeremiah's understanding of the Babylonian conquest:

Who is the wise man, that he may understand this? And who is he to whom the mouth of YHWH has spoken, that he may declare it? Why is the land perishing and laid waste like a wilderness, so that none passes through? And YHWH says: Because they have forsaken my law (*torati*) which I set before them, and have not hearkened to my voice, or walked therein (Jeremiah 9:11–12)

Habakkuk and Jeremiah both share a cosmic understanding of the law, its world-making (or world-maintaining) role, and the elemental devastation that will result from Israel's inability to commit to it. Yet beyond this,

Habakkuk parts ways rather severely with Jeremiah. Within the book of Jeremiah, the prophet remains committed to Deuteronomistic principles and advocates for the maintenance of the law in adjusted forms befitting new circumstances. But the book of Habakkuk moves in the opposite direction: Habakkuk 2 deemphasizes the place of the law in the reorganization of the world, opting instead to stress the majesty and power of the *kabod* YHWH, not the name/*šem* hypostasis associated with YHWH in the Deuteronomistic tradition.[51] It is that older concept which will enter Israelite consciousness and reaggregate the devastated nation.

The closing hymn in Habakkuk 3 makes this explicit, saturated as it is with mythological imagery of the divine warrior storming forth to restructure the natural order through his terrible might.[52] Habakkuk forms an intellectual model for dismantling the Deuteronomistic understanding of law. When the concept of law is abrogated—when its *mišpat* is rendered useless—YHWH reemerges in his full and furious nature. A finite corpus of legal literature such as Deuteronomy is inadequate in expressing the scope of YHWH's power. As such, YHWH commands Habakkuk to "write the revelation" (Hab. 2:2), to produce a prophetic book, that can effectively herald the full mythological range of what is to come.[53] The implication for the Book of the Twelve seems clear: a fixed, material Pentateuch cannot be the end-all of *torah* discourse.

The final passage in the Book of the Twelve involving a reference to *torah* once again returns us to the Malachi oracles:

> The true law (*torat 'emet*) was in his mouth, and unrighteousness was not found in his lips (*bi-sefatav*); he walked with me in peace and uprightness, and turned many away from iniquity. For the priest's lips (*siftei kohen*) should keep knowledge (*da'at*), and they should seek the law (*torah*) from his mouth (*mi-pihu*); for he is the messenger of YHWH of hosts. But you are turned aside out of the way; you have caused many to stumble (*hikhšaltem*) in the law (*ba-torah*); you have corrupted the covenant of Levi, says YHWH of hosts. (Mal. 2:6–8)

We have already observed that in relation to Moses, the Malachi oracles close the Book of the Twelve precisely because they so strongly advocate the worldview of the Levite redactors in the context of a predominantly Aaronide temple cult. The entire book is a testament to Levite thinking: the priesthood is held accountable to the "covenant of Levi" (Mal. 2:4, 8) and the oracles

86 AN EMPIRE FAR AND WIDE

conclude with the notice that they are the product of "YHWH fearers" (*yir'ei YHWH*) whose devotion leads to the distinction between "the righteous and the wicked" (Mal. 3:16–18).[54] This concluding unit is steeped in wisdom language that was common among Levite discourses of the Persian period, qualifying the entire prophetic contents of the book of Malachi as a discourse on wisdom.[55]

The focus on wisdom also characterizes the reference to law in Malachi 2:6–8. While written law collections were the province of the priesthood in the early Persian period, Malachi 2:6–8 makes no reference to any such written works. Law, in this passage, is not a matter of written regulations upon which one builds social policy or through which a cultic system is governed. In fact, despite the repeated references to the role of priests in these verses, there is no discussion of the cult at all. Rather, a priest serves one purpose: to orally teach the law. The repetition of the words "lips" (*siftei, bi-sefatav*) and "mouth" (*pihu*) make clear that law here is a matter of oral pronouncement and discussion, not textual transmission or scribal training. Yet it is a wisdom term (*da'at*) that is set in parallel with *torah* in the central verse of the unit (v. 7). The claim of stumbling (*hikhšaltem*) in the law not only puns on another wisdom term (*sekel*) but recalls the similar sapiential admonition closing Hosea's oracles (*yikašlu*) in Hosea 14:10. Law may well be preserved in literary form, but in the eyes of the author of Malachi, a priest's primary use of law is to cultivate wisdom.

A sense of competition is indeed implied in the phrase "true teaching" (*torat 'emet*) at the outset of the passage, raising the question of whether or not some other form of teaching or law was somehow deficient. The word *'emet* immediately suggests its antonym: *šeqer*, falsehood. This, of course, was the charge levied by Jeremiah throughout his career against those who advocated for empty institutions, gestures and ideas.[56] The coupling of the legal language here with an (implied) intertextual reference to Jeremiah and the Babylonian conquest points to a larger rift forming within the ranks of Jerusalem's priest-scribes at the time the Malachi oracles were composed or shaped to fit their literary setting.[57] This is not entirely surprising since the redactors of the Book of the Twelve were the same scribal group responsible for Chronicles, which features and amplifies the Jeremiah tradition in its closing chapters.[58] The choice to include this concept of *torah* and its attendant implications in the closing frame of the Book of the Twelve suggests a desire by the redactors to resuscitate this dramatic polemic to address the concerns of their own day.

Prophetic *Torah* and Imperial *Data*

The foregoing examples within the Book of the Twelve reflect prophetic attitudes regarding *torah* that spanned roughly three centuries. Each represents vastly different linguistic, economic, geographic and cultural settings, but what they share is a belief that *torah* is anything but fixed, statutory, or *de rigueur*. It is instead a concept with cultural fluidity, a *topos* connected to various mythologies (divine, Israelite, priestly, sapiential, etc.). These oracles claim that *torah* is not strictly a matter of Pentateuchal law but instead point to transcendent principles expressed in other literary genres such as prophetic texts. Law is not the end result of revelation, but material manifestations of a mythic reality, a point of conceptual departure that can—must—be factored into an ongoing history of revelation. It is telling that the prophetic texts in question appear at the outset, in the center, and at the end of the Book of the Twelve, akin to the Moses discourses I have discussed in this chapter. The redactors challenge the Pentateuch's presentation of Moses and his teachings as superior to other prophetic traditions by setting its references to Moses at the beginning, middle, and conclusion of their work; each prophetic unit within the work becomes an expression of "Mosaic" prophecy and thus placed on par with the Pentateuch. By deploying *torah* in the same way, the redactors present their rendition of the term as an alternative to prevailing understandings or qualifications of the same term.

This sets up a potent alternative to prevailing Aaronide concepts of *torah* and imperial *data* such as that found in Ezra-Nehemiah. I propose that the Achaemenid *data* model here is especially useful in determining why the oft-noted cross-references in the Book of the Twelve exist. Just as each prophet becomes an iteration of Moses, each prophet is also presented as declaring and even performing prophetic *torah* as an alloform of royal *data* shared across successive Achaemenid regnal periods. This delineates boundaries for an alternative realm across both time (eighth–fifth centuries BCE) and space (monarchic Israel, monarchic Judah, various regions in Mesopotamia, extra-Jerusalemite locales in Persian Yehud, etc.). In this, the repeated lemmas found throughout the book resemble the repeated use of stereotyped imagery and formulaic language found across the range of Achaemenid monumental inscriptions and reliefs.[59]

We also see the impulse for the textual interpolation of language across literary corpora witnessed with the Behistun copy at Elephantine, here manifested in the redators' own interpolation of language from one prophetic

88 AN EMPIRE FAR AND WIDE

book into another. If Moses is an alternative to the typological emperor (the "Persian Man"), and the prophets in the Book of the Twelve are prophets like Moses (Deut. 18:15–18), then these prophets are quasialternatives or parallels to the Achaemenid rulers. Each prophet and their words (so repeatedly critical of kingship and empire) may be read against the royal inscriptions of the Achaemenid emperors, forming another path of authoritative agency. The Achaemenid rulers may transmit the *data* of Ahuramazda; the prophets in the Book of the Twelve, by contrast, are agents of YHWH, entrusted with heavenly *torah* in both material and oral forms that derive from a figure long predating the rise of Persia (*torat moshe ʿabdi* in Mal. 3:22).

In Sum

In one fell swoop, the Levite redactors of the Book of the Twelve affirm their place within the imperial network of scribal elitism while simultaneously creating distance through burrowing deeper into their native, ancestral textual traditions. They use the common methods of scribes in other places but do so to highlight their stewardship not of imperial order but of a larger realm identified and illuminated by the succession of prophets in the work they redacted. Their efforts resulted in a textual monument that paralleled Achaemenid propaganda and the Myth behind it, but also opened new vistas for conceiving of their own ethnographic and religious identity. After centuries of navigating power structures rooted in monarchy and imperialism, the goal of this literature was not to polemicize against a still-indomitable political status quo but to highlight legacy Jewish traditions regarding Moses, prophecy, and *torah* that were compatible with it. This constitutes negotiation not only with the empire but with Jewish tradition; the texts used in the Book of the Twelve were most likely recruited for use within the Aaronide temple cult supported by the Achaemenids.[60] Redacting them into a discrete literary work provided a new avenue for sustaining prophecy alongside, rather than within, an imperial crucible.

5

Repudiating Empire

The Shemihazah/Asael Narrative (1 Enoch 6–11)

The Book of Watchers (1 Enoch 1–36) is generally dated to the early to mid–third century BCE, and all commentators agree that 1 Enoch 6–11 constitutes the oldest material therein. These chapters contain a narrative of the transgressive deeds of the angels Shemihazah and Asael (the "S/A Narrative"), who convene other angels—the titular "Watchers"—to reveal illicit knowledge to humanity. The S/A Narrative was redacted into a larger work where the legendary sage Enoch receives and transmits divinely revealed knowledge, offering the reader a way through the chaos wrought by the rebellious angels. Virtually all scholars of this material see a relationship between the Pentateuch's concept of Enoch and the Enoch of the Book of Watchers—the latter is an elaborated rendition of the former—but specifics remains debated.[1] The consensus view is that during the early Hellenistic era, the Enochian writers took up a mélange of cultural traditions and forged a discourse where Enoch's interaction with the Watchers became a basis for the ongoing composition of esoteric literature among elite scribes of the era.[2] According to this view, the connection between the figure of Enoch and the S/A Narrative originated with the production of this literature.

Most have seen the S/A Narrative against the background of the wars of the Diadochi in the late fourth century BCE; some scholars, however, place it earlier, toward the end of the Persian period.[3] In this chapter I will provide additional support for the latter view, but I challenge the common assumption that Enoch and the Watchers were never connected until the Book of Watchers began to form around the S/A Narrative in the early Hellenistic period. I propose that there was an older concept of Enoch that had strong points of contact with the myth of divine beings that was later annexed by the scribes behind the S/A Narrative. As I will show below, the scribes who constructed this narrative did so with full awareness of this earlier connection, and chose to engage this material as part of a challenge to the Aaronide-led cultic system that had laid claim to these earlier traditions. This challenge

---

An Empire Far and Wide. Mark Leuchter, Oxford University Press. © Oxford University Press 2024.
DOI: 10.1093/oso/9780197772744.003.0006

90 AN EMPIRE FAR AND WIDE

was not simply a critique of the Aaronide priesthood but a repudiation of the (now-compromised) Achaemenid mythology that had empowered it.[4]

Behind the Pentateuchal Enoch

References to Enoch are found scattered throughout the Hebrew scriptures, but the most important of these are found in the early chapters of the book of Genesis. In Genesis 4, we find genealogical information situating Enoch within a larger epic story spanning Genesis 1–11 stemming from a non-P source; Genesis 5 provides us with an alternative, where a P writer presents Enoch as a prominent figure in a different type of genealogy that contributes to another view of human history before the flood. A closer look at each Pentateuchal source will reveal that they have more in common than often assumed, and draw from a much older tradition regarding the figure of Enoch.

The Enoch of P (Genesis 5)

The P account of Enoch is more complex than the non-P rendition in Genesis 4, replete with clues that the P writers inherited traditions that granted Enoch particular privileges. These include the placement of Enoch as Seth's descendant of the seventh generation, his lifespan of 365 years, his ascent to the heavens, and the "Enoch walked with *ha-'elohim*" notices in Genesis 5:22,24.[5] All of these lemmas carry sacral connotations: his preheavenly lifespan matches the days of a calendrical year and his genealogical position aligns him with the cosmic significance of the number seven in Priestly thought.[6] These point to P's understanding of Enoch as far more than an ordinary human with an ordinary life or access to ordinary knowledge. By working Enoch's interaction with *ha-'elohim* into a tale that extended the relationship beyond the flood (through Noah and his lineage) and eventually intertwined it with Israel's ancestry as a cosmic institution (via the term *toledot* in Gen. 2:4a, 6:9, and eventually 12:3), the P author makes a case for Israelite/Judahite tradition as no less connected to special knowledge and wisdom from before the flood through the cosmological role of the priesthood.[7]

But the sophistication of this discourse has brought once-independent traditions into an ambitious project, and at least one dimension of an earlier Enoch tradition can be detected in the "walked with *ha-'elohim*" notices. Though identical language characterizes the description of Noah in Gen. 6:9, the terminology is not repeated there, which suggests that the repetition of this language related to Enoch is somehow different:

> v. 22: And Enoch walked with *ha-'elohim* after he begot Methuselah three hundred years ...
> v. 23: And all the days of Enoch were three hundred sixty and five years.
> v. 24: And Enoch walked with *ha-'elohim* and he was not; for *'elohim* took him.

The arrangement of this unit makes the focal point of Enoch's lifetime a matter of discerning the sacred divisions of time with which the authors of P were concerned, framing it with the *ha-'elohim* notices.[8] But that the "walked with *ha-'elohim*" is therefore twice-mentioned with regard to Enoch suggests that the phrase itself had a life *before* it was taken up by the Priestly writers. To be sure, P's usage of the term *'elohim* in Genesis 1 first associates the creation of time with the mysteries of spatial existence as part of a divine plan, and the P creation account imparts knowledge of this to the reader through reformulating existing myths.[9] The opening verses of Genesis 5 explicitly carry this forward into the present narrative.[10] Yet the sheer frequency of *'elohim* in vv. 22–24 is a red flag that the writer behind these verses has inherited an existing tradition. If, as Carr has argued, Genesis 5 draws from a pre-P *toledot*-book into which this lemma already figured,[11] then this tradition was long associated with Enoch's name by P's day.

Here, the ancestral-chthonic aspects of the term *'elohim* becomes important,[12] suggesting that Enoch the son of Jared (*yered*, Gen. 5:20–21), who is depicted as walking "with *ha-'elohim*, was known for having the power to descend (*yered*) into the realm of the underworld. Concomitant with the redefinition of myth elsewhere in their work,[13] the P writers reconfigured the *ha-'elohim* notices in their source where Enoch's "walking" with *ha-'elohim* was earlier understood as a reference to divination with the dead. Traces of the original tradition still linger within this chapter, as Enoch is literally surrounded by figures who are all dead—each strophe describing these figures ends with the notice that they meet their end (Gen. 5: 5, 8, 11, 14, 17, 20).

92   AN EMPIRE FAR AND WIDE

In P's recasting, Enoch no longer "walks" with the dead ancestors but literally sits among them on the page; they do not speak to him, nor he to them. In claiming Enoch for their narrative, the writers of P had to dismantle the pre-P tradition they knew, but the discursive parameters of that tradition persevere in plain sight. In the case of Enoch, the result is a discourse about a patriarch whose cosmic intimacy—and implicit knowledge of secret things—is disconnected from death. But the pre-P Enoch must have been steeped in a contrary tradition where Enoch's secret knowledge came through interaction with the dead and the crossing of boundaries between the realm of the living and the netherworld or afterlife.[14]

The Enoch of Non-P (Genesis 4:1–24; 6:1–4)

Genesis 4 is concerned with the development of human culture within the natural world, but this an expression of human agency and the quest for knowledge which already begins in Eden in the previous chapter. The first two humans make decisions out of their own agency as part of the tale's larger concern with human cognition. And as a consequence, they transform into beings closer to the divine (Gen. 3:5) as new forms of knowledge and awareness emerge from partaking of the forbidden fruit.[15] This motif undergirds the ensuing discourse on Cain and his descendants: urban settlements and the development of craft/trade are ultimately characterized by violence and vengeance with increasing intensity (Gen. 4:24).

The non-P Enoch appears in a seemingly inconspicuous place within this literary flow, depicted in brief terms as Cain's son and the namesake of a city that Cain built. The narrative then moves on to note that Enoch named his own son Irad (Gen. 4:18), whose subsequent progeny developed musical instruments, musicianship, and metalsmithing (vv. 20–22). Many have looked to the obvious wordplay between 'ir and Irad and in relation to the Mesopotamian city Eridu.[16] But the alignment of Genesis 4:18 with a specific or direct parallel misses the purpose of the wordplay with 'ir: associating Cain with urban life stands against the abundance of evidence in the biblical record for the Kenites (Cain's legendary descendants) as a transhumant group, something to which the narrator even tips his hat in the early verses of Genesis 4.

The place of the Kenites in Israelite tradition is inconsistent.[17] Alliances between Israelite and Kenite groups are attested in some places but they are viewed as outsiders, opponents and threats in others. This uneven picture reflects upon earlier periods of socioeconomic change in the Iron I–IIa periods, which David Schloen argued could be assigned to the shift to monarchy in Israel.[18] But the one thing that remains relatively consistent across most of these sources is the presentation of Kenites as tent-dwellers and nomads. These sources primarily depict the Kenites as being able to move across or remove themselves from specific territories; brief references to Kenite "cities" in 1 Sam. 30:29 speaks to changes in economic and material resources across wider population groups in the late eleventh century BCE rather than an inherent feature of Kenite culture from earlier times.[19] While the crediting of the first city to the Kenites breaks with the more consistent presentation of them elsewhere, the critique of urban centers, spaces, cultures and economies is very much at home in Israelite literary polemics, especially those addressing circumstances in the mid-ninth to late-eighth centuries BCE.[20] The rhetoric of Genesis 4 makes sense if this non-P narrative conveys a hostile memories regarding the Kenites and imports a similar antiurban sentiment.

A polemic against the Kenites may relate to the running theme associated with the development of culture within the chapter, namely, the transformation of time, space, and material through human initiative. This establishes the framework for making sense of the cultural creations listed in the chapter: musical instruments affect the perception of time by creating new sounds and rhythms, metallurgy yields entirely new compounds and shapes (including instruments of warfare),[21] and even the building of a city yields new communal spaces not limited strictly to kinship structures (something presented as a source of violence and disorder).[22] For the non-P writers, these new forms are replete with transgressive potential carrying forward the transgressions in the Eden tale, upsetting the order of things in their natural state and inviting disorder, chaos and violence. The implication is that these transformations-transgressions bring humanity ever closer to chaos and bloodshed.

We encounter here the theme of knowledge, even secret knowledge: Cain's descendants are associated with specialized crafts, the skills for which require careful training and even initiation. This alone obviously connects strongly to Enoch, whose name translates into "initiate" (*hanoch*). But in addition to this, we once again encounter a narrative where the Enoch is situated in a discourse about death, opening with the slaying of Abel and ending with Lamech's threat of a massacre,[23] and facilitated by the cultivation of esoteric

94 AN EMPIRE FAR AND WIDE

knowledge. We may even go further and propose that since Cain is clearly an embodiment of "the Kenites" in general, the non-P account in Genesis 4 is primarily built around an old tradition of Enoch as a Kenite patriarch (made more likely through the closely related details preserved in Gen. 25:4 and 1 Chr. 1:3, 33) remembered for a connection to transgressive knowledge. Consequently, the non-P writers have shaped records of genealogies associated with him to transmit themes begun in the Eden story with a condemnatory intent.[24]

These themes culminate in Genesis 6:1–4. We are informed in Genesis 6:4 that "the Nephilim were in the land" during the sexual/cosmic transgression. Whatever the original concept of the Nephilim may have been, the term itself, "fallen ones," carry connotations of death; as Hendel noted several years ago, the role of Nephilim in the texts where they appear is to die.[25] We may go one step further—they are embodiments of Death/Mot as a cosmological constant. Like Death/Mot in west Semitic mythology,[26] the Nephilim return even after the flood wipes out all living things possessing the "spirt of life" (as we are informed in Gen. 7:22). As embodiments of Death/Mot, the Nephilim are not living things but cosmic figures challenging YHWH's intentions for the created order.[27] Related to this is that the land inhabited by the Nephilim is not termed 'adamah (which is the dominant term for land/landscape in the non-P narrative until this point) but 'aretz, a term with chthonic overtones meaning "netherworld."[28]

Scholars are divided on whether or not Genesis 6:1–4 derives from the same writers who composed or transmitted the Eden story in Genesis 2–3 and the Kenite polemic in Genesis 4. In my view, there is sufficient evidence to see these episodes as part of a single source document, and both thematic and lexical connections across these episodes reinforce this view.[29] When the P genealogy in Genesis 5 is set aside, the linguistic commonalities and the rhetorical sequence makes the lineage of Enoch in Genesis 4 central to the flow of events and the rising thematic pitch of transformation-transgression that peaks in Genesis 6:1–4:

Eden story → Enoch's lineage → Nephilim episode

By implication, this positions Enoch himself as a facilitator of the emergence of Death/Mot within the created realm. As with P, Enoch is made central to a narrative discourse about esoteric knowledge (especially if the depiction of the Nephilim is influenced by the Mesopotamian apkallu sages, as some commentators suggest), boundary crossing, and death.[30]

These overlaps point to an even earlier common tradition revolving around the motif of specialized, esoteric knowledge defining the cosmic boundary between life and death, and that this was projected onto a legendary *patriarch* named Enoch and his (Kenite) progeny over the course of time. This esoteric knowledge was envisioned in terms of an Israelite patriarch's primary sacerdotal trait: authority derived from consulting the ancestral dead.[31] While necromancy was accessible beyond family religious structures (e.g., 1 Samuel 28), it was the heads of households who served as patrons of the family shrines where icons of the deified ancestors were stored and where devotional rites were carried out.[32] Furthermore, Nissim Amzallag has noted the connections between metallurgy and the netherworld in antiquity, with the images of furnaces, ash, heat, mythologically associated with concepts of postmortem existence.[33] It is not surprising, then, that interaction with the dead would be central to the traditions about a patriarch connected to the Kenites, known for their metallurgic trade.

If Gen. 6:1–4 is part of the same non-P source as Genesis 2–4, then an association between Enoch and the "divine beings" (i.e., Watchers) narrative is original to the source that was eventually redacted into the Pentateuch.[34] But even if Genesis 6:1–4 stems from a different compositional hand, the redactors who set it into its current place must have done so out of recognizing the relationship between the Nephilim as embodiments of Death and the chthonic dimensions of the Enoch lore standing behind Genesis 4. The P and non-P Enochs thus relate more strongly to each other than has been previously thought; P lacks the polemical attitude of non-P, but both are concerned with a common mythology that had evolved in different directions.[35] That a redactor archived these traditions together speaks to the persistence of this mythology and the redactor's awareness that it came from high antiquity—thus placing it primeval times.

The S/A Narrative as a Myth of Imperial Death

The S/A Narrative was formed with the foregoing Enoch themes in mind. Like Ezra-Nehemiah and the Book of the Twelve, its contents resonate with the circumstances of the late Persian period, and feature priestly thinking throughout (a trait that persists in the later development of 1 Enoch overall).[36] However, the S/A Narrative avoids any explicit mention of older Jewish literary sources, takes place in protological times rather than in an historically

96 AN EMPIRE FAR AND WIDE

experienced past (however reimagined or stylized), and envisions a world bereft of human political hierarchies. Rather than viewing this as evidence of temporal or cultural distance from these other Persian-period works, it is the *proximity* of this material to these other works that accounts for the divergences. They represent the efforts of a scribal group fully conversant with these other texts but engaged in dramatically reassessing their value and function.

Dating the S/A Narrative and its Component Sources

In a recent study, Alexandria Frisch notes that the narrative of transgressive angelic descent constitutes a mythologization of imperialism. Her analysis points to longstanding mythic typologies in Jewish thought used in the S/A Narrative to explain the instability wrought by these successive Greek military conflicts, and to critique the divine power claims made by their perpetrators.[37] That the S/A Narrative mythologizes imperial politics is clear and was applied to Hellenistic imperialism, but this does not demand an early Hellenistic background for its origins. Siam Bhayro has examined the extensive redaction history of the S/A Narrative, arguing that it originating as a shorter tale focusing on the figure of Shemihazah that was composed as a polemic against Babylonian forms of divination.[38] This was then supplemented by a once-separate tale regarding Asael that included critiques of metallurgy, cosmetics, and other disciplines, with references (including the prominent mention of Mt. Hermon in 1 En. 6:6) that suggest origination in northern Palestine.

Bhayro proposes a Babylonian exilic setting for the earliest layer of 1 Enoch 6–11 and thus a possible sixth century BCE date,[39] with the Asael narrative deriving from a later setting among a scribal group residing near the former northern sanctuary of Dan.[40] Bhayro is correct that these features do not demand a Hellenistic date, yet the critique of Babylonian manticism in the Shemihazah stratum does not demand an exilic setting or date either. Aramaic scholasticism promulgated throughout the Persian empire included a thorough intellectual engagement with Babylonian divination praxes.[41] The Shemihazah stratum could just as easily have been composed in the fifth century BCE in reaction to the conventions of Aramaic scribal enculturation of the era, so influenced by Babylonian curricula.[42] Further, while the Shemihazah stratum knows the non-P narrative in Genesis 6:1–4, it also knows the Pentateuch's P stratum—the oft-noted Jared/*yered* word-play in 1 Enoch 6:6 shows awareness of the P material in Genesis 5 identifying Jared as Enoch's father.[43]

The authors' critique of Babylonian manticism *alongside* the use of these Pentateuchal sources suggests that the Shemihazah stratum takes aim at a larger scribal culture that was not novel in his day, and one where the Pentateuch was viewed as part of a larger network of sacred scholarship that included Babylonian curricula. A *terminus a quo* for the Shemihazah stratum in the early to mid-fifth century is thus possible, particularly in relation to the failed revolt against Xerxes in 484 BCE and consequent spread of Aramaic-Babylonian scholarship throughout the ranks of the empire's priest-scribe classes (which featured the study of mantic literature).[44] The critical tones of the Shemihazah stratum identified by Bhayro appear pitched to critique aspects of this enculturation in Aramaic-Babylonian knowledge; the specificity of its contents indeed suggests it was written by an insider of this learned caste.

Similar factors attend the dating of the Asael stratum. According to Bhayro, the focus on metallurgy in the Asael stratum points to the authors' familiarity with the tradecraft in the region of Mt. Hermon, since archaeological evidence shows this region to be a long-duration base for metalsmithing.[45] While Bhayro sees this as evidence for where the narrative took shape, the polemical tone is that of an outsider criticizing a nearby population and its religious praxes and institutions.[46] Because this material ultimately found its way into a text that was curated among Jerusalemite scribal groups, we should view it as originating at a time when a rupture took place within the Jerusalem establishment leading to tension with northern communities—after which time, Jerusalemite writers set about composing this stratum. The formation of the Samaritan temple at Gerizim by a faction of Aaronide priests in the second half of the fifth century BCE provides the likely background for the composition of the Asael stratum, with Hermon as a coded stand-in for Gerizim or as a metonym for Samaria overall.[47] The invocation of a northern mountain also taps into much earlier Canaanite mythology regarding an access point to the heavens at Mt. Zaphon ("the northern peak") and the motif in the book of Jeremiah of cosmic calamity deriving from the enemy "of/from the north" (Jer. 1:13–14, 6:22–25; 25:8; 50:3).

All of this points to the Persian period as the background for the component parts of the S/A Narrative.[48] Yet in their redacted form, the whole is greater than the sum total of the parts. The Shemihazah stratum notes that

98 AN EMPIRE FAR AND WIDE

illicit knowledge is conveyed to human women, but it is only in the Asael stratum that human women are depicted as taking this knowledge and cultivating it within society. Together, these strata show that the chain of cosmic corruption begins with the departure of the Watchers from heaven and continues into the human realm.

The apocalyptic form in the S/A Narrative diverges from the literary forms of the other texts we have considered. One of the fundamental features of apocalyptic literature is its periodization of history and its emphasis on the era of the writer as the closure of the last of these historical periods, with an eye to an impending cosmic cataclysm and eventual resolution.[49] That this is so central a feature of the S/A Narrative points to a time when the redactors perceived this taking place, that is, the chaotic final days of the Persian empire. The murder of Artaxerxes III by his own servant (Bagohi), followed by the tumultuously brief reign of Artaxerxes IV (also assassinated!) and finally the reign of Darius III—whose credentials as an Achaemenid were tenuous at best—could only exacerbate anxieties about the impending end of the empire with Alexandrian forces looming on the horizon.[50] Sanders's observation that "anxiety about rupture was a source of enormous productivity" on the literary level applies in this case: a centuries-old status quo was experiencing just such a rupture, inviting a textual reaction.[51]

The narrative as a myth of imperialism along the lines of Frisch's discussion is thus correct, but a closer examination of its features reveals that it *is the death of Persian imperialism*, and what it revealed, that is being mythologized. The S/A Narrative should thus not be set in the days of the Diadochi but in the closing days of the Achaemenids; it is not a polemical discourse on the foibles of a new imperial system being set in place but on the failure of a longstanding Achaemenid mythology. The narrative, as we will see, takes up the Achaemenids' own mythology of the empire as protological in nature, but turns it upside down: the imperial landscape was not an extension of a perfect cosmos but hopelessly corrupted from the very outset of time.

Language and Textuality

Why would the perception of Persia's imperial death throes compel a group of scribes to redact the Shemihazah and Asael sources as a revelatory statement in its current form? The answer is not simply a matter of a priestly partisan complaint; there is certainly a polemical tone to its message, but polemical interest alone does not account for its textualization. As Jacqueline Vayntrub as argued, textualization can arise from anxiety surrounding the prospect of death. A titular character ponders death and the survival of knowledge; the redactor then transmutes the character's accumulated wisdom into a text that might survive his demise.[52] Vayntrub's work applies not only to individual writers but, I would argue, to entire scribal cultures. Facing the prospect of cultural demise, a writer or group of writers may use text to transmute their own identities into a form that can persist beyond the implosion or fragmentation of the culture or society in which they live.

The redaction of the Shemihazah and Asael material is factored into a metaliterary exhortation on this theme. Within the story-world of the S/A Narrative, the Watchers transmit knowledge across various boundaries (heavenly vs. earthly, cosmic vs. social) but little is said about the written-ness of the illicit knowledge that corrupts human society and unleashes destructive chaos and bloodshed. Under a long-duration empire so characterized by writing as a sign of power and authority (both cosmic and political), it is nigh well impossible that the silence within the text on writing and documents is *not* a deliberate choice. Sophisticated literacy is a hallmark of the scribes who produced this material, but it is not granted to the characters within the tale.[53]

Here, it is significant that the S/A Narrative originated not in Hebrew but in Aramaic. This might seem like an affirmation of Persian scribal convention since Aramaic was the imperial *lingua franca*. But as Sanders has noted, Aramaic was suitable for this purpose precisely because it was not a culturally or geographically fixed system of communication. Hebrew was the language of Israelite and Judahite kingdoms, but Aramaic "does not remember native kingship,"[54] and this may be applied to the identity of emperors and empires as well. The composition of the S/A Narrative in Aramaic challenges the very use of Hebrew texts as *part* of the Aramaic scribal system,[55] and the purging of Hebrew from the S/A Narrative signals a rejection of this convention altogether. The literary/linguistic form of the S/A Narrative is a statement on how authoritative knowledge may be transmitted beyond the boundaries of cultural death: through the dutiful writing of a physical scroll, but not one steeped in Hebrew literary tradition that barely registered as a blip on the radar of history.[56]

Here, the redactors assert their own authority as trustees of scribal methods that they deny the Watchers in the narrative. The knowledge that

100 AN EMPIRE FAR AND WIDE

Shemihazah, Asael and the other Watchers reveal to humanity is not provided in much detail; it is only *reported* (1 En 8:1–4). The readers do not know the specifics of the illicit knowledge passed along by the Watchers, but the redactors of the S/A Narrative imply that *they* do, which creates a boundary between the danger conveyed to human beings in the narrative and the reader's awareness of it. The materiality of the texts they produced "contains" the danger posed by the contents of the narrative, enabling the reader to obliquely encounter it in a material form that is delimited by discernible, controllable substances and processes: parchment, ink, pens/penstrokes, script, orthography, syntax and grammar, lexical style, intertextual references, hermeneutical puns and even literary genre. The phenomenological character of the scribal process forces a narrative of lethal danger to abide by rules and order *through the act of material text-production*. The scroll containing the S/A Narrative insulates the reader from the destructive knowledge reported within the story.

Women's Bodies, Priests, and Landscapes

Virtually all scholars recognize that the material in 1 Enoch 6–7 builds upon the mythic fragment attested in Genesis 6:1–4. Yet the Promethean motifs within the S/A Narrative also draw from aspects of the Eden tale in Genesis 2–3 and the lineage of Cain provided in Genesis 4.[57] What was the result of human enterprise in Genesis is now credited to the initiative of the Watchers in the assignment of a heavenly origin to human evil. But there is a crucial change in the S/A Narrative: in Genesis 4, the human agents of dangerous knowledge are men, while the S/A Narrative emphasizes the role of women, a feature that has drawn no shortage of scholarly attention.[58] Much of this attention has positioned the S/A Narrative (and the Book of Watchers more generally) within a consideration of Hellenistic-era literature.[59] What has not been adequately considered is the interface with a persistent concern in Persian period biblical compositions that the status of women might pose potential threats to elite men. One of the most telling examples of this is the depiction of "Woman Folly" in the closing verses of Proverbs 9, whose words are quoted:

> "Stolen waters are sweet, and bread eaten in secret (*leḥem setarim*) is pleasant."

> But [the unsuspecting victim] does not know that the death demons are there;
> that her guests are in the depths of the netherworld (*be-ʿimqei šeʾol*) (Prov. 9:13–18)

This woman is presented by the writer of these verses as a source of danger, and the language is saturated with sexual euphemism.[60] The author of these verses warns the reader to be on the lookout for women who arouse their lust but whose clutches will be their undoing: earlier visitors to her home become her unwitting victims. The implication is that they, too, were sexually seduced, but the sexual union is cosmic in its dimensions and funnels the victims into *ʿimqei šeʾol*, the cosmic realm of Death.[61]

"Woman Folly" is the inverse parallel of "Woman Valor" in the closing frame of the book (Prov. 31:10–31);[62] the latter demonstrates an ideal Jewish type operating within Persian Yehud. Kelli Anne Gardner is correct to draw attention to the social spaces where these (and other) women in Proverbs can be found,[63] but it is the *public* status of "Woman Valor" and her interaction with socioeconomic norms regulated by the imperial economy that grant her social and sacral legitimacy.[64] "Woman Folly," by contrast, beckons her would-be victim to meet with her and "dine" privately (*leḥem setarim*). For Proverbs' redactors, it is engagement with imperial society (including its economic and intellectual institutions) that secures blessing, while withdrawal from public life leads to the victim's fate in the hands of Woman Folly and the death-demons residing in her domicile.

In Proverbs 9, then, we find a woman's (sexualized) body as a source of cosmic destabilization in relation to space (domicile, *ʿimqei šeʾol*) when set away from the reaches of imperial society—away from public spaces, administrative hierarchies, and especially priestly institutions and their *halakhot* regarding sexuality and bodily purity.[65] The S/A Narrative focuses on this motif but inverts how Proverbs and other texts express it. Against the assumptions of Proverbs (where Lady Wisdom is the inspiration for YHWH's cosmic creation at the heart of the P creation account) and Ezra 9–10 (where the "pious" *haredim* and the priest-scribe Ezra present themselves as trustees of Israel's holiness), it is at the very hands of the priestly figures (the Watchers) that women's bodies become sources of chaos and bloodshed, and that women themselves participate in the proliferation of evil across the landscape.

102 AN EMPIRE FAR AND WIDE

The motif of the landscape is also an important point of inversion within the S/A Narrative in relation to the focus on women, their bodies, and their social location in Yehudite society.[66] There is a strong connection between humans and the land as victims of the Watcher's conduct, as both cry out in protest at the injury they endure (1 En. 7:6; 8:4; 9:2, 10). The connection between women's bodies and the land is well attested in earlier Israelite and Judahite geomythology (Hos. 1–3; Judg. 11:37; 19; Gen. 38; Jer. 31:14; etc.)[67] and the city of Jerusalem is presented as a woman in various ways (2 Kgs. 19:21//Isa. 37:22; Isa. 1:8; Lam. 2:1; 4:22; Zech. 2:10; 3:14; Mic. 4:13; Jer. 6:2 Ps. 9:14, etc.) along with the smaller nearby towns identified as its "daughters" (Song. 1:5; 2:7; 3:5; 8:4). Achaemenid geomythology strongly affected the way these texts were transmitted or read.[68] But the concept of an imperial landscape manifesting divine order is undercut by Mt. Hermon— part of the Persian province of Samaria—as the entry-point for the Watchers to enact their plans for wickedness and destruction on Earth.

The S/A Narrative subverts Achaemenid geomythology, where every people resided in their own land: here, a Samarian location is used as part of a critique of Yehudite priestly leadership, providing a comment on the collapsing of a myth of every people being fixed in their "proper" place, a reversal of the imperial situation reflected in works like Ezra-Nehemiah and thus characterizing the Aaronide priestly worldview.[69] To sharpen this point, the pact made between Shemihazah and the other Watchers (1 En. 6:5) takes on the tone of an imperial *bandaka* pact, but one that ensures disorder.[70] In the S/A Narrative, the mechanisms of *aša* are revealed to be sites of *Drauga*'s dominance over the landscape and its inhabitants.

The Watchers, the Giants, and the Imperial Self-Image

This brings us to the relationship between the Watchers and the Giants (parallel to the Nephilim in Gen. 6:1–4) in the S/A Narrative. Scholars often attempt to navigate taxonomical problems when viewing the depiction of the Watchers and Giants as a product of the era of the Diadochi; if we attempt to align the tropes of the S/A Narrative with aspects of Persian rule in a one-to-one manner, similar taxonomical problems persist. But that is the point: the impossible alignment of taxonomies precludes the easy establishment of ordered parallels. Two centuries of Persian imperialism and Aramaic scholasticism led so many Jewish text collections to abide by such parallels or conform to governing intellectual models.[71] By contrast, the redactors of the S/A Narrative rejected this curated literary pattern of alignment and moved in the other direction. Their engagement of Gen 6:1–4 is engineered to yield a text that makes it impossible to see such familiar or fixed categories function within their own narrative. Alongside the decimation of the Persian empire, the S/A Narrative decimates extant literary tropes, smashing the edifice and rebuilding their own from the broken pieces.

With this in mind, we should look to no less than *the Achaemenid rulers themselves* to understand the symbolic function of the Watchers and the Giants.[72] Our purpose here is to read the confluence of motifs, images, conventions and values characterizing their collective reign that the redactors of the S/A Narrative annexed and rearranged in their work. We should begin with perhaps the most obvious trait regarding the Achaemenid rulers, namely, their physical and figurative stature. In Achaemenid iconography, a persistent motif that distinguishes each emperor from his subjects is his physical size. Beginning with Darius, each emperor towers over not only their vanquished enemies but servants, administrators and other supplicants. We must recall Root's observation that this iconography creates a mythic image of Achaemenid kingship over against the particulars of a given ruler's actual stature or accomplishments.[73]

Imperial language follows suit. Every royal inscription introduces the Achaemenid rulers not simply as kings but as "the Great King," "king of the world," etc. This locution is a legacy of earlier Mesopotamian empires, used already by the neo-Assyrians in their own decrees and inscriptions. Yet the "Great King" trope in Assyrian contexts was more limited, used as a rhetorical or propagandistic power-play against other kings who either had yet to be fully conquered or who stood as vassals but still retained local power.[74] Achaemenid rule replaced native kingship entirely, and thus an international scope of royal tradition was projected onto the ruler. The "Great King" language emphasizes the Achaemenid emperors as ultimate kings with supernatural traits against which all other forms of monarchic officeholders of the past paled by comparison.[75] Their vision and reach are depicted as being over entire cities and nations, satraps and provinces. In this way, Achaemenid literary sources also depicts the emperors as giants.

The parentage of the Watchers to the Giants critiques the idea of dynastic lineage and the order it purported to secure. The S/A Narrative suggests that despite the appearance of sustained order/*aša* through imperial *data* and priestly *halakha*, each successive emperor and generation of priests only made matters successively worse as part of corrosive feedback loop.[76] As to the military depiction of the Watchers and the bloodlust of the Giants, we must recall that bloody rebellions were regular occurrences throughout virtually the entirety of the Achaemenid period. So too was endocide, with brothers killing brothers and sons killings fathers to lay claim to the throne. Jewish scribes would have been aware of this reality behind the Myth even as they took it up in their own text-building. In the S/A Narrative, the bloodlust of the Giants reflects this, and it is not too distant a leap to see how the chthonic ideas in Genesis 6:4 served as a prism through which the scribes behind the S/A Narrative viewed the entirety of Achaemenid dynastic history. This also skewers the Achaemenid postmortem geomythology—a type of anagnorisis where the imperial landscape is indeed full of dead beings, but precisely the opposite of the "order" that inscriptions like XPh ("Xerxes at Persepolis") had in mind.

The very figure of the enduring "Great King" across the history of imperial reliefs and epigraphic records is thus fragmented into different types: the Giants *and* the Watchers, that latter of whom are imprisoned in the depths of the Earth (1 En. 10:12) but—at least in the traditions preserved in the subsequent text in 1 En. 15:8–9—the former of whom persist as demon-spirits throughout the land.[77] If Jewish textual formation during the Persian period was bound to the power of Achaemenid rulers, then the appeal to demons in the formation of texts *after* Persia's demise may be the result of the mythic transmutation of these rulers into demon-spirits or the fallen angels imprisoned in the bowels of the Earth in the early reception of the S/A Narrative. The mythic power of the Persian emperors did not vanish but was shuttled into more hermetic regions of culture that learned sages could access—at their own risk.

In Sum

The S/A Narrative is not simply a complaint, a critique, or an indictment. Like the other texts we have considered, it is intimately connected to the Myth, but it stands as a witness to its impotence and its initial implosion. A culture enduring an imploding social structure demands a new mythology to define the terms of its own survival. In the case of earlier Jewish communities, this took place almost entirely in emic terms. The Exodus myth emerges against the background of the Late Bronze Age collapse and emergent Israel's hinterland birth, the Davidic myth arises following the intergroup conflicts that traumatized early Israel's clans and tribes, etc. Achaemenid mythology, however, was superimposed over the Jewish world, folding relics of earlier emic mythologies into a vista far beyond anything local, internal, or insular. From the perspective of the redactors of the S/A Narrative, this injured Jewish identity nearly beyond repair. It is no wonder that in mythologizing the Persian empire's death, these Jewish scribes created a myth that once again turns toward the emic, focusing on an extant legacy mythology and developing it in light of international events. It is a reminder to the reader that moving within an imperial universe demands caution, as the demon-spirits of the slaughtered Watchers may take on new shapes and await them on the approaching horizon.

Conclusion

The texts surveyed in this study evidence a wide spectrum of reactions to Achaemenid mythology, ranging from accommodation (the redaction of the Pentateuch and Ezra-Nehemiah) to negotiation (the Book of the Twelve) to repudiation (the S/A Narrative). Despite their differences, all of these texts evidence a full enculturation in the terms of the Myth; in that sense, the Achaemenid imperial project was quite successful in Yehud, controlling the way these scribes mapped out time, space, memory, and identity. Yet these varieties of interactions with the Myth are not indications of wider social responses to Persian imperialism.[1] We cannot use them to make claims on broad demographic trends or ideologies that characterized populations well beyond the literati throughout the Yehudite countryside. Emerging from a culture where the production of material text extended heavenly patterns, the sources we have examined evidence a community of scribes who did not produce sociological mandates or political propaganda but instead burrowed deeply into a hermetic world of letters.[2] But the question remains *why* they did this.

Scholars frequently assign the varieties of literary tones and forms in these works to groups of priests or scribes polemicizing against each other, which presupposes factions who worked in different social and even geographic spaces.[3] To a degree, this is a reasonable position, and there are precedent conditions for seeing such a dynamic at work when we consider the late-monarchic or exilic eras.[4] But as we have seen, the situation changes under Persian hegemony; scribes in Yehud may have functioned beyond the Jerusalem temple, but all scribal groups revolved around the temple in one way or another by virtue of the economic and administrative organization of Achaemenid rule. By the late Persian period especially, the Jerusalem temple and its priesthood held political and economic primacy. Scribal activity could only really flourish as part of a network based in the temple, its infrastructure for the production and preservation of texts, and the authority of the Aaronides who oversaw its operation.[5]

An Empire Far and Wide. Mark Leuchter, Oxford University Press. © Oxford University Press 2024.
DOI: 10.1093/oso/9780197772744.003.0007

CONCLUSION   107

The temple's social, ritual, and economic resources exerted such control by the end of the Persian period that we must view the diversity of perspectives in the texts we have discussed not as polemics between priestly scribal communities but as a conversation within one.[6] In this, one might default to the axiom that in antiquity scribes wrote their work for themselves or for other scribal elites as performances of intellectual and sacral authority. This would render text-making as rather insular in scope—one could see this as a matter of the literati seeking to sustain their place in an imperial bureaucracy simply by demonstrating that they possessed the intellectual privilege and prerogative to produce such works.[7] But this is not the only reason for writing literature, especially under the aegis of an imperial power where texts convey an ideology that weaved together politics, society, and the cosmos. We have evidence that texts were written at least in part for public dissemination or performance,[8] but additional dimensions of the text may have served other purposes more suited to elite scholarly and even numinous interests.

As I discussed in Chapter 4, the oracles of Hosea (whose words are indeed a polemic against Assyrian imperial hegemony), evidence the inscribing of written texts as an expression of a decidedly partisan divine power. For Hosea, YHWH conveys his power and hegemony through material text production, an idea echoed in Isaiah's Jerusalemite oracles a few decades later. Given the influence of Assyrian tradition on Achaemenid mythology, we may see the textual conversation among Jewish scribes in the late Persian period as carrying a similar function with regard to affirming the potency of texts, and we have seen that this accounts in part for Hosea's position within the redaction of the Book of the Twelve. Yet unlike Hosea's older oracles (in their independent form), the Book of the Twelve overall does not carry a sharp repudiation of an empire. The S/A Narrative does carry that trait, but the other texts examined above do not, nor do related works like Chronicles or collections like the Psalms that developed around the same time.[9] Even though these texts were produced within the same scribal community, there is no cohesive scribal "party line" in these works. So what did these scribes believe they were doing by giving voice to such an array of reactions to Achaemenid mythology?

From a postcolonial perspective, the reproduction of the empire's terms (in this case, aspects of the dynastic mythology of the Achaemenids) might be a claim on social authority within a scribal community that sensed encroaching instability.[10] Even the S/A Narrative, replete with its rejection of the Myth, still deploys linguistic and methodological strategies characterizing the elite

108   AN EMPIRE FAR AND WIDE

scribal culture promulgated under the Achaemenids. But without dismissing this sociological function of literary production, I would argue that another possibility emerges. The intertextuality of these works constituted a type of ritual or mantic phenomenon inspired by the concept of numinous textuality that flourished under the rule of the Achaemenids. By the end of the Persian period, royal inscriptions/decrees and the Aramaic-Babylonian curriculum had dominated scribal culture for two centuries as sources of revelation and heavenly power. And as the combination of material in DB Aram suggests, that accessibility came through the intertextual countenancing of these texts.

A later text, Daniel 9, provides some helpful perspective. Though this episode was composed in the 2nd century BCE, the continuity of Aramaic scholarship into this later era permits us to mine it for a sense of how Jewish scribes in the late Persian period regarded their textual products. At the very least, it shows how Jewish scribes perceived or remembered their Persian period forebears. The episode presents Daniel struggling to make sense of Jeremiah's famous Seventy-Year oracle regarding the end of the Babylonian exile and the restoration of Israel. Yet Daniel does not only consult Jeremiah's written oracle; rather, Daniel 9:2 relates that he "meditated upon the scrolls" (*binoti ba-sefarim*) where Jeremiah's oracle has been subjected to literary exegesis in the hopes of receiving new revelation. A closer examination of the language in Daniel 9 further suggests that the scrolls Daniel consults are meant to be understood as the work of the Chronicler.[11] The narrative thus presents Daniel as a devotee of the scribal craft of the late Persian period as much as a devotee of the prophetic tradition that scribes such as the Chronicler took up in their work.

Within the episode, Daniel's scribal enterprise fails and the new revelation he obtains comes through an angelic intercessor following his penitential prayer.[12] But the episode presupposes two important aspects of Persian period textuality and scribalism, the first of which is that material texts were sources of revelation, a point I have highlighted throughout this book. The second is that consulting these material sources of revelation in dialogue with each other could lead to tangible outcomes. The revelation Daniel gets from the angelic intercessor leads to the visions of Daniel 10–12, which address the forthcoming unfurling of cosmic shifts in human history. If the angelic intercession is presented as a replacement for meditating upon "the scrolls," then Daniel 9 implies that Jewish scribes in the Persian period produced and consulted such texts to affect religious and social life. It is not just texts that held power; the study, discussion, teaching, and exegesis of texts did as well.[13]

CONCLUSION   109

If the traditions preserved in Daniel are any indication, the Yehudite scribal conversation of the late Persian period was not simply a matter of affirming elite identity through textual performance but of harnessing supernatural power for utilitarian or social purposes. We will recall that according to Achaemenid mythology, royal inscriptions were indexes of Ahuramazda's will, and scribal works that copied these inscriptions carried forward their numinous potency. We will also recall that this concept of Achaemenid textuality was combined with the venerable legacy of Aramaic-Babylonian scribalism and its connection to the heavens. This is attested at the outset of Achaemenid rule already in DB, which we have seen presents its own inscribed materiality as a method for dispelling *Drauga*.[14] I propose that the Yehudite scribal conversation be viewed in light of this framework. The Jewish scribes of the late Persian period may not have produced their texts in a coordinated manner, but they did compose their materials as intertexts that acknowledged each other's discursive contents as a practical way to survive the social and cosmic turbulence of the era. Following Vayntrub's argument that text-production represented a way for an individual to navigate mortality, these scribes produced literature to find ways to navigate the mortal threats confronting Persian stability.[15]

An important antecedent to this may be discerned in the exilic-era development of the Jeremiah tradition. In an earlier study, I noted that the scribal dynamics within that material suggest that for its authors, prophetic texts served as surrogate sanctuaries, with physical space replaced by textual space.[16] Just as YHWH's presence resided in a temple, it could now also reside in a scroll or a collection of scrolls, and the scribes who curated these works served as gatekeepers and facilitators just as priests serve in a physical sanctuary. The encounter with the divine took place on the page; writing and reading was devotional/ritual in orientation and function. There can be little doubt regarding the prominence of Jeremiah in the Persian period given the deference to his prophetic legacy throughout major works of *Schriftprophetie* like the book of Zechariah, the reference in Ezra 1:1–4, in the closing verses of Chronicles (which of course repeat much of Ezra 1:1–4),[17] as remembered by the authors of Daniel 9, and possibly even in the development of the S/A Narrative.[18] This suggests that the Jewish scribes in Yehud did not only view their texts through the lens Achaemenid mythology, they viewed Achaemenid mythology through the lens of this Jeremianic scribal tradition.

With this in mind, we may arrive at a better understanding of how the Yehudite scribal community understood themselves and their work. The production of these texts was, in essence, the creation of an alternative "sanctuary"—a new place where the divine voice could be discerned, where scribal agents could be empowered to mediate holiness, and where protection and stability could be secured. This is not altogether surprising given the priestly profile of these scribes and their common enculturation in the esoteric crafts of elite scribalism under Persian imperialism. Yet this was not a matter of creating competing textual works but of creating a collective textual macrostructure. The work of these scribes yielded an intellectual environment where texts could mutually affect each other, be read with and against each other, stimulate new frameworks for conceiving of how the past weighed upon the present, and how this itself constituted YHWH's own self-disclosure. If YHWH was understood as a deity who worked through the unfolding of history,[19] these texts built a space where the manifold rituals, linguistic formulae, and memories of that history could be conveyed anew.

I do not wish to suggest a type of utopian situation within this scribal community; tensions between and within priestly groups had always existed and would continue to exist down to the end of the Second Temple period. But with a growing recognition that Achaemenid mythology might not be the end-all of historical and cultural determinants, these various works created a crucible for envisioning not only a way forward but multiple ways forward under divine auspices—a distant forerunner to the later rabbinic aphorism *'elu ve-'elu dibrei 'elohim hayyim* (e.g., y. *Berakhot* 1:2; y. *Kiddushin* 1:1; b. *Eruvin* 13b). We may identify this scribal activity as an affirmation of the mythological power of scribalism at a time when the imperial mythology that had sustained it was compromised. The scribal engagement of the Myth in these texts used it not as a teleological milestone but as a stepping-stone, a building block in the textual sanctuary resulting from their mediation of written heavenly power.

A certain irony should not be lost on us. These scribes created a literary sanctuary that depended upon the centrifugal power of a physical sanctuary (the Jerusalem temple), and the former was ultimately incorporated into the ritual and pedagogical system of the latter in the Hellenistic period. During this time, scribal power was increasingly dissociated from the prevailing foreign imperial culture and increasingly annexed by the priesthood, which continued to lay authoritative claim to the texts from earlier eras.[20] By this point, the dynastic myth of the Achaemenids was no longer active, but a pivotal aspect of it remained, namely, the idea that texts functioned as spaces for encountering supernatural forces standing behind the ordinary, indeed waiting to flood into the ordinary world. This was an outgrowth of centuries of scribal text-building as a vehicle for Achaemenid hegemony, which viewed itself as the bridge between the cosmic and the mundane. The Achaemenid empire may have faded, but this idea of textuality as a vehicle for world-making did not.

But this also meant that a connection to the now-fallen Achaemenid empire was a residual trait of this concept of scribalism—it was powerful but inherently unstable, conditioned as it was by ideas of imperialism that were themselves unstable. Again, the book of Daniel gives us a sense of how anxiety toward imperialism affected the concept of scribalism. The dream interpreted in Daniel 2 critiques the durability of empires, yet still sees them as extensions of each other, a contiguous edifice with distinctions that at the same time combine into a single statue of a single ruler. The statue in the dream analyzed by Daniel may contain an ongoing memory of the "Persian Man" motif within Achaemenid mythology that folded one emperor into another as symbols of an enduring divine prototype. With the benefit of hindsight, the second century BCE authors of Daniel 2 extend this from individual emperors to entire empires, but this also implies that texts produced under such imperialism contain both the cosmic power standing behind these empires and the chaotic power that eventually brough each regime to an end. Scribalism could create the world *and* destroy it. This is also the implications of Daniel 5, where a heavenly scribal hand creates a text within the Persian court itself, only to literally spell out its doom.[21]

Within the Aaronide temple cult of the Hellenistic period, the claim over this type of text-production was levied to support priestly social and ritual dominance over the Jewish world. In time, this would lead to the Aaronide text par excellence, the Pentateuch, serving as a basis for ritual and legal thought in Jewish communities well beyond Jerusalem. But such a development was predicated on the concept of texts serving as gateways into a a supernatural world, one characterized by the potential for danger. As James Watts has discussed, part of the Pentateuch's compelling rhetoric is that the ritual texts it contains are dangerous and even deadly; only priests were capable of containing such power.[22] This concept extended to texts incorporated into the Aaronide ritual matrix during the Hellenistic period, including those produced by the late Persian period Yehudite scribes. But because these texts were produced under Persian imperialism, their connection to Achaemenid mythology—and to the chaos resulting from its failure—persisted.

112 AN EMPIRE FAR AND WIDE

In a recent study, Annette Yoshiko Reed proposed that scribes in the third to second centuries BCE saw their work as channels to invoke both angels and demons.[23] Demonology, in particular, evolved as scribes developed literary discourses to identify the sources of chaos, destruction and evil in an effort to redirect dangerous supernatural forces toward productive ends. Pursuant to Reed's argument, I would suggest that this concept of demonology and textuality is rooted in the lingering memory of Achaemenid mythology, especially in the Enochian texts that Reed examines. In Chapter 5, I noted that the monstrous giants of the S/A Narrative were cyphers for the Achaemenid rulers; their depiction in that narrative reveals their fundamental essence as destructive, cannibalistic creatures that herald death and chaos. And as I noted in that chapter, the subsequent Hellenistic development of the Book of Watchers relates that the giants were transformed into demons whose dangerous spirits continued to reside throughout the (post-Achaemenid) landscape (1 En. 15:8–9).

At least one major criteria Reed describes for demonic invocation, the mantic power of composing and studying written lists (*Listenwissenschaft*),[24] parallels the prominence of lists in Achaemenid royal inscriptions and administrative material, both of which were part of the Myth's functional expression in ordering the landscape. It was also a feature of the late Persian Jewish texts surveyed in this study. Nehemiah, especially, is presented as drawing knowledge and pious authority from the generation of the pact register in Nehemiah 10 and his study of repeated lists of priestly figures of various sorts in Nehemiah 11–12—leading to his ability to "purify" society (Neh. 13:30).[25] Notable, too, is the appearance of the population list in Ezra 2/Nehemiah 7 immediately before the rebuilding of the temple site in Ezra 3 and again immediately before the *torah*-reading ceremony in Nehemiah 8. Implicit in this structure is that the list, which details the inhabitants of the local imperial landscape across various generations, is deeply connected to sites of divine encounter, be it a physical altar or a cosmic text.

Chronicles, emerging from the same late Persian setting, also uses lists in relation to sacral activity, boundaries and, notably, in containing the danger connected to the contact between terrestrial and celestial forces.[26] The Levite genealogies are deployed in relation to the fixtures and spaces of the temple, which passages like 2 Chronicles 30:27 reveal to be the portal to heaven where the Levites' prayers are directed. Yet the lists of the Levites are *themselves* counted as prayers; such is the implication of the famous passage in 1 Chronicles 25:4, which fuses a Levite genealogy to an actual Levite prayer.

CONCLUSION   113

This is a deliberate attempt by the Chronicler to transform the lists of Levites into a category of prayer, consciously eradicating the distinction between sacerdotal figures and a ritual incantation. In this case, the Levitical lists are vehicles for reaching the heavens, just as 2 Chronicles 30:27 tells us that Levite prayers reached heaven through the temple. Yet this is the very same space where YHWH's destroying agent continued to abide, as 1 Chronicles 21 strongly implies.[27] And we should bear in mind that the generating circumstance behind 1 Chronicles 21 is that an agent of chaos—a *satan*—influences David to take a census (1 Chr. 21:1), that is, to produce a list that brings about cosmic violence and introduces the need for punishment and expiation. Again, list-production can invoke a supernatural presence.

As early as the redaction of the Pentateuch in the mid-fifth century BCE, the function of lists are used to mediate the power of heavenly creation alongside the forces of Death and the netherworld. The *toledot* formulae weave the Aaronide priesthood into a celestial network; as David L. Petersen observes, the final *toledot* formula regarding the Aaronide lineage connects it to the *toledot* "of the Heavens and the Earth" in Genesis 2:4a.[28] But the Hebrew term for "Earth," *'aretz*, leaves open the possibility that the *toledot* in question relate not only to the land but to the netherworld so often depicted using the very same locution. Even if this was not the linguistic intent of the P writer who composed this passage, the later Pentateuchal redactors no doubt recognized this illocutionary tone, as suggested by the fact that the P genealogical list in Genesis 5 (following, notably, on the heels of *another* list in Genesis 4) leads directly to the account of cosmic transgression and the Nephilim in Genesis 6:1–4 and the catastrophic deluge that follows. The literary device also surfaces in postdiluvian narrative, where the account of descent into Egypt—a long-duration symbol of the netherworld and Death—is heralded by a listing of the children of Israel, tribe by tribe (Exod. 1:1–7).[29]

The Hellenistic-era practice of *Listenwissenschaft* discussed by Reed thus appears to follow a practice that emerged already in Persian period Jewish texts. Indeed, this draws from even earlier priestly understandings of lists as a way to delineate the order and structure of the natural and supernatural worlds, as Liane Feldman writes.[30] By the Hellenistic period, this was perhaps an example of fighting fire with fire, pitting Jewish scribal values against the hubris of post-Achaemenid emperors who successively laid claim to the same landscapes and produced literature pushing their own ideology.[31] As the Enochian writers and other priestly scribes of the Hellenistic period recognized, those cycles did not come to an end but continued unabated.

114   AN EMPIRE FAR AND WIDE

New emperors would arise to take the place of the old, the bloodthirsty giants would continue to consume everything before them, and the land would again cry out. It is no wonder that practitioners of the scribal craft developed systems to control the chaotic forces of the demonic landscape while turning to the heavens for inspiration.

That later Jewish intellectual traditions would return to *terra firma* for exploring revelation (b. *Bava Metziah* 59b) and connect learned figures with the landscape (y. *Avodah Zarah* 3:1, 42c; b. *Moed Qatan* 25b) points to the complications that accompanied Enochian reactions to imperial geomythology as the era of empires continued across the horizons of history. When theorizing the nature of scriptural composition and transmission, the Rabbis envisioned a process full of contradiction. Rebecca Scharbach Wollenberg has recently discussed how rabbinic literature conceives of scripture as originating in heaven and wrought from unearthly, supernatural materials.[32] The scripture that reaches human hands, however, is unstable and even unreliable; it is imperfect and corrupted by the shortcomings of human language, social hierarchies, political agendas and moral uncertainty. The celestial materials on which divine scripture originated stand in stark contradistinction to the organic, perishable materials upon which human-transmitted scripture was inscribed, materials derived from mundane activity rooted in physical labor rather than sacral, esoteric prognostication.[33]

These rabbinic sages viewed scripture as a compromised enterprise. Revelation could be transmitted in material form but the result was a meager approximation of an original heavenly prototype that could never be fully recovered. The ontology of these sages living under Roman rule could not be more different from that of scribes who lived under Persian rule and whose textual products carried the force of heavenly/imperial prototypes. Yet the rabbinic passages expressing much of this anxiety and ambivalence revolve around institutions and events either expressly or implicitly connected to the Persian period. These texts regularly return to the figure of Ezra, the trope of the Great Assembly, the shifts from a Hebrew script and language to an Aramaic one, and so forth.[34] And most significantly, the anxiety regarding texts as sites of power and danger persisted. The oral *torah* and the ritual system the Rabbis developed insulated the community from the threats of an unstable text that imparted communal holiness when its contents were *not* directly read.[35]

It is for this reason that upon looking back to a protological era, the redactors of Avot 1.1 characterize *torah* as a concept that is meant to be

CONCLUSION 115

a "fence" around *the* Torah. The Torah in this case refers not solely to the Pentateuch but to the canon of Jewish scripture as a material text that possessed dangerous potential. In the introduction to this study, I proposed that the Rabbis behind Avot 1 were hesitant to say much about the Great Assembly due to viewing the Persian period as distinct from the their own era. I would further suggest that this reflects trepidation on their part to embrace an era they remembered as the time in which the dangers of written scripture originated. The Rabbis remembered that Jewish scripture emerged from an imperial myth and its ultimate failure, pointing to a volatile cosmos standing behind the semblance of an ordered imperial reality in which they still lived. They remembered that scripture was forged through the fires of imperialism and had been used, time and again, to accommodate the dangers of foreign cultures. They could not reject a text that provided a dim reflection of the heavens, but to approach it without due caution would risk unleashing its potential to rupture the delicate balance they endeavored to maintain.

Notes

Introduction

1. Though the last Achaemenid emperor Darius III died in 330 BCE, I choose 332 as the final year of Achaemenid hegemony before the conquest of Alexander permanently altered the balance of international power in west Asia (332/331 BCE).

2. This issue was broached in a paper by Azzan Yadin-Israel presented at the 2022 AJS meeting (Boston, MA) entitled "Second Temple Judaism: Periodization and Ideology." I place the Hellenistic and Roman periods in a different category than the Persian period not because there were no other Jewish sanctuaries at that time but because the Jerusalem temple and its priesthood had emerged as the most powerful and important site of ritual authority in ancient Judaism by then—something that began to take shape during the Persian period but which was not yet fully the case at that time. The Gerizim sanctuary in Samaria outshined that of Jerusalem at various points throughout the Persian period and was likely viewed by many Jews in Yehud and elsewhere as a serious contender as the primary temple site for devotion to YHWH. See Gary Knoppers, *Jews and Samaritans: The Origins and History of Their Early Relations* (New York: Oxford University Press, 2013), 102–134.

3. See, e.g., Bob Becking, *Israel's Past as Seen from the Present* (BZAW; Berlin: De Gruyter, 2021), 130; Herbert Niehr, "Religio-Historical Aspects of the 'Early Post-Exilic' Period," in *The Crisis of Israelite Religion: Transformation of Religious Tradition in Exilic & Post-Exilic Times*, ed. Bob Becking and Marjo C. A. Korpel (Leiden: Brill, 1999), 244.

4. Mark Leuchter, "The Book of the Twelve and the 'Great Assembly' in History and Tradition," in *Perspectives on the Formation of the Book of the Twelve*, ed. Rainer Albertz et al. (Berlin: De Gruyter, 2012), 337–353. See also Joachim Schaper, *Priester und Leviten im Achaemenidischen Juda: Studien zur Kult- und Sozialgeschichte Israels in Persischer Zeit* (FAT; Tübingen: Mohr Siebeck, 2000), 307, on the connection between scribal methods of the late Persian period and subsequent Pharisaic interpretive traditions. This is relevant given the prominence of Pharisaic pairs within Avot 1.

5. See further Amram Tropper, *Wisdom, Politics, and Historiography: Tractate Avot in the Context of the Graeco-Roman Near East* (Oxford: Oxford University Press, 2004).

6. See Tropper, *Tractate Avot*, especially ch. 5.

7. See the discussion by Charles E. Carter, *The Emergence of Yehud in the Persian Period: A Social and Demographic Study* (Sheffield: Sheffield Academic Press, 1999), 31–35.

8. I follow the definition provided by Jon L. Berquist that an empire is a central power primarily motivated to dominate peripheral cultures and territories through colonization for the purpose of extracting resources ("Postcolonialism and Imperial Motives for Canonization," *Semeia* 75 [1996]: 16–17). See also the definition of Katell Berthelot that imperialism constitutes the practical and ideological conquest of distant territories by a metropolitan center: *Jews and Their Roman Rivals* (Princeton, NJ: Princeton University Press, 2021), 17). A case study is provided by John Ma, "Aršama the Vampire," in *Aršama and His World: The Bodleian Letters in Context* (Vol. 3), ed. Christopher Tulpin and John Ma (Oxford: Oxford University Press, 2020), 190–208.

9. See among others Carter, *The Emergence of Yehud*; Mary Joan Winn Leith, "Israel Among the Nations: The Persian Period," in *The Oxford History of the Biblical World*, ed. Michael D. Coogan (New York: Oxford University Press, 1998), 276–316; Rainer Albertz and Bob Becking (ed.), *Yahwism After the Exile: Perspectives on Israelite Religion in the Persian Era* (Assen: Van Gorcum, 2003); Oded Lipschits and Manfred Oeming (ed.), *Judah and the Judeans in the Persian Period* (Winona Lake, IN: Eisenbrauns, 2006).

10. I describe below the reasons for identifying this period as the historical setting for the shaping of these texts.

11. Seth L. Sanders, *From Adapa To Enoch* (TSAJ; Tübingen: Mohr Siebeck, 2017), 3, 236.

118   NOTES

12. The question is addressed by Marc Z. Brettler, "Judaism in the Hebrew Bible? The Transition from Ancient Israelite Religion to Judaism," *CBQ* 61 (1999): 429–447.
13. Yonatan Adler, *The Origins of Judaism: An Archaeological-Historical Reappraisal* (New Haven, CT: Yale University Press, 2021), 189–236.
14. Karel van der Toorn, *Becoming Diaspora Jews: Behind the Story of Elephantine* (New Haven, CT: Yale University Press, 2019), 14–18.
15. Van der Toorn, *Becoming Diaspora Jews*, 15–20.
16. Joachim Schaper, "Torah and Identity in the Persian Period," in *Judah and the Judeans in the Achaemenid Period*, ed. Oded Lipschits et al. (Winona Lake: Eisenbrauns, 2011), 27–36.
17. Roland Boer, "Thus I Cleansed Them from Everything Foreign: The Search for Subjectivity in Ezra–Nehemiah," in *Postcolonialism and the Hebrew Bible: The Next Step*, ed. Roland Boer (Atlanta: SBL, 2013), 224–227.
18. Lawrence M. Wills, "Jew, Judean, Judaism in the Ancient Period: An Alternative Argument," *JAJ* 7 (2016): 169–193.
19. Wills, "Alternative Argument."
20. Homi K. Bhabha, *The Location of Culture* (London: Routledge, 1994), 19–39.
21. Bhabha, *Location of Culture*, 53.
22. See further Inchol Yang, "Nehemiah as a Mimic Man under the Achaemenid Empire: A Postcolonial Reading of Nehemiah 5," *The Expository Times* 133 (2022): 409–420.
23. R. S. Sugirtharajah, *Postcolonial Criticism and Biblical Interpretation* (Oxford: Oxford University Press, 2002), 11–13, 60.
24. See further Chapter 3.
25. Victor Turner, *Ritual Process: Structure and Anti- Structure* (Chicago: Aldine, 1969); Victor Turner, *The Forest of Symbols: Aspects of Ndembu Ritual* (Ithaca, NY: Cornell University Press, 1967), 93–111.
26. Mark S. Smith, *The Origins of Biblical Monotheism* (New York: Oxford University Press, 2002), 27–29.
27. Ezekiel, for example, make the distant homeland the new locus of chaos, danger, and recompense. See C. A. Strine and C. L. Crouch, "YHWH's Battle Against Chaos in Ezekiel: The Transformation of Judahite Mythology for a New Situation," *JBL* 132 (2013): 883–903.
28. See the more detailed discussion on this matter in Chapter 1.
29. George Lakoff and Mark Turner, *More Than Cool Reason: A Field Guide to Poetic Metaphor* (Chicago: University of Chicago Press, 1989); Nuwan Leitan and Lucian Chaffey, "Embodied Cognition and Its Applications: A Brief Review," *Sensoria: A Journal of Mind, Brain and Culture* 10 (2014): 3–10; Barbara Tversky and Birdgette Martin Hard, "Embodied and Disembodied Cognition: Spatial Perspective- Taking," *Cognition* 110 (2009): 124–129; Ayelet Landau, Lisa Aziz- Zadeh, and Richard B. Ivry, "The Influence of Language on Perception: Listening to Sentences about Faces Affects the Perception of Faces," *The Journal of Neuroscience* 30 (2010): 15254–15261.
30. Ronald Langacker, *Foundations of Cognitive Grammar: Theoretical Prerequisites* (Stanford, CA: Stanford University Press, 1987), 183.
31. George Lakoff and Marc Johnson, *Philosophy in the Flesh: The Embodied Mind and its Challenge to Western Thought* (New York: Basic, 1999).
32. George Lakoff, personal email correspondence, June 26, 2023.
33. Daniel O. McClellan, *YHWH'S Divine Images: A Cognitive Approach* (Atlanta: SBL, 2022) 14.
34. Barbara Tversky and Elizabeth J. Marsh, "Biased Retellings of Events Yield Biased Memories," *Cognitive Psychology* 40 (2000): 1–38.
35. Michael A. Arbib, "Schemas vs. Symbols: A View from the 90s," *Journal of Knowledge Structures and Systems* 2 (2021): 70; David Tuggy, "Schematicity," *The Oxford Handbook of Cognitive Linguistics* (ed. Dirk Geeraerts and Hubert Cuyckens; Oxford: Oxford University Press, 2007) 82–116.
36. On social memory and cognition, see Aaron Beim, "The Cognitive Aspects of Collective Memory," *Symbolic Interaction* 30 (2007): 7–26.
37. Deborah Scoggins Ballentine, *The Conflict Myth and the Biblical Tradition* (New York: Oxford University Press, 2015) 8–13. A relatively recent example of this perspective is provided by Fritz Graf in his own understanding of Israelite religious literature, where YHWH's revelation precludes the "place for myth." See Fritz Graf, "Myth," in *Religions of the Ancient World: A Guide*, ed. Sarah Iles Johnston (Cambridge: Cambridge University Press, 2004), 53.
38. Ballentine, *Conflict Myth*, 5–6.

NOTES 119

39. Ballentine, *Conflict Myth*, 8.
40. Leonard Steinhorn, "The Fundamental Flaw in 'Make America Great Again,'" *The Washington Post*, July 26, 2022.
41. Fran Schor, *Weaponized Whiteness: The Constructions and Deconstructions of White Identity Politics* (Leiden: Brill, 2020), 32–43.
42. The MAGA phrase itself takes on the role of Ultimate Sacred Postulate, governing how all other features of the communities abiding by it conceive of holiness. See Roy A. Rappaport, *Ritual and Religion in the Making of Humanity* (Cambridge: Cambridge University Press, 1999), 430–436.
43. Ehud Ben Zvi, *Social Memory among the Literati of Yehud* (BZAW; Berlin: de Gruyter, 2019).
44. On the economic prosperity of this period, see Leo Mildenberg, "Artaxerxes III Ochus (358–338 B.C.): A Note on the Maligned King," *ZDPV* 115 (1999): 213–218.
45. John W. Betlyon, "Egypt and Phoenicia in the Persian Period: Partners in Trade and Rebellion," in *Egypt, Israel and the Ancient Mediterranean World*, ed. Donald B. Redford, Gary Knoppers, and Antoine Hirsch (Leiden: Brill, 2004), 471–472; Lloyd Llewellyn Jones, "The Achaemenid Empire," in *King of the Seven Climes: A History of the Ancient Iranian World, 3000 BCE–651 CE*, ed. Touraj Daryaee (Leiden: Brill/Jordan Center for Persian Studies, 2017), 78.
46. Oded Lipschits and Orel Tal, "The Settlement Archaeology of the Province of Judah: A Case Study," in *Judah and the Judeans in the Fourth Century B.C.E.*, ed. Oded Lipschits et al. (Winona Lake, IN: Eisenbrauns, 2007) 45–46.
47. Mildenberg, "Maligned King," 213–218; Matt Waters, *Ancient Persia: A Concise History of the Achaemenid Empire 550–330 BCE* (Cambridge: Cambridge University Press, 2014), 209. There is some reason to believe that Artaxerxes I was in view as a model for the goals and policies of Artaxerxes III, since it is during the reign of his earlier namesake that the use of the Old Persian language itself came in direct contact with Yehudite society. See Aren Wilson Wright, "From Persepolis to Jerusalem: A Reevaluation of Old Persian-Hebrew Contact in the Achaemenid Period," *VT* 65 (2015): 152–167.
48. The situation, however, had roots in the ill-conceived policies of Artaxerxes II; see Mildenberg, "Maligned King," 222.
49. Schaper, *Priester und Leviten*, 139–141.
50. I discuss the Yehudite scribal community in Chapter 2 below.

Chapter 1

1. Pierre Briant, *From Cyrus to Alexander: A History of the Persian Empire* (Winona Lake, IN: Eisenbrauns, 2002), 39–44.
2. Amélie Kuhrt, "Cyrus the Great of Persia: Images and Realities," in *Representations of Political Power: Case Histories from Times of Change and Dissolving Order in the Ancient Near East*, ed. M. Heinz and M.H. Feldman (Winona Lake, IN: Eisenbrauns, 2007) 169–191.
3. Briant, *Cyrus to Alexander*, 31–49.
4. Briant, *Cyrus to Alexander*, 40–41.
5. Amélie Kuhrt, "Making History: Sargon of Agade and Cyrus the Great of Persia," in *A Persian Perspective: Essays in Memory of Heleen Sancisi-Weerdenburg*, ed. Wouter Henkelman and Amélie Kuhrt (Leiden: Nederlands Institute voor het Nabije Oosten, 2003), 347–361. On the influence of neo-Assyrian iconography in Persian period propagandistic reliefs, see Root, *King and Kingship*, 27–34, 38, 58 n. 38.
6. See further Katell Berthelot, *Jews and their Roman Rivals: Pagan Rome's Challenge to Israel* (Princeton: Princeton University Press, 2021), 55, for explicit engagement of neo-Assyrian language in Persian propaganda.
7. Amélie Kuhrt, *The Persian Empire: A Corpus of Sources from the Achaemenid Period* (London: Routledge, 2010), 104.
8. Briant, *Cyrus to Alexander*, 56–59.
9. Joseph P. Blenkinsopp, "The Mission of Udjahorresnet and Those of Ezra and Nehemiah," *JBL* 106 (1987): 409–414. This runs contrary to Herodotus' description of Cambyses as "half insane" and slaying the sacred Apis Bull (Herodotus, *Hist* 3.27–29).
10. Laurie E. Pearce and Cornelia Wunsch, *Documents of Judean Exiles and West Semites in Babylonia in the Collection of David Sofer*. Cornell University Studies in Assyriology and Sumerology (Bethesda, MD: CDL Press, 2014) §§74–76, 100.
11. See Briant, *Cyrus to Alexander*, 108–138, for an analysis of Darius's turbulent ascent to power.
12. See the discussion by Briant, *Cyrus to Alexander*, 113–114.

120 NOTES

13. See the recent study by Melissa Benson, "Violence in the Behistun Monument: Construction and Cohesion of Achaemenid Imperial Rule under Darius I (522–519 BCE)," PhD Dissertation, University College London, 2020, which is the most thorough and up to date examination of the inscription's materiality, rhetoric, and sociopolitical characteristics, and contains a comprehensive summary of the most relevant history of scholarship.

14. Branislaw Malinowski, *Magic, Science, Religion and Other Essays* (Glencoe: Free Press, 1948), 120–121. Charter myths apply to group identity formation and fall into the category of adaptive myths; see Vito Signorile, "Acculturation and Myth," *Anthropological Quarterly* 46 (1973): 120.

15. John J. Collins, "Cosmology: Time and History," in *Ancient Religions*, ed. Sarah Iles Johnston (Cambridge, MA: Harvard University Press, 2007), 59–70 (see especially pp. 66–68 for a discussion of ancient Persian usage of these mythic patterns).

16. Jason Silverman, "Was There an Achaemenid Theology of Kingship? The Intersections of Mythology, Religion, and Imperial Religious Policy," in *Religion in the Achaemenid Persian Empire: Emerging Judaisms and Trends*, ed. Diana Edelman et al. (Tubingen: Mohr Siebeck, 2016), 188–189; "From Remembeing to Expecting the 'Messiah': Achaemenid Kingship as Reformulating Apocalyptic Expectations of David," in *Political Memory in and after the Persian Empire*, ed. Jason M. Silverman and Caroline (Waerzeggers; Atlanta: SBL, 2015), 428–429.

17. Item #NM 2003.3, Chau Chak Museum, Nicholson Collection, University of Sydney.

18. Native Lydian leadership was entirely replaced with Persian officialdom upon the transformation of Lydia from a kingdom into a satrapy. See Eduard Rung, "The End of the Lydian Kingdom and the Lydians After Croesus," in *Political Memory in and after the Persian Empire*, ed. Jason M. Silverman and Caroline Waerzeggers (Atlanta: SBL, 2015), 7–22.

19. Andrew Nichols, "The Iranian Concept AŠA and Greek Views of the Persians," in *Studi classici e orientali: LXII, 2016* (Pisa: Pisa University Press, 2016), 61–86.

20. Udjahorresnet narrates this turn of events in his own inscription.

21. Nichols, "The Iranian Concept," 61–62.

22. Nichols, "The Iranian Concept," 62 n. 9.

23. On the place of Darius within an Achaemenid theology of creation, see Christine Mitchell, "The Politics of Judahite Creation Theologies in the Persian Period," in *Political Theologies in the Hebrew Bible* (JAJSup), ed. Mark G. Brett and Rachelle Gilmour (Paderborn: Brill Schöning, 2023), 28–31. I will not speculate here on whether the Teispid or Achaemenid rulers practiced Zoroastrian religion, which is a matter of ongoing debate. It will suffice to note that at least as far as the Achaemenids are concerned, devotion to Ahuramazda implies some connection to Zoroastrian theology as it developed across the latter centuries of the first millennium BCE. At the very least, Achaemenid imperial religion contributed significantly to the character of Zoroastrian religious thought and practice in ensuing centuries.

24. Nichols, "The Iranian Concept," 62.

25. Darius's own desperate proclamation "I was not a liar" (DB 63) is one indication of the severity and commonality of the charge against him.

26. The use of Elamite, in particular, may be an attempt to reinforce Darius's claim of a family connection to Cyrus, who many scholars view as emerging from an Elamite background. See Daniel L. Potts, "Cyrus the Great and the Kingdom of Anshan," in *The Idea of Iran: Birth of the Persian Empire*, ed. V. S. Curtis and S. Stewart (London: Tauris, 2005), 7–28.

27. See Margaret Cool Root, "Defining the Divine in Achaemenid Persian Kingship: The View from Bisitun," in *Every Inch a King: Comparative Studies on Kings and Kingship in the Ancient and Medieval Worlds*, ed. Lynette Mitchell and Charles Melville (Leiden: Brill, 2013), 49–50. On the figure as a representation of *farnah*, see Silverman, "Theology of Kingship," 177–178. The promotion of Ahuramazda in Achaemenid inscriptions is connected to attempts to distinguish the lineage from earlier Elamite religious traditions, despite the role of Elamite in DB; see Manfred Hutter, "Probleme iranischer Literatur und Religion unter den Achämeniden," *ZAW* 127 (2015): 547–564.

28. Clarisse Herrenschmidt, "Les créations d'Ahuramazda," *Studia Iranica* 6 (1977): 17–58. See further below for more on Achaemenid concepts of landscape.

29. For the theological implications of this imagery, see Bertholet, *Jews and their Roman Rivals*, 57.

30. Jason M. Silverman, "Achaemenid Sources and the Problem of Genre," in *Conceptualizing Past, Present, and Future*, ed. S. Fink and R. Rollinger; Melammu Symposia 9 (Münster: Ugarit-Verlag, 2018), 265. The summary rehearsals of DB in subsequent inscriptions indicate its perception as a mythological charter (Mitchell, "Judahite Creation Theologies," 27–28).

NOTES 121

31. Sanders, *From Adapa to Enoch: Scribal Culture and Religious Vision in Judea and Babylon* (Tübingen: Mohr Siebeck, 2017), 166–183.
32. Anne Fitzpatrick-McKinley, *Empire, Power and Indigenous Elites: A Case Study of the Nehemiah Memoir* (JSJSup; Leiden: Brill, 2015), 8–38.
33. Sanders, *From Adapa to Enoch*, 183–186.
34. Sanders, *From Adapa to Enoch*, 183–195.
35. Donald C. Polaski, "What Mean These Stones? Inscriptions, Textuality and Power in Persia and Yehud," in *Approaching Yehud: New Approaches to the Study of the Persian Period*, ed. John L. Berquist (Atlanta: SBL, 2007), 38.
36. See Louis C. Jonker, "Anything New under the Sun?! Exploring Further Avenues for Writing Another Commentary on Chronicles," *Acta Theologica* 26 (2018): 330. In Jonker's words: "the actual wording and contents of inscriptions were not as important as the fact that they were written down."
37. Because scribal groups so often were found among the ranks of priesthoods, the Persian break with previous concepts of the monarch-priest relationship must have factored into the new role that scribes would play within this new paradigm. See Jason Silverman, "From Remembering to Expecting the 'Messiah': Achaemenid Kingship as (Re)Formulating Apocalyptic Expectations of David," in *Political Memory in and After the Persian Empire*, ed. Jason M. Silverman and Caroline Waerzeggers (Atlanta: SBL, 2015), 430–431.
38. Scribes trained in Aramaic rose to far greater local prominence under Persian imperialism even before the time of Darius; see Michael Jursa, "Ein Beamter flucht auf Aramäisch: Alphabetschreiber in der spätbabylonischen Epistolographie und die Rolle des Aramäischen in der babylonischen Verwaltung des sechsten Jahrhunderts v. Chr.," in *Leggo! Studies Presented to Frederick Mario Fales on the Occasion of His 65th Birthday*, ed. Giovanni Lanfranchi et al. (Wiesbaden: Harrasowitz, 2012), 390.
39. Paul-Alain Beaulieu, "Official and Vernacular Languages: The Shifting Sands of Imperial and Cultural Identities in First-Millenium B.C. Mesopotamia," in *Margins of Writing, Origins of Culture*, ed. Seth L. Sanders (Chicago: Oriental Institution, 2006), 207.
40. See Chapter 2 of the present study for further discussion.
41. Sanders, *From Adapa To Enoch*, 192–194.
42. The propagandistic rhetoric of Persian iconography and inscriptions throughout the empire make this clear, from the visual depiction of Cambyses as a Pharaoh to the substitution of Ahuramazda's name with that of Bel-Marduk on the Babylonian version of DB.
43. See Mitchell's discussion of the creation formula as summary-rehearsals of DB ("Judahite Creation Theologies," 27–28).
44. Root, "Defining the Divine," 58.
45. Margaret Cool Root, *The King and Kingship in Achaemenid Art* (Leiden: Brill, 1979), 309–311.
46. See the example discussed by Jennifer Hilder, "Masterful Missives: Form and Authority in Arsama's Letters," *Aršāma and His World: The Bodleian Letters in Context*, Vol. III, ed. Christopher Tulpin and John Ma (Oxford: Oxford University Press, 2020), 99.
47. Mitchell, "Judahite Creation Theologies," 27–28.
48. Robert Rollinger, "Thinking and Writing about History in Teispid and Achaemenid Persia," in *Thinking, Recording, and Writing History in the Ancient World*, ed. Kurt Raaflaub (Malden: Wiley Blackwell, 2014), 195–200.
49. Johannes Haubold, "The Achaemenid Empire and the Sea," *Mediterranean Historical Review* 27 (2012): 4–23.
50. So also Mitchell, "Judahite Creation Theologies," 29.
51. Mark B. Garrison, *The Ritual Landscape at Persepolis: The Glyptic Imagery from the Persepolis Fortification and Treasury Archives* (Chicago: Oriental Institute, University of Chicago, 2017), 410–412.
52. Mehr Azar Soheil, *The Concept of Monument in Achaemenid Empire* (New York: Routledge, 2019), 127–136.
53. Soheil, *Monument*, 129–131; Gojko Barjamovic, "Propaganda and Practice in Assyrian and Persian Imperial Culture," in *Universal Empire: A Comparative Approach to Imperial Culture and Representation in Eurasian History* (Cambridge: Cambridge University Press, 2012), 47–50.
54. Mitchell, "Judahite Creation Theologies," 29–31.
55. Mitchell, "Judahite Creation Theologies," 27.
56. Root, *Kingship*, 160.

122 NOTES

57. Mitchell ("Paradeisos") has shown that the most prominent Jewish prophet of the period, Zechariah, developed his oracles at Ramat Rahel, the Achaemenid administrative center in Yehud, its imperial iconography prompting his visions and their earliest stages of interpretation.

58. Gad Barnea, "Interpretatio Ivdaica in the Achaemenid Period," forthcoming in *JAJ*.

59. Sanders notes some relevant information in the scholarship addressing these sources (*From Adapa To Enoch*, 153 n. 3).

60. Laurie E. Pearce, "'Judean': A Special Status in Neo-Babylonian and Achemenid Babylonia?" in *Judah and the Judeans in the Achaemenid Period*, ed. Oded Lipschits et al. (Winona Lake, IN: Eisenbrauns, 2011), 271.

61. Oded Lipschits, "Persian Period Finds From Jerusalem: Facts and Interpretations," *Journal of Hebrew Studies* 9, no. 20 (2010): 18.

62. William M. Schniedewind, *Who Really Wrote the Bible? The Story of Scribal Communities* (Princeton, NJ: Princeton University Press, forthcoming). See also Ian Douglas Wilson, "Yahweh's Anointed: Cyrus, Deuteronomy's Law of the King, and Yehudite Identity," *Political Memory in and After the Persian Empire*, 332–333.

63. Mitchell, "Paradeisos." For an overview of Ramat Rahel as an administrative center, see Oded Lipschits, Yuval Gadot, and D. Langgut, "The Riddle of Ramat Raḥel: The Archaeology of a Royal Persian Period Edifice," *Transeuphrates* 41 (2012): 57–79.

64. Mizpah had functioned as an administrative site since the early sixth century BCE under Babylonian control and continued to hold a similar position into the Persian period. See the summary discussion by Patrick-McKinley, *Indigenous Elites*, 43–44, 47–49.

65. Mark Leuchter, "The Levites in Exile: A Response to L.S. Tiemeyer," *VT* 60 (2010): 586–589.

66. Boccaccini, *Roots of Rabbinic Judaism*, 61–72. On Joshua 24, see Jeremy M. Hutton, "The Levitical Diaspora (II): Modern Perspectives on the Levitical City Lists (A Review of Opinions)," in *Levites and Priests in History and Tradition*, ed. Jeremy M. Hutton and Mark Leuchter (Atlanta: SBL, 2011), 45–82.

67. David Janzen, "The Cries of Jerusalem: Ethnic, Cultic, Legal and Geographic Boundaries in Ezra-Nehemiah," in *Unity and Disunity in Ezra-Nehemiah*, ed. Mark J. Boda and Paul L. Redditt (Sheffield: Sheffield Phoenix Press, 2008), 117–135. Scholars who downplay the severity of the Babylonian conquest do not reckon with the evidence of significant social disruption; see Oded Lipschits, "Demographic Changes in Judah between the Seventh and the Fifth Centuries B.C.E.," in *Judah and the Judeans in the Neo-Babylonian Period*, ed. Oded Lipschits and Joseph Blenkinsopp (Winona Lake, IN: Eisenbrauns, 2003), 323–376.

68. For a full examination of the *golah* worldview and competing perspectives in Yehud see Dalit Rom-Shiloni, *Exclusive Inclusivity: Identity Conflicts between the Exiles and the People Who Remained (6th–5th Centuries BCE)* (London: Bloomsbury, 2013).

69. Caroline Waerzeggers, "The Babylonian Revolts against Xerxes and the 'End of Archives,'" *AfO* 50 (2003/2004): 150–173. See also the overview by Eleanor Robson, *Ancient Knowledge Networks: A Social Geography of Cuneiform Scholarship in First-Millennium Assyria and Babylonia* (London: UCL Press, 2020), 174–176; Michael Jursa, "The transition of Babylonia from the Neo-Babylonian Empire to Achaemenid Rule," *Proceedings of the British Society* 136 (2007): 90–91. The shift challenged old standards of more insular forms of information transmission within priestly circles; see Hartmut Waetzoldt, "Keilschrift und Schulen in Mesopotamien und Ebla," in *Erziehungs und Unterrichtsmethoden im historischen Wandel*, ed. Lenz Kriss-Rettenbeck and Max Liedtke (Bad Heilbrunn: Linkhardt, 1986), 30.

70. Waerzeggers, "The Babylonian Revolts," 162–163; Seth L. Sanders, *From Adapa To Enoch: Scribal Culture and Religious Vision in Judea and Babylon* (Tübingen: Mohr Siebeck, 2017), 231.

71. Sanders, *From Adapa To Enoch*, 183, 191.

72. It is for this reason that Ezra 7:6,10 specifies that Ezra's own variety of priesthood is primarily qualified by his scribal skill rather than his Aaronide pedigree (*pace* Koch, "Origins of Judaism," 190–193).

73. Mark Leuchter, "Ezra's Mission and the Levites of Casiphia", in *Communal Identity in Judean Historiography*, ed. Gary N. Knopper and Kenneth A. Ristau (Winona Lake: Eisenbrauns, 2009), 179–183.

74. Chapter 2 of this study discusses this phenomenon in greater detail.

NOTES   123

Chapter 2

1. Gerhard von Rad, "The Beginning of History Writing in Ancient Israel," in *The Problem of the Hexateuch and Other Essays* (London: SCM, 1984), 166–204.

2. For an overview, see Bob Becking, *Israel's Past as Seen from the Present* (BZAW; Berlin: De Gruyter, 2021), 24–29. On pre-ninth century script and text production, see Daniel Pioske, "The Scribe of David: A Portrait of a Life," *Maarav* 20 (2013): 176–178; Matthieu Richelle, "Elusive Scrolls: Could any Hebrew Literature Have Been Written Prior to the Eighth Century BCE?" *VT* 66 (2016): 556–594.

3. Pioske, "Scribe of David," 179–182.

4. William M. Schniedewind, *Who Really Wrote the Bible: The Story of the Scribes* (Princeton: Princeton University Press, 2024), ch. 7.

5. Jack R. Lundbom, "Baruch, Seraiah, and Expanded Colophons in the Book of Jeremiah," *JSOT* 36 (1986): 89–114 (here, 107–108).

6. Karel van der Toorn, *Family Religion in Babylonia, Syria and Israel* (Leiden: Brill, 1996), 355–357.

7. See further Heath Dewrell, "Textualization and the Transformation of Biblical Prophecy," in *Scribes and Scribalism*, ed. Mark Leuchter (London: T & T Clark, 2021), 95–106.

8. Mark Leuchter, *The Polemics of Exile in Jeremiah 26–45* (New York: Cambridge University Press, 2008), 145–176.

9. Despite different perceptions of its role in communal and ethnic organization in the Persian period, it is clear that by the mid-fifth century BCE, the Jerusalem temple became a principal hub of religious and administrative activity in Yehud. This is indicated by the attention paid to the structure and its priestly groups in the Nehemiah Memoir, the assignment of interest in temple restoration by the local 'am ha'aretz in Ezra 4:4, and the deference to its priestly leadership evidenced in Jedaniah's letter at Elephantine in TAD 4.7–4.8.

10. Kenneth Ristau, *Reconstructing Jerusalem: Persian Period Prophetic Perspectives* (Winona Lake, IN: Eisenbrauns, 2016), 113–115 (including discussion of Trito-Isaiah), 139–141.

11. See the ensuing discussion of DB Aram at Elephantine.

12. See the implications of Ayelet N. Landau et al., "The Influence of Language on Perception: Listening to Sentences about Faces Affects the Perception of Faces," *Journal of Neuroscience 30* (2010): 15254–15261.

13. George Lakoff, *Don't Think of an Elephant: Know Your Values and Frame the Debate* (White River Junction, VT: Chelsea Green, 2004).

14. Christine Mitchell, "Berlin Papyrus P. 13447 and the Library of the Yehudite Colony at Elephantine," *JNES* 76 (2017): 146–147.

15. See Jason M. Silverman, "From Remembering to Expecting the 'Messiah': Achaemenid Kingship as (Re)Formulating Apocalyptic Expectations of David," *Political Memory in and After the Persian Empire*, ed. Jason M. Silverman and Caroline Waerzeggers (Atlanta: SBL, 2015), 420, 425–432.

16. I differ here somewhat from Sanders, who suggests that Aramaic scribal scholarship overtook the "dignity" of royal decrees, rendering them little more than subjects of its more prestigious curriculum (Seth L. Sanders, *From Adapa To Enoch: Scribal Culture and Religious Vision in Judea and Babylon* (Tübingen: Mohr Siebeck, 2017), 185). Viewed through the multifaceted lens of the Myth, the working of such decrees into an Aramaic scholarly curriculum provides reinforcement to their position in local myths of sacral power and knowledge, creating a more intricate intertwining of subject cultures into the imperial project.

17. Gard Granerod, "'By the Favour of Ahuramazda I am King': On the Promulgation of a Persian Propaganda Text among Babylonians and Judaeans," *JSJ* 44 (2013): 455–480; Karel van der Toorn, *Becoming Diaspora Jews: Behind the Story of Elephantine* (New Haven, CT: Yale University Press, 2019), 89–114. Van der Toorn's overall assessment is compelling, though Tawny Holm draws attention to some weaknesses in his discussion of the community's connection to a period spent in Palmyra, "Papyrus Amherts 63 and the Arameans of Egypt: A Landscape of Cultural Nostalgia," *Elephantine in Context*, ed. Reinhard G. Kratz and Bernd U. Schipper (Tübingen: Mohr Siebeck, 2022), 328–329. But a connection to earlier Israelite communities is not in doubt, especially given the strong points of contact the manuscript evidenced with various psalms. See M. Rosel, "Israels Psalmen in Agypten? Papyrus Amherst 63 und die Psalmen xx und lxxv," *VT* 50 (2000): 81–99.

124 NOTES

18. Mitchell, "Berlin Papyrus."
19. Gard Granerod, *Dimensions of Yahwism in the Persian Period* (BZAW; Berlin: De Gruyter, 2016), 132.
20. Gard Granerod, "YHW the God of Heaven: An *interpretatio persica et aegyptiaca* of YHW in Elephantine," *JSJ* 52 (2021): 22.
21. Granerod, *Dimensions of Yahwism*, 136–140.
22. On priesthood as a traditional locus of scribal skill David M. Carr, *Writing on the Tablet of the Heart* (New York: Oxford University Press, 2005), 33, 53, 116–120.
23. See further Nathan Hayes, "Yedaniah's Identity as Priest or Layperson and the Rhetoric of the Letter from the Judean Garrison of Elephantine to Bagavahya," *JBL* 139 (2020): 521–541.
24. Anselm Hagedorn puts the matter succinctly and clearly by observing that the formation of the Pentateuch took place within Jewish elite circles in response to the empire and not as an external imposition of the empire's decrees or policies: "this shaping was done by the biblical authors themselves, who created a legal corpus that functioned in a wider imperial context . . . that allowed postexilic Israel to operate as part of the Persian Empire without entering into conflict with it." ("Local Law in an Imperial Context: The Role of Torah in the (Imagined) Persian Period," *The Pentateuch as Torah: New Models of Understanding its Promulgation and Acceptance* [ed. Gary N. Knoppers and Bernard M. Levinson; Winona Lake, IN: Eisenbrauns, 2007], 58). On the formation of local laws (there is no reason to except Yehud from this widespread system of imperial regulation), see Jeremiah W. Cataldo, *A Theocratic Yehud? Issues of Government in a Persian Province* (LHBOTS; New York: T & T Clark, 2009), 39–40.
25. Sanders, *From Adapa To Enoch*, 195.
26. David Lambert, "Tôrâ as Mode of Conveyance: The Problem with 'Teaching' and 'Law,'" in *Torah: Function, Meaning and Diverse Manifestations in Early Judaism and Christianity*, ed. William M. Schniedewind et al. (Atlanta: SBL, 2021), 61–80.
27. See "The Date and Scope of P" for additional comments regarding the dating of this material.
28. Scholars are divided on whether these verses were composed for their current setting or were once part of the end of a pre-Pentateuchal source. The issue is not relevant to the current discussion; irrespective of their origins, we are concerned here with their rhetorical function as the closing verses of a redacted Pentateuch. Whether they were lifted from an extant source or composed for their current setting, the verses close-off the Pentateuch and establish temporal dynamics for conceiving of its material reception and preservation.
29. Some of what follows draws from my article "Moses between the Pentateuch and the Book of the Twelve," *HUCA* 90 (2021): 163–183; sections taken from that article appear here with permission.
30. Mark Leuchter, *The Levites and the Boundaries of Israelite Identity* (New York: Oxford University Press, 2017), 180–187.
31. Karel van der Toorn, *Scribal Culture and the Making of the Hebrew Bible* (Cambridge, MA: Harvard University Press, 2007), 126–127, 208–209.
32. See, e.g., Num. 5:11–31.
33. Leuchter, *The Levites*, 187.
34. Thomas C. Romer and Marc Z. Brettler, "Deuteronomy 34 and the Case for a Persian Hexateuch," *JBL* 119 (2000): 401–419.
35. Eckart Otto's view that the Pentateuch's formation is a concession to diaspora Jewish communities (*Deuteronomium im Pentateuch und Hexateuch: Studien zur Literaturgeschichte von Pentateuch und Hexateuch im Lichte des Deuteronomiumsrahmen* [FAT; Tübingen: Mohr Siebeck, 2000] 247–248) does not consider the possibility of Achaemenid mythological schemas informing the mythopoeic function of the work.
36. See Yishai Kiel, "Reinventing Mosaic Torah in Ezra-Nehemiah in the Light of the Law (*dāta*) of Ahura Mazda and Zarathustra," *JBL* 136 (2017): 323–345, who notes how the Moses/YHWH dynamic in the Pentateuch aligns with the Zarathustra/Ahuramazda dynamic in Avestan tradition.
37. A single torah-scroll did not likely emerge until the Hellenistic period. See Liane Feldman, *The Consuming Fire* (Oakland: University of California Press, 2023), 3.
38. Menahem Haran, "Book-Scrolls at the Beginning of the Second Temple Period: The Transition From Papyrus to Skins," *HUCA* 14 (1983): 11–22. See also the more recent discussion by David S. Vanderhooft, "'El-mědînâ ûmědînâ kiktābāh: Scribes and Scripts in Yehud and in Achaemenid Transeuphratene," *Judah and the Judeans in the Achaemenid Period*, 529–544.

NOTES   125

39. On the significance of script for and material representations of language in imperial contexts, see Catherine E. Bonesho, "Aesthetic of Empire: Material Presentation of Palmyrene Aramaic and Latin Bilingual Inscriptions," *Maarav* 23 (2019): 207–228.

40. In a recent study, Jason M. Silverman critiques earlier arguments I made along these lines ("Imperialism, Identity, and Language Choice in Persian Yehud: Towards Understanding the Socio- Political Implications in the Achaemenid Empire," *AABNER* 1 [2021]: 145– 192). Silverman's critique holds in relation to his discussion of Aramaic script within the matrix of imperial administrative documentary production and the question of spoken language practices (the principal focus of his study). But Silverman does not consider the important distinctions between scribes working in administrative capacities and priest- scribes working in sacral-scholarly capacities less concerned with shifts in vernacular linguistic trends. For the latter, the adoption of Aramaic script in the transmission of pre-Persian legacy traditions would carry a different symbolic, mantic, and ritual function than the utilitarian role it played in the production of documents primarily concerned with facilitating communication between different language communities in the course of business-as-usual imperial administration.

41. Brian Peckham, "Writing and Editing," in *Fortunate the Eyes that See*, fs. D.N. Freedman, ed. Astrid Beck et al. (Grand Rapids, MI: Eerdmans, 1995), 364–383.

42. For the Mesopotamian context for this sacral scribal discourse, see Sara Milstein, *Tracking the Master Scribe: Revision Through Introduction in Biblical and Mesopotamian Literature* (Oxford: Oxford University Press, 2016), 208–209.

43. Caroline Waerzeggers, "The Babylonian Revolts Against Xerxes and the 'End of Archives'," *AfO* 50 (2003/2004).

44. Sanders, *From Adapa to Enoch*, 46.

45. Sanders, *From Adapa to Enoch*, 57–58.

46. John L. Berquist, "Postcolonialism and Imperial Motives for Canonization," *Semeia* 75 (1996): 15–35, 23.

47. We should not, however, assume that the Pentateuch carried statutory power that was implemented as a basis for regulating religious and social life throughout Yehud. The evidence for this type of role played by the Pentateuch points to a later era, that of the Hasmoneans, as the time when the Pentateuch's laws took on such a role. See Yonatan Adler, *The Origins of Judaism: An Archaeological- Historical Reappraisal* (New Haven, CT: Yale University Press, 2021), 189–236, 234–236.

48. Jonathan Vroom, *The Authority of Law in the Hebrew Bible and Ancient Judaism* (JSJSup; Leiden: Brill, 2018), 182–201 explains this phenomenon in relation to Ezra, but it applies equally well to the Aaronides whose social and religious power strongly affected the literary presentation of Ezra, as I describe in Chapter 3 of this study.

49. Elsie Stern, "Royal Letters and Torah Scrolls: The Place of Ezra- Nehemiah in Scholarly Narratives of Scripturalization," *Contextualizing Israel's Sacred Writings*, 239–262.

50. See the discussion by Lauren A. S. Monroe, *Josiah's Reform and the Dynamics of Defilement* (New York: Oxford University Press, 2011), 130– 132. Liane Feldman has recently challenged the common model of categorizing Leviticus 17–26 into a distinct "Holiness Code," in *The Story of Sacrifice: Ritual and Narrative in the Priestly Source* (FAT; Tübingen: Mohr Siebeck, 2020), 170–193, situating these chapters within a more contiguous literary work of mostly common authorship. In this case, distinctions between P and H may reside more on the level of concept and language than strictly as a matter of text/composition with a linear direction of development or dependence.

51. Christophe Nihan, "The Torah between Samaria and Judah: Shechem and Gerizim in Deuteronomy and Joshua," in *The Pentateuch as Torah*, ed. Gary N. Knoppers and Bernard M. Levinson, 187– 223; Konrad Schmid, *The Scribes of the Torah* (Atlanta: SBL, 2023). For a range of arguments in this direction, see Jakob Wöhrle, "Frieden durch Trennung: Die priesterliche Darstellung des Exodus und die persische Reichsideologie," in *Wege der Freiheit: Zur Entstehung und Theologie des Exodusbuches*, fs. Rainer Azlbertz, ed. Reinhard Achenbach et al. (Zürich: Theologischer Verlag Zürich, 2014), 87–111; S. David Sperling, "Pants, Persians and the Priestly Source," in *Ve-Eileh Divrei David* (Leiden: Brill, 2017), 196–209; Joseph P. Blenkinsopp, "An Assessment of the Alleged Pre-Exilic Date of the Priestly Material in the Pentateuch," *ZAW* 108 (1996): 495–518.

126   NOTES

52. Schmid, *Scribes*, 237, 254, 481–482; Albert de Pury, "Pg as the Absolute Beginning," in *Les Dernières Rédactions du Pentateuque, de l'Hexateuque et de l'Ennéateuque*, ed. Thomas Romer and Konrad Schmid (Leuven: Peeters, 2007), 99–128.
53. Schmid, *Scribes*, 481.
54. Leuchter, The Levites, 42–51; Robert D. Miller II, "When Pharaohs Ruled: On the Translation of Judges 5:2," *Journal of Theological Studies* 59 (2008): 650–654; Gary A. Rendsburg, "Merneptah in Canaan," *Journal of the Society for the Study of Egyptian Antiquities* 11 (1981): 171–172.
55. Leuchter, *Polemics of Exile*, 135, 160.
56. *Contra* Schmid, who argues that the focus on Egypt's military is a reflection of Persian confrontations with Egyptian military forces.
57. Pursuant especially to Dalit Rom-Shiloni's observations about Jeremiah's pre-exilic familiarity with P language and traditions ("'How can you say, "I am not defiled . . .?"' (Jeremiah 2:20–25): Allusions to Priestly Legal Traditions in the Poetry of Jeremiah," *JBL* 133 [2014]: 757–775), any reconstruction of text-building in Israelite/Judahite or Jewish antiquity must reckon with the very dynamic interaction between scribal groups and an active cult where their formulations were worked into a living, and evolving, orally performed liturgy that in turn exerted influence on textualization praxes.
58. Van der Toorn, *Scribal Culture*, 154; Leuchter, *The Levites*, 171–172.
59. Feldman, *Story of Scripture*.
60. See Feldman's critique of correlative dating in *Consuming Fire*, 48–49.
61. In this sense, the centralized cult in P should be viewed alongside the theoretical rituals depicted in P's legislation—they are both rhetorical in orientation and not indexes of actual praxes or institutions (as per Watts, *Ritual and Rhetoric*).
62. Christophe Nihan, *From Priestly Torah to Pentateuch* (FAT; Tübingen: Mohr Siebeck, 2007); "Between Samariah and Judah," 191, 223. Much of Nihan's argument is rooted in the assignment of P to the fifth century (*Priestly Torah*, 195–197) and the composition of Leviticus 10 as part of a late redactional stratum connected to the overall redaction of the Pentateuch (576–607, 617–618), but there are grounds for questioning this view. See the review of Nihan's monograph by James W. Watts in *Biblica* 91 (2010): 597–598.
63. See Jeremy M. Hutton, "The Levitical Diaspora (I): A Sociological Comparison with Morocco's Ahansal," in *Exploring the Longue Durée* (Fs. Lawrence E. Stager, ed. J. David Schloen (State Park: Pennsylvania State University Press, 2009), 227–228; Leuchter, *The Levites*, 127.
64. Andre Lemaire, "Administration in Fourth-Century B.C.E. Judah in Light of Epigraphy and Numismatics," *Judah and the Judeans in the Fourth Century B.C.E.*, 53–74.
65. Schmid, *Scribes*, 124–125.
66. Brian Rainey, *Religion, Ethnicity, and Xenophobia in the Bible: A Theoretical, Exegetical and Theological Survey* (London: Routledge, 2018) 106–111.
67. See Jurg Hutzli, *The Origins of P* (FAT; Tübingen: Mohr Siebeck, 2023), 133–137.
68. Note, again, how Schmid uses DB to support his view of P's reliance on Persian imperial ideology that he implies was already in place in Cambyses's time (*Scribes*, 124), but does not account for the dramatic *break* that DB creates between Darius' reign and that of Cambyses.
69. Evidence for earlier points of origin is discussed by Rom-Shiloni, "'How Can You Say"; Alice Mandell, "Writing as a Source of Ritual Authority: The High Priest's Body as a Priestly Text in the Tabernacle-Building Story," *JBL* (2022) 141: 43–64, especially Mandell's concluding observations; Feldman, *Consuming Fire*, 49.
70. The thematic points of contact between the P creation account and the Achaemenid creation theology may point to why a particular chronological logic guides the Pentateuchal narrative. On these points of contact, see Christine Mitchell, "'The Politics of Judahite Creation Theologies in the Persian Period," in *Political Theologies in the Hebrew Bible* (JAJSup), ed. Mark G. Brett and Rachelle Gilmour (Paderborn: Brill Schöning, 2023), 23–41 The P creation account may not be product of Persian influence, but its theology lends itself to serving as the opening canto of a larger document forged under Persian rule.
71. Cataldo provides a concise synopsis of the regularity of these revolts (*A Theocratic Yehud*, 34–37).

Chapter 3

1. Laura Carlson Hasler, "Persia Is Everywhere Where Nothing Happens: Imperial Ubiquity and Its Limits in Ezra-Nehemiah," *The Bible and Critical Theory* 16 (2020): 140–154. Recent work has demonstrated that the narrative is informed by the long-term effects of imperialist

NOTES 127

violence, social identity dissolution, and the desperate need to reconstruct communal identity boundaries. See Lisa J. Cleath, "Rebuilding Jerusalem: Ezra-Nehemiah as Narrative Resilience," *JSQ* 30 (2023): 1–27. Cleath's observations help provide context for the book's narrative structure and thematic emphases as a bid for stability by Achaemenid standards.

2. Bob Becking, "'We All Returned as One!': Critical Notes on the Myth of the Mass Return," In *Judah and the Judeans in the Persian Period*, ed. Oded Lipschits and Manfred Oeming (Winona Lake, IN: Eisenbruans, 2006), 12–13.

3. There is bountiful evidence for late Persian redactional work in these sources, including the attempt to adjust earlier discourse to fit the understandings of the late scribes who sought to recycle their sources. See Ingo Kottsieper, "'And They Did Not Care To Speak Yehudit': On Linguistic Change in Judah during the Late Persian Era," in *Judah and the Judeans in the Fourth Century B.C.E.*, ed. Oded Lipscits et al. (Winona Lake: Eisenbrauns, 2007), 99–101.

4. H. G. M. Williamson, "The Composition of Ezra i–vi," *JTS* 34 (1983): 1–30, though the final form of the work should not be set in the early Hellenistic era as Williamson argued. See David M. Carr, *The Formation of the Hebrew Bible: A New Reconstruction* (Oxford: Oxford University Press, 2011), 208–209.

5. Melody D. Knowles, "Pilgrimage to Jerusalem in the Persian Period," in *Approaching Yehud: New Approaches to the Study of the Persian Period*, ed. Jon L. Berquist (Atlanta: SBL, 2007), 11–12, 14.

6. The variety of lists, for example, call attention to their once-independent archival status; so too the various letters in Ezra 4–6 and, obviously, the Artaxerxes Rescript in Ezra 7. On the consistent emphasis on *torah* that cumulatively points to the Pentateuch, see Jonathan Vroom, *The Authority of Law in the Hebrew Bible and Early Judaism* (Leiden: Brill, 2018), 176–177.

7. Yishai Kiel, "Reinventing Mosaic Torah in Ezra-Nehemiah in the Light of the Law (*Data*) of Ahura Mazda and Zarathustra," *JBL* 136 (2017): 323–345. This further weakens the argument for separating *torah* and *data* as made by Rolf Rendtorff, "Esra und das 'Gesetz,'" *ZAW* 96 (1984): 165–184.

8. On the postbiblical *Nachleben* of Ezra, see Rebecca Scharbach Wollenberg, *The Closed Book: How the Rabbis Taught the Jews (Not) to Read the Bible* (Princeton, NJ: Princeton University Press, 2023), 29–39.

9. For an overview of these positions, see H. G. M. Williamson, *Ezra, Nehemiah* (Waco, TX: Word, 1985), xxxix–xliv. More recent advocates of the late-dating of Ezra include Joachim Schaper, "The Temple Treasury Committee in the Time of Nehemiah and Ezra," *VT* 47 (1997): 201; Saul M. Olyan, "Purity Ideology in Ezra–Nehemiah as a Tool to Reconstitute the Community," *JSJ* 35 (2004): 14; Lisbeth Fried, *Ezra and the Law in History and Tradition* (Columbia: University of South Carolina Press, 2014), 40–41; see also Fried's "Ezra's Use of Documents in the Contexts of Hellenistic Rules of Rhetoric," *New Perspectives on Ezra-Nehemiah: History and Historiography, Text, Literature and Interpretation* (Winona Lake, IN: Eisenbrauns, 2012), 11–26.

10. For an overview see the recent monograph of Philip Y. Yoo, *Ezra and the Second Wilderness* (Oxford: Oxford University Press, 2017), 7–9.

11. David Janzen has discussed these issues in his article "The 'Mission' of Ezra and the Persian Period Temple Community," *JBL* 119 (2000): 619–643.

12. Janzen, "The 'Mission' of Ezra," 643.

13. Some scholars opt to assign the Rescript a post-Persian date altogether. See Sebastian Grätz, *Das Edikt des Artaxerxes: Eine Untersuchung zum religionspolitischen und historischen Umfeld von Ezra 7,12–26* (Berlin: de Gruyrter, 2004), 134. Fried argues for a Ptolemaic date: *Ezra and the Law*, 11, 28.

14. Such is the view of Israel Finkelstein, "Jerusalem in the Persian (and Early Hellenistic) Period and the Wall of Nehemiah," *JSOT* 32 (2008): 501–520.

15. See Lester L. Grabbe, "The 'Persian Documents' in the Book of Ezra: Are They Authentic?," in *Judah and the Judeans in the Persian Period*, ed. Oded Lipschits and Manfred Oeming (Winona Lake, IN: Eisenbrauns, 2006), 53–570 (summary material on 561–563); Janzen, "The 'Mission' of Ezra," 629. A more nuanced position is that of James D. Moore, "Who Gave You a Decree? Anonymity as a Narrative Technique in Ezra 5:3, 9 in Light of Persian-Period Decrees and Administrative Sources," *JBL* 140 (2021): 69–89, who notes a combination of administrative and nonadministrative forms in Ezra 4–6. Moore suggests that the nonadministrative forms derive from Hellenistic-era writers intent on obscuring dimensions of historical memory for the purpose of amplifying the legendary status of Cyrus (89). But the departures from strict administrative forms aligns with the ethos of scribal adaptation very much at home in the Persian period,

128   NOTES

and the deliberate obscuring of certain details can be explained by the effect of Achaemenid mythology on the author.

16. I am more amenable to the proposal of Nissim Amzallag, who notes ideological and lexical differences within the Ezra material and the Nehemiah material and posits that these materials developed independently before being redactionally set in relation to each other and, indeed, to support the Nehemian ideology within the finished work ("The Authorship of Ezra and Nehemiah in Light of Differences in Their Ideological Background," *JBL* 137 [2018]: 271–297). Though my position in this study is that the "books" of Ezra and Nehemiah *did not* develop in isolation from each other, I will argue in this chapter that various Ezra traditions existed before incorporation into Ezra- Nehemiah. The peculiar ideological and linguistic conventions noted by Amzallag may be viewed as relics of the early growth of these traditions (both oral and textual).

17. The latter view is also adopted by scholars who allow for the earlier composition of Ezra materials, but who argue that those materials remained entirely separate from a book of Nehemiah that these Hellenistic era authors knew. The most thorough argument for this scenario is that of Dieter Böhler, *Die heilige Stadt in Esdras und Ezra–Nehemia: Zwei Konzeptionen der Wiederherstellung Israels* (Freiburg: Universitätsverlag; Göttingen: Vandenhoeck & Ruprecht, 1997). See also Samuel L. Adams, "Where Is Ezra? Ben Sira's Surprising Omission and the Selective Presentation in the Praise of the Ancestors," in *Sirach and Its Contexts: The Pursuit of Wisdom and Human Flourishing*, ed. Samuel L. Adams et al. (Leiden: Brill, 2021), 151– 176; Jürgen- Christian Lebram, "Die Traditionsgeschichte der Esragestalt und die Frage nach dem historischen Esra," in *Sources, Structures, Synthesis: Proceedings of the Groningen 1983 Achaemenid History Workshop*, ed. Heleen Sancisi-Weerdenburg (Leiden: Nederlands Instituut voor het Nabije Oosten, 1987), 126–132.

18. Benajmin D. Sommer, "Dating Pentateuchal Texts and the Perils of Pseudo- Historicism," in *The Pentateuch: International Perspectives on Current Research*, ed. Thomas B. Dozeman et al. (Tübingen: Mohr Siebeck, 2011), 86–108.

19. H. G. M. Williamson, "The Aramaic Documents in Ezra Reconsidered," *JTS* 59 (2008): 54–62.

20. Seth L. Sanders, "Enoch's Imaginary Ancestor: From Ancient Babylonian Scholarship to Modern Academic Folklore," *JAJ* 9 (2019): 176; *From Adapa to Enoch: Scribal Culture and Religious Vision in Judea and Babylon* (Tübingen: Mohr Siebeck, 2017), 183– 187; Polaski, "What Mean These Stones? Inscriptions, Textuality and Power in Persia and Yehud," in Berquist (ed.), *Approaching Yehud*, 40, 48.

21. Laura Carlson Hasler, *Archival Historiography in Jewish Antiquity* (New York: Oxford University Press, 2020). See also Amélie Kuhrt, "The Achaemenid Persian Empire (c. 550–c. 330 BCE): Continuities, Adaptations, Transformations," in *Empires: Perspectives from Archaeology and History*, ed. Susan E. Alcock et al. (Cambridge: Cambridge University Press, 2009), 115.

22. On the close reliance of Nehemiah 8 on Persian ritual iconography, see Mark Whitters, "The Persianized Liturgy of Nehemiah 8:1–8," *JBL* 136 (2017): 63–84.

23. Michael Austin, *The Hellenistic World from Alexander to the Roman Conquest: A Selection of Ancient Sources in Translation* (Cambridge: Cambridge University Press, 2006), 271; Josef Wiesehöfer, *Die 'dunklen Jahrhunderte' der Persis: Untersuchungen zu Geschichte und Kultur von Fars in frühhellenistischer Zeit (330– 140 v. Chr.)* (Munich: Beck, 1994), 107–108; Stephen Mitchell, "In Search of the Pontic Community in Antiquity," in *Representations of Empire: Rome and the Mediterranean World*, ed. A. K. Bowman et al. (Oxford: Oxford University Press, 2002), 57.

24. On Esther as a Hellenistic work, see Beate Ego, "The Book of Esther: A Hellenistic Book," *JAJ* 1 (2010): 279–302; Lawrence Wills, "Jewish Novellas in a Greek and Roman Age: Fiction and Identity," *JSJ* 42 (2011): 141–165. Hasler also notes a significant rhetorical distinction in the uses of Hebrew and Aramaic found between Daniel and Ezra-Nehemiah; the former employs linguistic shifts to signal the fall of an empire, while the latter does not (*Archival Historiography*, 68).

25. I have discussed the existence of oral lore regarding the scribal figure Baruch already by the end of the exilic period; see "The Name 'Berechiah' in Sach 1," *ZAW* 134 (2022): 58–61. Extratextual traditions regarding such figures circulated in antiquity beyond the boundaries of fixed text traditions. See Jacqueline Vayntrub, "Before Authorship: Solomon and Prov. 1:1," *BibInt* 26 (2018): 182–206; Eva Mroczek, *The Literary Imagination in Jewish Antiquity* (New York: Oxford University Press, 2016), 51–83.

NOTES   129

26. Aaron Demsky, "Who Came First, Ezra or Nehemiah? The Synchronistic Approach," *HUCA* 65 (1994): 1–19. For an alternate proposal, see David Janzen, "Politics, Settlement, and Temple Community in Persian-Period Yehud," *CBQ* 64 (2002): 497.

27. See, e.g., Williamson, *Ezra, Nehemiah*, xxviii–xxxi; Sara Japhet, "Composition and Chronology," in *From the Rivers of Babylon to the Highlands of Judah* (Winona Lake, IN: Eisenbrauns, 2006), 251; Juha Pakkala, *Ezra the Scribe* (Berlin: De Gruyter, 2004), 227–230; Yoo, *Ezra and the Second Wilderness*, 1–5. Ezra 7 is often viewed as part of this Ezra source, but I will argue below that its relationship to traditions about Ezra, and the very formation of those traditions, is more complicated.

28. Anselm Hagedorn, "Local Law in an Imperial Context: The Role of Torah in the (Imagined) Persian Period," in *The Pentateuch as Torah*, ed. Gary N. Knoppers and Bernard Levinson (Winona Lake, IN: Eisenbrauns, 2007), 57–76, 70–71.

29. Hasler, *Archival Historiography*, 94.

30. Sanders, *From Adapa to Enoch*, 154–155, 183–187.

31. This relies on two aspects of Achaemenid ideology: the idea of royal decree as a matter of heavenly disclosure (e.g., the equation between *torah* and *data* in Ezra-Nehemiah; see Janzen, *Politics of Davidic Restoration*, 217–219) and the provision in the closing section of DB that scribal copies/adaptations of royal decrees carried the force of the original compositions (DB 70); see Polaski, "What Mean These Stones?" 38, 40, 48.

32. On Nehemiah's annexation of Ezra traditions, see Mark Leuchter, "Ezra's Mission and the Levites of Casiphia," in *Communal Identity in Judean Historiography*, ed. Gary Knoppers and Kenneth R. Ristau (Winona Lake, IN: Eisenbrauns, 2008), 190.

33. Pakkala, *Ezra the Scribe*, 73–81.

34. Christopher M. Jones, "Embedded Written Documents as Colonial Mimicry in Ezra-Nehemiah," *BibInt* 26 (2018): 180–181. The distinctions Jones notes present Nehemiah's documents as Yehudite subsets or instances of the schema established within the Ezra section of the book.

35. Oded Lipshits, *The Fall and Rise of Jerusalem* (Winona Lake, IN: Eisenbrauns, 2005), 160–168.

36. Jason M. Silverman, "Sheshbazzar, a Judean or a Babylonian? A Note on His Identity," in *Exile and Return: The Babylonian Context*, ed. Jonathan Stökl and Caroline Waerzeggers (Berlin: De Gruyter, 2015), 308–321.

37. Japhet, "Composition and Chronology," 260.

38. For a related discussion regarding literary reframing of Nehemiah, see Lisbeth S. Fried, "Who Was Nehemiah ben Hacaliah?," *Journal of Hebrew Scriptures* 21 (2021): 6.1–14. Fried argues that Nehemiah's title *ha-tirshata* is a corruption of the proper name Attirshata ("Who Was Nehemiah," 7–9). She notes the linguistic problem with the term *tirshata* (from the OP *tarša*) pertaining to his gubernatorial status. However, *ha-tirshata* roughly translates into "the trembler," which associates him with the *haredim* prominent in Yehud in the late sixth to fifth centuries BCE, a group that regarded Ezra as their leader; see Joseph Blenkinsopp, "A Jewish Sect of the Persian Period," *CBQ* 52 (1990): 16–19. This partially explains why Nehemiah and his supporters developed traditions about Ezra to promote Nehemiah's own policies. On the addition of Nehemiah's titles to an older narrative by partisan redactors committed to the legacy of his policies, see Deirdre N. Fulton, "What Kind of Governor was Nehemiah? The Titles פחה and תרשתה in MT and LXX Ezra-Nehemiah," *ZAW* 130 (2018): 252–267. The term *ha-tirshata* may thus be a matter of a redactor's wordplay.

39. These chapters represent the latest unit to enter the work; see Peter R. Bedford, *Temple Restoration in Early Achaemenid Judah* (Leiden: Brill, 2001), 87–110.

40. Yoo, *Ezra and the Second Wilderness*, 81, 209.

41. The common view of Ezra 7:1–5 as distinct from vv. 6ff. should be revised to see a break between vv. 1b–6 and vv. 7ff. On vv. 1–10 as a rhetorical unit, see Williamson, *Ezra, Nehemiah*, 89–91. On the unit as part of a narrative that overall reflects a redactor's implied favoring of a fifth-century setting, see Pakkala, *Ezra the Scribe*, 245. While I agree that this is the intended *peshat* implication of the narrative, I will attempt to show below that the semiotics within the narrative point to a more elaborate literary goal.

42. Pakkala, *Ezra the Scribe*, 24n7.

43. Lester L. Grabbe, *Ezra-Nehemiah* (London: Routledge, 1998), 24–25. But see Yoo, *Ezra and the Second Wilderness*, 83, on vv. 7ff. as separate from vv. 1–6.

130 NOTES

44. Yoo views the final portion of v. 6 as inconsistent with material in Ezra 8 and thus identifies it as secondary (*Ezra and the Second Wilderness*, 83). This, however, is predicated on the view that Ezra 8 is part of an original Ezra memoir from which much of Ezra 7:1b–6 was drawn. In what follows I will propose a different way to evaluate the origins of what we find in Ezra 7:1b–6 that does not require their origination in an extant Ezra memoir whence Ezra 8 originated.

45. Pakkala (*Ezra the Scribe*, 28) suggests that the reference to the king in v. 6 is secondary. Yet this is based on a redaction-critical evaluation of Ezra 7 that assumes a dependence on the Artaxerxes Rescript, which is not demanded by the implications of vv. 1b–6 when read independently.

46. That we encounter a concept of *torah*, priesthood and scribalism in Ezra 7:1b–6 that shows no evidence of such hybridity suggests that the tradition preserved in these verses has origins in a period before Persian imperialism had fully hybridized Jewish institutional self-perception.

47. Mark Leuchter, *The Polemics of Exile in Jeremiah 26–45* (Cambridge: Cambridge University Press, 2008), 145–175.

48. Dalit Rom-Shiloni, "From Ezekiel to Ezra-Nehemiah: Shifts of Group Identities within Babylonian Exilic Ideology," in *Judah and the Judeans in the Achaemenid Period*, ed. Oded Lipschits et al. (Winona Lake, IN: Eisenbrauns, 2011), 127–151; "Ezekiel as the Voice of the Exiles and Constructor of Exilic Ideology," *HUCA* 76 (2005): 1–45. See also Joseph P. Blenkinsopp, *Judaism: The First Phase* (Grand Rapids, MI: Eerdmans, 2009) 127–128.

49. The exilic development of P and H as textual works builds upon antecedent discourses circulating among the priestly circles of Jerusalem well before the end of the exile. Jeffrey Stackert observes features of H that are identifiably exilic in origin and orientation ("Political Allegory in the Priestly Source: The Destruction of Jerusalem, the Exile, and their Alternatives," in *The Fall of Jerusalem and the Rise of the Torah* [FAT], ed. Peter Dubovský et al. [Tübingen: Mohr Siebeck, 2016], 211–223, esp. 222). These concepts may have further developed in the early Persian period, but they originate before that time.

50. Leuchter, *Polemics of Exile*, 177–184.

51. Klaus Koch, "Ezra and the Origins of Judaism," *JSS* 19 (1974): 184; Richard J. Clifford, "The Unity of the Book of Isaiah and its Cosmogonic Language," *CBQ* 55 (1993): 4–5, 9–11.

52. See Yoo's summarized discussion in *Ezra and the Second Wilderness*, 203–205.

53. References to the Exodus in Deuteronomy saturate the entire book, from the Decalogue (Deut 5:6, 14) to the closing curse in Deuteronomy 28. On the significance of the Exodus in the structure of P within the Pentateuch, see Konrad Schmid, "Exodus in the Pentateuch," in *The Book of Exodus: Composition, Redaction, and Interpretation* (FIOTL), ed. Thomas Dozeman et al. (Leiden: Brill, 2014) 33–36. Telling is the Holiness Legislation's culmination in Lev 26:13,45 with references to the Exodus as a boundary marker for maintaining Israel's ethnological cohesion.

54. Gary N. Knoppers, "Ethnicity, Genealogy, Geography and Change: The Judean Communities of Babylon and Jerusalem in the Story of Ezra," *Judean Historiography*, 150–156.

55. Knoppers, "Ethnicity," 156–158; Mark Leuchter, "The Medium and the Message, or, What is Deuteronomistic About the Book of Jeremiah?" *ZAW* 126 (2014): 208–227 (on the movement of Deuteronomistic discourse to prophetic rather than legal genres, yet still retaining an emphasis on *torah*).

56. Sara Japhet, "Periodization between History and Ideology II: Chronology and Ideology in Ezra–Nehemiah," *From the Rivers of Babylon*, 426–427.

57. Pierre Briant, *From Cyrus to Alexander* (Winona Lake, IN: Eisenbrauns, 2002), 43–44; Caroline Waerzeggers,"Very Cordially Hated in Babylonia? Zēria and Rēmūt in the Verse Account," *Altorientalische Forschungen* 39 (2012): 316–320.

58. Joseph Blenkinsopp, "The Mission of Udjahorresnet and Those of Ezra and Nehemiah," *JBL* 106 (1987): 409–421.

59. Karel van der Toorn, "Ezra in Egypt? The Significance of Hananyah's Mission," *VT* 67 (2017): 609–610; Reinhard G. Kratz, "Judean Ambassadors and the Making of Jewish Identity: The Case of Hannaniah, Ezra, and Nehemiah," in *Judah and the Judeans in the Achaemenid Period*, ed. O. Lipschits et al. (Winona Lake, IN: Eisenbrauns, 2011), 437.

60. Juha Pakkala, *Ezra The Scribe* (BZAW; Berlin: De Gruyter, 2004), 42, 135, 179, who views the addition of "priest" only as a late accretion motivated by the cultic interests of later redactional additions to the Ezra story.

61. Most scholars for the last several decades have seen the material in chs. 4–6 as drawn from archival source documents of different types. See A. H. J. Gunneweg, "Die aramaische und die hebraische Erzahlung tiber die nachexilische Restauration-ein Vergleich," *ZAW* 94 (1982): 299;

NOTES 131

Williamson, *Ezra, Nehemiah*, xxiii–xxiv; Richard C. Steiner, "Bishlam's Archival Search Report in Nehemiah's Archive: Multiple Introductions and Reverse Chronological Order as Clues to the Origin of the Aramaic Letters in Ezra 4–6," *JBL* 125 (2006): 641–685. But see now Hasler's evaluation in *Archival Historiography*.

62. Bedford has drawn attention to the tendentiousness of Ezra 1–6 (and especially Ezra 1:1–4:5) as historically reliable resources (*Temple Restoration*, 30–31). But if these chapters are driven by theological interest, then the lack of any mention of Ezra alongside the figures associated with Darius' and Cyrus' reigns is all the more telling.

63. Indeed, the inscription carrying the details of Udjahorresnet's charge under Darius makes clear that the decay of the temple to Neith was the result of Cambyses' reign, and that it was only under Darius that restoration was possible (lines 43–44).

64. Such a rhetorical strategy reflects the degree to which notable portions of the golah community traced their social institutions to the time of Cambyses.

65. The phrase is elsewhere used as a device to compensate for temporal abstraction or ambiguity; see Philip Yoo, "'After These Things' and its Composition in Genesis," *VT* 68 (2018): 660–672.

66. The use of time as a thematic or hermeneutical device in the structuring of biblical narratives was identified many years ago by Brian Peckham, "History and Time," in *Ki Baruch Hu: Ancient Near Eastern, Biblical, and Judaic Studies in Honor of Baruch A. Levine*, ed. Robert Chazan et al. (Winona Lake, IN: Eisenbrauns, 1999), 298, 314.

67. On this last point, see Whitters, "Persianized Liturgy." The chief deity is of course identified with YHWH in Ezra-Nehemiah, but Jews under Achaemenid rule recognized pairings between YHWH and Ahuramazda. See Barnea, "Interpretatio Ivdaica," and David Janzen, *Chronicles and the Politics of Davidic Restoration* (London: Bloomsbury, 2017), 212–224 for the wider spectrum of Achaemenid inscriptional ideologies and the shape of Ezra-Nehemiah.

68. Moore, "Who Gave You A Decree?."

69. Moore, "Who Gave You A Decree?," 71, 87–88.

70. Moore, "Who Gave You A Decree?," 89.

71. Silverman, "Sheshbazzar."

72. Udjahorresnet Inscription, lines 43–44; Blenkinsopp, "Udjahorresnet," 411.

73. This is invariably connected to support in Yehudite circles for Darius' earlier policy of shifting power to the east; see Jason M. Silverman, *Persian Royal-Judaean Elite Engagements in the Early Teispid and Achaemenid Empire: The King's Acolytes* (LHBOTS; London: T & T Clark, 2021), 196. For the adoption of this idea in Ezra-Nehemiah, see P. R. Bedford, "Homeland: Diaspora Relations in Ezra-Nehemiah," *VT* 52 (2002): 147–165.

74. Fried, *Ezra and the Law*, 45–50; Reinhard G. Kratz, "Ezra: Priest and Scribe," in *Scribes, Sages, and Seers: The Sage in the Eastern Mediterranean World* (FRLANT), ed. L. Perdue (Göttingen: Vandenhoeck & Ruprecht, 2008) 163–188.

75. Briant, *From Cyrus to Alexander*, 681–690. The brief and troubled reign of Artaxerxes IV is unlikely to have provided conditions under which Ezra-Nehemiah would have been produced. For additional evidence on the redaction of Ezra-Nehemiah during this general period, see Paul L. Redditt, "The Census List in Ezra 2 and Nehemiah 7: A Suggestion," *New Perspectives on Ezra-Nehemiah*, 240; Pakkala, *Ezra the Scribe*, 58–59; Kottsieper, "Yehudit," 99–101.

76. Hasler, *Archival Historiography*, passim.

77. Blenkinsopp, "Jewish Sect."

78. The episode, however, also points to a self-perpetuating cycle resulting from the application of the Achaemenid mythic framework to Jewish life in Yehud. The recurrence and ostensible resolution of the problem in Nehemiah 13 projects the problem into the realm of myth or cosmic pattern, with Nehemiah's declaration of purification (Neh. 13:30) constituting a rehearsal of Darius' or Xerxes' triumphs over adversity on a stereotyped level. Boer reads this as a "spiral of exclusion" ("Ezra-Nehemiah," 224) in his sociological and socio-economic critique of the narrative. I do not disagree that the text carries this trait, but the function of these patterns and responses in antiquity derives from colonial mimicry among scribes enculturated in the imperial myth.

Chapter 4

1. Mark Leuchter, *The Levites and the Boundaries of Israelite Identity* (New York: Oxford University Press, 2017), chs. 2–4.

2. Mark Leuchter, "Inter-Levitical Polemics in the Late 6th Century BCE: The Evidence from Nehemiah 9," *Biblica* 85 (2014): 269–279.

132 NOTES

3. Ehud Ben Zvi, "Levites of Memory in Chronicles and Some Considerations about Historical Levites in Late-Persian Yehud," in *Chronicles and the Priestly Literature of the Hebrew Bible*, ed. Jeyoung Jeon and Louis C. Jonker (BZAW; Berlin: De Gruyter, 2021), 293, with related observations on p. 299.
4. On the Levite authorship of Chronicles, see Leuchter, *The Levites*, 220, 237, 249–253. On evidence of Aramaic scribal enculturation within the work, see Christine Mitchell, "The Testament of Darius (DNa/DNb) and the Construction of Kings and Kingship in 1–2 Chronicles," in *Political Memory In and After the Persian Empire*, ed. Jason M. Silverman and Caroline Waerzeggers (Atlanta: SBL, 2015), 364–365.
5. For a detailed examination of one episode in the work displaying the range of these methodologies, see my article "The Census Crisis Episode and the Chronicler's Mythological Agenda in 1 Chronicles 21," *VT* 23 (2023): 707–735.
6. I agree with the position of Martin Leuenberger that the redaction of the Book of the Twelve was also strongly influenced by political conditions within the empire that would lead to increased theological interest in prophetic oracles containing judgement of foreign nations ("Time and Situational Reference in the Book of Haggai: On Religious- and Theological-Historical Contextualizations of Redactional Processes," *Perspectives on the Formation of the Book of the Twelve*, 166). The discussion I offer here seeks to complement the focus on legacy Jewish (prophetic) tradition in Leuenberger's study with a view to the weight of Achaemenid mythology on *how* such a theological critique would be formed.
7. An overview of scholarly positions is provided by Jakob Wöhrle, *Der Abschluss des Zwölfprophetenbuches: Buchübergreifende Redaktionsprozesse in den späten Sammlungen* (BZAW; Berlin: de Gruyter, 2008) 2–14.
8. Mika S. Pajunen and Hanne von Weissenberg, "The Book of Malachi, Manuscript 4Q76 (4QXIIa), and the Formation of the 'Book of the Twelve,'" *JBL* 134 (2015): 731–751.
9. Mark Leuchter, "Another Look at the Hosea/Malachi Framework in the Twelve," *VT* 64 (2014): 249–265.
10. A minority of scholars date the work to the early Hellenistic period. As I will show , however, a late Persian period setting better accounts for the rhetorical shape and scope of the work (in keeping with the dating proposed by most commentators).
11. Mark Leuchter, "Another Look at the Hosea/ Malachi Framework in The Twelve," *VT* 64 (2014): 249–265.
12. James D. Nogalski, "One Book of Twelve Books? The Nature of the Redaction Work and Implications of the Cultic Source Material in the Book of the Twelve," in *Two Sides of a Coin*, ed. Thomas C. Römer (Piscataway, NJ: Gorgias Press, 2010), 40–46.
13. On the MT sequence of Jeremiah as informed by the Moses tradition overall, see Christopher M. Seitz, "The Prophet Moses and the Canonical Shape of Jeremiah," *ZAW* 101 (1989): 3–27.
14. Leuchter, *The Levites*, 86–92.
15. Scholars are divided on the antiquity of material in the book of Hosea, with some seeing substantial compositions deriving from redactors/ authors who long postdate Hosea's time; for this view, see Martti Nissinen, *Prophetie, Redaktion, und Fortschreibung im Hoseabuch* (AOAT; Neukirchen-Vluyn: Neukirchener, 1991); Roman Vielhauer, *Das Werden des Buches Hosea: Eine redaktionsgeschichtliche Untersuchung* (BZAW; Berlin: de Gruyter, 2007), 178–79; James M. Bos, *Reconsidering the Date and Provenance of the Book of Hosea: The Case for Persian-Period Yehud* (LHBOTS; London/New York: Bloomsbury, 2013). However, as Marvin Sweeney has observed, the book of Hosea does not make any references to the Babylonian exile ("A Form Critical Re-Reading of Hosea," *Journal of Hebrew Scriptures* 2 [1998]: 1.3.8—1.3.9), and other features in the book derive from sociological factors that a late redactor could not have invented (see further below). The position I adopt here is that while some of the material in Hosea arises from Judahite redaction and scribal transmission, the overwhelming amount of material in the book is authentic to a pre-721 social setting.
16. Hans Walter Wolff, "Hoseas Geisteige Heimat," *TLZ* 81 (1956), 83– 90, 94, n. 71; Joseph Blenkinsopp, *A History of Prophecy in Israel* (Louisville: Westminster John Knox, 1996), 84–85; van der Toorn, *Family Religion in Babylonia, Syria and Israel* (Leiden: Brill, 1996), 314. On Hosea's Levitical lineage see Cook, *Social Roots*, 233–261.
17. For a full treatment of the book of Hosea as an artifact of northern Israelite society, see Adina Levin, "Hosea and North Israelite Tradition" (Ph.D. Dissertation, University of Toronto, 2009), with an overview of scholarship on 1–9.

NOTES 133

18. Rainer Albertz, *A History of Israelite Religion in the Old Testament Period*. 2 vols. (Louisville: Westminster John Knox, 1994), 1: 141–43; Karel van der Toorn, *Family Religion in Babylonia, Syria and Israel* (Leiden: Brill, 1996), 300–301; John J. Collins, "The Development of the Exodus Tradition," in *Religious Identity and the Invention of Tradition*, ed. Jan Willem van Henten and Anton Houtenpen (Assen: Van Gorcum, 2001), 145–155; Michael Oblath, "Of Pharaohs and Kings: Whence the Exodus?" *JSOT* 87 (2000): 23–42.

19. On the divisions of Hosea 4– 11 and 12– 14, see Hans W. Wolff, *Hosea* (Hermeneia; Philadelphia: Fortress Press, 1974), xxix–xxxi; Dwight R. Daniels, *Hosea and Salvation History* (BZAW; Berlin: De Gruyter, 1990), 28–31.

20. Yair Hoffman, "A North Israelite Typological Myth and a Judean Historical Tradition: The Exodus in Hosea and Amos," *VT* 39 (1989): 169–182.

21. The Deuteronomic concept of a succession of Mosaic prophets (Deut. 18:15–18) find a point of origin in Hosea's oracles. See Wolff, *Hosea*, 216; Blenkinsopp, *A History of Prophecy in Israel*, 50; Christophe Nihan, "'Moses and the Prophets': Deuteronomy 18 and the Emergence of the Pentateuch as Torah," *SEA* 75 (2010): 33–34.

22. Mark Leuchter, "The Royal Background of Deut 18,15–18," *ZAW* 130 (2018): 364–383.

23. William Schniedewind, *How the Bible Became a Book: The Textualization of Ancient Israel* (New York: Cambridge University Press, 2004), 94–95.

24. On the overlaps between Micah and the Deuteronomistic tradition, see Jack R. Lundbom, *Deuteronomy: A Commentary* (Grand Rapids, MI: Eerdmans, 2013), 35; Blenkinsopp, *A History of Prophecy in Israel*, 143– 146. In at least one case, the Deuteronomists deliberately invoke the Micah tradition in an explicit intertextual manner; see Keith Bodner, "The Locutions of 1 Kings 22:28: A New Proposal," *JBL* 122 (2003): 533–546.

25. On the connection between the Levites, the Deuteronomists, and the redactors of Jeremiah, see Leuchter, *The Levites*, 189–217.

26. Stephen L. Cook, *The Social Roots of Biblical Yahwism* (Atlanta: SBL, 2004), 216–217, 221–227.

27. Aaron Schart, *Die Entstehung des Zwolfprophetenbuchs* (BZAW; Berlin: De Gruyter, 1998), 317; Burkhard M. Zapff, *Redaktionsgeschichtliche Studien zum Micahbuch im Kontext des Dodekapropheten* (BZAW; Berlin: De Gruyter, 1997), 12, 223; Hans Walter Wolff, *Dodekapropheten: Micha* (BKAT; Neukirchen-Vluyn: Neukirchener Verlag, 1982), 144–145.

28. The predominance of the Moses traditions is already presupposed by the early traditions regarding Samuel (especially 1 Samuel 1– 7, which allude to Moses traditions with relative frequency) and standing behind the development of the early northern Exodus narrative; see Carr, *The Formation of the Hebrew Bible: A New Reconstruction* (Oxford: Oxford University Press, 2011), 477–478.

29. Karel van der Toorn, *Scribal Culture and the Making of the Hebrew Bible* (Cambridge, MA: Harvard University Press, 2007), 253–255.

30. David Lambert, "Tôrâ as Mode of Conveyance: The Problem with 'Teaching' and 'Law,'" in *Torah: Function, Meaning and Diverse Manifestations in Early Judaism and Christianity*, ed. William M. Schniedewind et al. (Atlanta: SBL, 2021).

31. For other resonances in Malachi that are designed to recall Hosea, see David L. Petersen, *Zechariah 9–14 and Malachi* (OTL; Louisville: Westminster John Knox, 1995), 233.

32. Aaron Schart, "The First Section of the Book of the Twelve Prophets: Hosea— Joel— Amos," *Interpretation* 61 (2007): 146–147, observes that the opening section of the Book of the Twelve places material from the Pentateuch in the mouths of the first few prophets within the work.

33. Lambert, "Mode of Conveyance."

34. Leuchter, "Royal Background."

35. Elijah, of course, factors into the closing colophon of the Book of the Twelve; see the ensuing discussion.

36. See similarly Christine Mitchell, "Achaemenid Persian Concepts Pertaining to Covenant in Haggai, Zechariah, and Malachi," in *Covenant in the Persia Period: From Genesis to Chronicles*, ed. Richard J. Bautch and Gary N. Knoppers (Winona Lake, IN: Eisenbrauns, 2015), 304.

37. See, re., the Levite orientation of Hosea's oracles.

38. David Noel Freedman, *The Unity of the Hebrew Bible* (Ann Arbor, MI: University of Michigan Press, 1991), 26– 27; John Goldingay, "Hosea 4 and 11 and the Structure of Hosea," *TynBul* 71 (2020): 181–190; Brian Peckham, "The Composition of Hosea," *HAR* 11 (1987): 337.

39. Timothy Hogue, "The Monumentality of the Sinaitic Decalogue: Reading Exodus 20 in Light of Northwest Semitic Monument-Making Practices," *JBL* 138 (2019): 79–99.

134 NOTES

40. Shalom Spiegel, "A Prophetic Attestation of the Decalogue: Hosea 6:5 with some Observations on Psalm 15 and 24," *HTR* 27 (1934): 105–144 (here, 136–139).
41. The (arguably) premonarchic Song of Deborah already associates YHWH with the Sinai motif (Judg. 5:5).
42. A parallel is found in the near-contemporaneous oracles of Isaiah in Judah as reactions to neo-Assyrian propagandistic rhetoric. See Shawn Zelig Aster, "The Image of Assyria in Isaiah 2:5–22: The Campaign Motif Reversed," *JAOS* 127 (2007): 249–278.
43. Schniedewind, *How the Bible Became a Book*, 24–34.
44. Van der Toorn, *Scribal Culture*, 206–221.
45. Frank R. Polak, "Style Is More than the Person: Sociolinguistics, Literary Culture and the Distinction between Written and Oral Narrative," in *Biblical Hebrew: Studies in Chronology and Typology*, ed. Ian Young (JSOTSup; London: T & T Clark, 2003), 52, 87–98.
46. For an overview of Habakkuk's activity in this era, see Robert D. Haak, *Habakkuk* (VTSup; Leiden: Brill, 1992), 130–149. See also David S. Vanderhooft, "Habakkuk," in *The Oxford Encyclopedia of the Books of the Bible*, ed. Michael D. Coogan (Oxford: Oxford University Press, 2011), 351–352.
47. Moshe Weinfeld, *Deuteronomy and the Deuteronomic School* (Oxford: Clarendon, 1972), 244–274.
48. Leuchter, *The Levites*, 175–177.
49. The view that these units are rhetorically independent cannot be sustained. See the trenchant discussion by Csaba Balogh, "Survival of the Fittest: Habakkuk and the Changing Trail of the Prophetic Tradition," in *Wichtige Wendepunkte: Verändernde und sich ändernde Traditionen in Zeiten des Umbruchs/ Pivotal Turns: Transforming Traditions in Times of Transition*, ed. Hodossy-Takács Előd (Leipzig: Evangelische Verlagsanstalt, 2014), 34–36. His argument that Hab. 1:5–11 was once an oracle penned by an author other than the prophet-scribe behind the rest of the chapter, however, rests on too slender threads. It is better viewed as an author's invocation of motifs either known from Jeremiah's oracles or which served as a common source for both Jeremiah and Habakkuk.
50. Haak, *Habakkuk*, 14.
51. See also the discussion by Vanderhooft, "Habakkuk," in *The Oxford Encyclopedia of the Books of the Bible*, ed. Michael D. Coogan (Oxford: Oxford University Press, 2011), 355.
52. The provenance of the hymn in Habakkuk 3 is a matter of ongoing debate. The majority view is that it draws from conventional and archaic styles of hymnic literature, but there are signs that it was composed in a specifically scribal setting. See especially Michael L. Barre, "Newly Discovered Literary Devices in the Prayer of Habakkuk," *CBQ* 75 (2013): 446–462..
53. Michael H. Floyd, "Prophecy and Writing in Habbakuk 2,1-5," *ZAW* 105 (1993): 479–480.
54. On the origins of the "covenant of Levi" in the Malachi oracles as a fusion of motifs from earlier traditions, see Robert R. Kugler, *From Patriarch to Priest* (Atlanta: Scholars Press, 1996), 18–19.
55. Leuchter, *The Levites*, 246–247. I take this material as the final oracular unit proper, though the book obviously includes concluding colophons.
56. For a full study of this motif, see Thomas J. Overholt, *The Threat of Falsehood: A Study in the Theology of the Book of Jeremiah* (London: SCM Press, 1970).
57. The reliance on Jeremiah from the very outset of the Persian period is strongly suggested by Ezra 1:1–4, which presents the rise of Persia itself as licensed by Jeremiah's oracles, and Zephaniah's use of Jeremiah's oracles presume their authoritative position in the developing canon of the repatriated community's sacred literature. See Mark J. Boda, *The Book of Zechariah* (NICOT; Grand Rapids: Eerdmans, 2016), 76–79, 192, 199, 255, 399–400, 421, 428–429.
58. Baruch Halpern, "Why Manasseh Is Blamed for the Babylonian Exile: The Evolution of a Biblical Tradition," *VT* 48 (1998):511–512.
59. Margaret Cool Root, *The King and Kingship in Achaemenid Art* (Leiden: Brill, 1979), 309–311.
60. Leuchter, *The Levites*, 247.

Chapter 5

1. For an overview, see by Siam Bhayro, *The Shemihazah and Asael Narrative in 1 Enoch 6–11: Introduction, Text Translation and Commentary with Reference to Ancient Near Eastern and Biblical Antecedents* (Münster: Ugarit Verlag, 2005), 1–6. The proposal of Jozef T. Milik that the *Book of Watchers* predates Genesis (*The Books of Enoch: Aramaic Fragments from Qumran Cave 4* [Oxford: Clarendon, 1976], 30–32) has not enjoyed wide scholarly acceptance.

NOTES   135

2. See Helge Kvanvig, *Primeval History: Mesopotamian, Biblical, and Enochic: An Intertexual Reading* (JSJSup; Leiden: Brill, 2011).

3. For a Hellenistic setting, see George Nickelsberg, *1 Enoch* (Hermeneia; Minneapolis: Fortress Press, 2001), 170–171; Anathea Portier-Young, "Symbolic Resistance in the Book of the Watchers," in *The Watchers in Jewish and Christian Tradition*, ed. Angela Harkins et al. (Minneapolis: Augsberg Fortress Press, 2014), 39–49. For a late Persian setting, see Gabriele Boccaccini, *Roots of Rabbinic Judaism: An Intellectual History from Ezekiel to Daniel* (Grand Rapids, MI: Eerdmans, 2002), 100–103. Other discourses within the early Enochian literature may have developed, at least in an embryonic form, during the late Persian period as well. See Jonathan Ben Dov, "A Jewish Parapegma? Reading 1 Enoch 82 in Roman Egypt," in *Time, Astronomy, and Calendars in the Jewish Tradition*, ed. Sacha Stern and Charles Burnett (Leiden: Brill, 2013), 3; Jason M. Silverman, "Iranian Details in the Book of Heavenly Luminaries (1 Enoch 72–82)," *JNES* 72 (2013): 199–200, 204–208.

4. Boccaccini's characterization of the narrative as a priestly polemic (*Roots of Rabbinic Judaism*, 99–103) should thus be qualified and expanded; see the ensuing discussion.

5. For reasons that will become clear below, I do not translate this phrase as "god," as there are additional connotations to its function in these verses.

6. David M. Carr, *The Formation of Genesis 1–11: Biblical and Other Precursors* (Oxford: Oxford University Press, 2020), 107. Many credit this position to influence from the Mesopotamian traditions about Enmeduranki on the P writers during the postmonarchic period (e.g., Day, "The Enochs of Genesis 4–5," 300), but Sanders makes a stronger case that the traditions about Adapa were far more influential on evolving concepts of Enoch leading to the sources in 1 Enoch (*From Adapa To Enoch*).

7. David L. Petersen, "Genesis and Family Values," *JBL* 124 (2005): 10–11.

8. On P's presentation of time as a scholastic discourse, see Seth Sanders, *From Adapa to Enoch: Scribal Culture and Religious Vision in Judea and Babylon* (Tübingen: Mohr Siebeck, 2017), 138–142. Day notes that the P writers knew the 365 day solar calendar ("The Enochs of Genesis 4 and 5," 299–300).

9. The P creation story clearly draws from an existing mythology about creation, using the same language found in non-Priestly sources like Hos. 4:3; Jer. 4:23–26.

10. Carr, *Formation*, 93–94.

11. Carr, *Formation*, 84–92.

12. Alan Cooper and Bernard R. Goldstein, "The Cult of the Dead and the Theme of Entry into the Land," *BibInt* 1 (1993): 294–296. The term might also reflect a kinship term applied to a revered departed figure beyond familiar lineage groups as a type of honorific (1 Sam. 28:13); see Kerry Sonia, *Caring for the Dead in Ancient Israel* (Atlanta: SBL, 2020) 72–73 n. 13; 77–78. See also van der Toorn, *Family Religion in Babylonia, Syria and Israel* (Leiden: Brill, 1996), 236–265.

13. Baruch Halpern, *From Gods to God: The Dynamics of Iron Age Cosmologies* (FAT; Tübingen: Mohr Siebeck, 2009), 417, 440, 450–452, 473–476.

14. The necromantic aspects of Enoch found in the *toledot*-book source would have been at home in the priestly and cultic infrastructure of Jerusalem down to P's day. Evidence within the book of Kings indicates that space was reserved in/around the temple precincts in Jerusalem for rites associated with the elusive *'am ha-'aretz*, "the people of the land," i.e., the rural elites who were able to intervene in matters of court and cult in Jerusalem (2 Kgs. 11; 15; 16:15; 21:24; 23:30). If the members of this caste were the heads of hinterland clans/families, then the authority of these elites must have included hegemony over the ancestral cult (reading *'am ha-'aretz* idiomatically as "mediators [lit: "kin"] of the underworld"). P's demythologization of the ancestral cult should be seen as part of what Halpern terms a broader "state assault" on traditional praxes, projected back onto the historiographic account of Hezekiah's own reign in 2 Kings 18 but originating in the late seventh century in the wake of Josiah's activity (Halpern, *From Gods to God*, 402). Before this time, however, the Jerusalem cult would not have considered ancestral devotion to be a cultural or theological allergen, and necromantic dimensions of the Enoch-patriarch tradition would naturally be acknowledged in a *toledot*-book with earlier compositional origins.

15. Marc Zvi Brettler notes, however, that the very opposite is also implied in the Eden tale: YHWH's warning to the man is that eating the forbidden fruit will in fact make him (and, eventually, his female partner) mortal (*How To Read The Bible* [Philadelphia: JPS, 2005], 46). The transformation works in the other direction than what the serpent claims in Genesis 3:5. The presence of both within the same story is suggestive of the boundary between divinity and mortality as a

136 NOTES

permeable, which not only points ahead to the "divine beings" narrative in Genesis 6:1–4 but which also reverberates with the ideas underlying the reformulations in P's rendition of Enoch.

16. Kvanvig, *Primeval History*, 418.
17. The recent treatment by Robert D. Miller II, *Yahweh: Origin of a Desert God* (Göttingen: Vandehoeck & Ruprecht, 2021), 18–41 provides a thorough overview of the issue and of the history of research.
18. J. David Schloen, "Caravans, Kenites, and Casus Belli: Enmity and Alliance in the Song of Deborah," *CBQ* 55 (1993): 38.
19. On the eleventh century demographic shifts, Ann E. Killebrew, "Israel during the Iron Age II Period," in *The Oxford Handbook of the Archaeology of the Levant: C. 8000–332 BCE*, ed. Margreet Steiner and Ann E. Killebrew (Oxford: Oxford University Press, 2013), 733–734.
20. Especially in the prophetic tradition (Amos 3–5; Hos. 5:13–14; 7:10–11; 10:7; Mic. 1–3; Isa. 1:21; 26:5; 28:1). See William M. Schniedewind, *How the Bible Became a Book: The Textualization of Ancient Israel* (New York: Cambridge University Press, 2004), 76–77.
21. The connection between Kenites and metallurgy has long been recognized. See John Day, "Cain and the Kenites," *Homeland and Exile: Biblical and Ancient Near Eastern Studies in Honor of Bustenay Oded* (VTSup), ed. Gershon Galil et al. (Leiden: Brill, 2009), 343; Carr, *Formation*, 74–76; Joseph P. Blenkinsopp, "The Midianite-Kenite Hypothesis Revisited and the Origins of Judah," *JSOT* 33 (2008): 140; Miller, *Origin of a Desert God*, 33.
22. Robert Kawashima, "On The Yahwist's Leviathan," *Near Eastern Archaeology* 78 (2015): 264–271.
23. Kawashima, "Leviathan," 268.
24. Carr, *Formation*, 72–73.
25. Ronald S. Hendel, "Of Demigods and the Deluge: Toward an Interpretation of Genesis 6:1–4," *JBL* 106 (1987): 21–22.
26. KTU 1.6 V 11–12, 24–25.
27. The LXX Genesis 6:3 indicates that the Nephilim (rendered "giants," γιγαντες) did not survive the flood, thus including the Nephilim among the living. But this is most likely a later adjustment that knows the Enochic version of the event where the Nephilim are the progeny of the divine beings and human women. This departs from an original reading that is consonant with a larger mythic agenda spanning the non-P material.
28. Mark S. Smith, "The Baal Cycle," in *Ugaritic Narrative Poetry*, ed. S. B. Parker (Atlanta: Scholars Press, 1997), 165n. 10. So also the clear meaning of the term in 1 Sam. 28:13 and the chthonic aspects of the term in Hos. 2:2 (Leuchter, *The Levites*, 143–144).
29. Mark S. Smith, *The Genesis of Good and Evil* (Louisville: Westminster John Knox, 2019), 75–78.
30. On the Nephilim and the *apkallu*, see Carr, *Formation*, 107–108, n. 66; Ronald S. Hendel, "The Nephilim Were On The Earth: Genesis 6:1-4 and its Ancient Near Eastern Context," in *The Fall of the Angels*, ed. C. Auffarth and L. Stuckenbruck (Leiden: Brill, 2004), 28–29.
31. On the paterfamilias within family structures as the principle cultic mediator between the living family and the deified dead ancestors, see Lewis, "Ancestral Estate," 608–609; most of the cases Lewis discusses position the paterfamilias of a family or clan as the principal authority over rites and obligations to departed ancestors connected to the family estate.
32. Priestly function at the family shrine is part of the background to obtaining the position as paterfamilias, at which point the paterfamilias becomes the patron of the shrine and its cult overall. Alan Cooper and Bernard R. Goldstein identify both features of the ancestral cult and access to divine knowledge as firmly associated with the paterfamilias characters in Genesis "The Cult of the Dead and the Theme of Entry into the Land," *BibInt* 1 (1993): 201–215; "At the Entrance to the Tent: More Cultic Resonances in Biblical Narrative," *JBL* 116 [1997]: 208–210).
33. Nissim Amzallag, "Furnace Remelting as the Expression of YHWH's Holiness: Evidence from the Meaning of *qannā'* (קנא) in the Divine Context," *JBL* 134 (2015): 242–243.
34. It is beyond the scope of this study to address the *terminus ante quo* of Enoch's place in the myth behind Genesis 6:1–4, but some tentative observations can be made. If the P narrative derives from the late monarchic or exilic period, the non-P narrative must predate it sufficiently to account for the linguistic differences between them (on which see Carr, *Formation*, 78–81; on further distinctions, see Hendel, "Nephilim," 12–17). A late eighth century BCE date for non-P seems reasonable, supported by the similar date for the composition of the non-P Judah-Tamar episode in Genesis 38 that exhibits both a similar linguistic profile and a criticism of urban elitism; see Mark Leuchter, "Genesis 38 in Social and Historical Perspective," *JBL* 132 (2013): 209–227.

NOTES 137

35. See the similar observation of Hendel, "The Nephilim," 20, 22, 30, re., the "bricolage" of traditions shared between these sources.
36. Annette Yoshiko Reed, "Heavenly Ascent, Angelic Descent, and the Transmission of Knowledge in 1 Enoch 6–16," in *Heavenly Realms and Earthly Realities in Late Antique Religions*, ed. Annette Yoshiko Reed and Ra'anan Boustan (Cambridge: Cambridge University Press, 2004), 58–59.
37. Alexandria Frisch, "The Empirical Empire: Perceptions of Empire in Second Temple Literature" (Ph.D. Dissertation, NYU, 2013), 151–170.
38. Bhayro, *1 Enoch 6–11*, 25–27; as well as 12–18, 227–259 on the interactive redactional strata. Kvanvig offers a critique of the finer points of Bhayro's approach (*Primeval History*, 351–354, 432), but it is the overall identification of two major sources underlying 1 Enoch 6–11 that concerns us here.
39. See the similar position by Henryk Drawnel, "Knowledge Transmission in the Context of the Watchers' Sexual Sin with the Women in 1 Enoch 6–11," *The Biblical Annals* 59 (2012): 128–136.
40. Bhayro, *1 Enoch 6–11*, 42–43.
41. Bhayro notes this possibility (*1 Enoch 6–11*, 244–245).
42. The "Babylonian Matrix" for Apocalyptic thought overall is discussed by John J. Collins, *The Apocalyptic Imagination* (Grand Rapids, MI: Eerdmans, 2016 [3rd ed.]), 32–36. Sanders draws attention to the centuries-long intertwining of Akkadian and Aramaic text, language and literature (*From Adapa to Enoch*, 167–183).
43. Kvanvig, *Primeval History*, 2, 354.
44. See the discussion in Chapter 1.
45. Bhayro, *1 Enoch 6–11*, 42 n. 10.
46. On metalsmithing as a long duration feature of some corners of Yahwism in both Israel and Judah, see Blenkinsopp, "Midianite-Kenite Hypothesis," 140; Miller, *Origin of a Desert God*, 33.
47. James W. Watts, "Scripturalization and the Aaronide Dynasties," *Journal of Hebrew Scriptures* 13 (2013): 6.5.
48. Annette Yoshiko Reed notes that the redactors of these materials did not view the respective distinctions between the sources as incompatible or problematic for mutual submersion (*Fallen Angels and the History of Judaism and Christianity: The Reception of Enochic Literature* [Cambridge: Cambridge University Press, 2005], 30–34).
49. John J. Collins, *Daniel* (Hermeneia: MN: Fortress Press, 1994), 55, 59, 352. Collins' discussion of Daniel 11 (377–394) elucidates the degree to which apocalyptic writers aligned their compositions with the cosmic aspects of temporal hinges within periods of history; the discussion addresses Hellenistic-era compositions but carries implications for the authors/redactors of 1 Enoch 6–11 and their view of one such historical hinge.
50. For an overview of these events, see Pierre Briant, *From Cyrus to Alexander* (Winona Lake, IN: Eisenbrauns, 2002), 695–726.
51. Sanders, *From Adapa to Enoch*, 101.
52. Jacqueline Vayntrub, "Ecclesiastes and the Problem of Transmission in Biblical Literature," in *Scribes and Scribalism*, ed. Mark Leuchter (London: Bloomsbury, 2021), 82–92.
53. This idea is developed in the later discourses regarding Enoch in the surrounding chapters; see Frisch, "Empirical Empire," 156–157.
54. Sanders, *From Adapa to Enoch*, 186.
55. Menahem Haran, "Book-Scrolls at the Beginning of the Second Temple Period: The Transition From Papyrus to Skins," *HUCA* 14 (1983): 11–22.
56. Seth L. Sanders notes that ancient Hebrew, as a literary language, could claim not even a three-century lifespan over against countless centuries of Akkadian literature ("Enoch's Imaginary Ancestor: From Ancient Babylonian Scholarship to Modern Academic Folklore," *JAJ* 9 [2019]: 174).
57. Mark Leuchter, "The Pre-Pentateuchal Enoch," *CBQ* 86 (2024): 48–51.
58. Rebecca Lesses, "They Revealed Secrets to Their Wives: The Transmission of Magical Knowledge in 1 Enoch," in *With Letters of Light— Otiyot Shel Or: Studies in Early Jewish Apocalypticism and Mysticism in Honour of Rachel Elior*, ed. Dafna Arbel and Andrei Orlov (Berlin: De Gruyter, 2010), 199–202, 211–214. On the ongoing significance of passages dealing with women in the variant versions of the Watchers texts, see Kelley Coblentz Bautch, "What Becomes of the Angels' Wives? A Text-Critical Study of 1 Enoch 19:2," *JBL* 125 (2006): 766–780.

138 NOTES

59. For an overview see Lesses, "Transmission of Magical Knowledge," 214–221. Lesses notes a connection to Proverbs (on which, see the ensuing discussion in the present study) but does not address it in detail with regarding to 1 Enoch 6–11.

60. See Kelli Anne Gardner, "The Figure and Figuration of Women in the Hebrew Bible: Proverbs 1–9, 31 and Lamentations 1–2" (PhD Dissertation, University of Chicago, 2020), 218 n. 288.

61. This connects the "Woman of Folly" to the "Strange Woman" throughout Proverbs 1–9, who is similarly connected to death (Gardner, "Figuration," 163).

62. Lady Wisdom herself, of course, functions as the literary prefiguration of the Woman Valor; see Gardner, "Figuration," 141.

63. Gardner, "Figuration," 141.

64. See especially Christine Roy Yoder, "The Woman of Substance (אשת־חיל): A Socioeconomic Reading of Proverbs 31:10–31," *JBL* 122 (2003): 427–47.

65. The body as a site of holiness—and thus a potent locus for undoing or transgressing it—was noted already by Mary Douglas, "The Abominations of Leviticus," in *Purity and Danger: An Analysis of Pollution and Taboo* (London: Routledge, 1984), 41–57.

66. Gardner, "Figuration," 5–26, for an overview of scholarship.

67. Gardner, "Figuration," 38–39; Rhiannon Graybill, *Are We Not Men? Unstable Masculinity in the Hebrew Prophets* (Oxford: Oxford University Press, 2016), 50–51, 62–69; Alice A. Keefe, *Woman's Body and the Social Body in Hosea* (JSOTSup; Sheffield: Sheffield Academic Press, 2001), 16–18.

68. Shin-Ichi Anzai observes that the assertion of control over the landscape as feminine/Other is a feature of colonialism ("Transplantation of the Picturesque: Emma Hamilton, English landscape, and redeeming the Picturesque," in *Gender and Landscape: Renegotiating Morality and Space*, ed. Lorraine Dowler et al. [London: Routledge, 2005], 60–65). We may cautiously apply this to the reordering of subordinate foreign lands under ancient Mesopotamian imperialism; see Gardner, "Figuration," 20, 39–40.

69. See further Thomas B. Dozeman, "Geography and History in Herodotus and Ezra-Nehemiah," *JBL* 122 (2003): 462–464, on imperial space as an ordering principle.

70. On the *bandaka* see Christine Mitchell, "Achaemenid Persian Concepts Pertaining to Covenant and Haggai, Zechariah and Malachi, in *Covenant in the Persian Period: From Genesis to Chronicles*, ed. Richard J. Bautch and Gary N. Knoppers (Winona Lake, IN: Eisenbrauns, 2015), 295–301.

71. One thinks, for example, of the *Book of the Twelve*, generally regarded as redacted during the late Persian period, and which folds the prophetic figures within it into the prototype of Moses akin to the way all the Achaemenid emperors were folded into the typology established by Darius as the "Persian Man" at Behistun.

72. In what follows I differ with Anathea Portier-Young's reading of the giants as renditions of Hellenistic imperial forces ("Constructing Imperial and National Identities: Monstrous and Human Bodies in Book of Watchers, Daniel, and 2 Maccabees," *Interpretation* 74 [2020]: 163), though her observation that the monstrousness of the Giants present "occupation, and domination as disordered, distorted, and out of control . . . [i]t also betrays anxiety about Judean/Jewish identity in the shadow of empire" applies equally well to a view of failing Achaemenid imperialism.

73. Margaret Cool Root, *The King and Kingship in Achaemenid Art* (Leiden: Brill, 1979), 309–311.

74. E.g., famously, 2 Kgs. 18:19.

75. Eran Almagor, "The Political and the Divine in Achaemenid Royal Inscriptions," *Ancient Historiography on War and Empire* (ed. Timothy Howe et al; Philadelphia: Oxbow, 2017) 38–41.

76. Boccaccini, *Roots of Rabbinic Judaism*, 91, 165–167. But the critique extends to the Achaemenids as well. Indeed, the Giants are called *mamzerim* ("bastards") in 1 En. 10:9, an acute stab at Achaemenid dynastic connections to the heavens.

77. For an analysis of this and related traditions, see Matthew Goff, "Monstrous Appetites: Giants, Cannibalism and Insatiable Eating in Enochic Literature," *JAJ* 1 (2010): 40–42.

Conclusion

1. Just as the archaeological record does not support the picture in Ezra-Nehemiah presented in Ezra-Nehemiah, the less accommodationist ideologies we have surveyed seem to reside only on the page as well, and continuity in settlement and economy persists even into the post-Achaemenid period. See Oded Lipschits and Oren Tal, "The Settlement Archaeology of the

NOTES 139

Province of Judah: A Case Study," in *Judah and the Judeans in the Fourth Century B.C.E.*, ed. Oded Lipschits et al. (Winona Lake, IN: Eisenbrauns, 2007), 33–52.

2. See similarly Ehud Ben Zvi, "Levites of Memory in Chronicles and Some Considerations about Historical Levites in Late-Persian Yehud," in *Chronicles and the Priestly Literature of the Hebrew Bible*, ed. Jeyoung Jeon and Louis C. Jonker (BZAW; Berlin: De Gruyter, 2021), 289.

3. Paul D. Hanson, *The Dawn of Apocalyptic: The Historical and Sociological Roots of Jewish Apocalyptic Eschatology* (Minneapolis: Fortress Press, 1975); Gabriele Boccaccini, *Roots of Rabbinic Judaism: An Intellectual History from Ezekiel to Daniel* (Grand Rapids, MI: Eerdmans, 2002) (but see his important qualification on 99); Benedikt Rausche, "The Relevance of Purity in Second Temple Judaism According to Ezra-Nehemiah," in *Purity and the Forming of Religious Traditions in the Ancient Mediterranean World and Ancient Judaism*, ed. Christian Frevel and Christophe Nihan (Leiden: Brill, 2013), 457–475.

4. Mark Leuchter, *The Polemics of Exile in Jeremiah 26–45* (Cambridge: Cambridge University Press, 2008), 159–176.

5. James W. Watts, *Ritual and Rhetoric in Leviticus: From Sacrifice to Scripture* (New York: Cambridge University Press, 2007), 145–169.

6. This is most clearly illustrated by the doublet in Ezra 1:1–4/2 Chr. 36:22–23, where the texts are not only in conversation with each other but with the prophetic tradition represented by Jeremiah, and all under the auspices of Persian imperial authority. But S/A Narrative's engagement with the Pentateuch (and subsequent Enochian reliance on P materials) is also suggestive of this interaction. See Seth L. Sanders, *From Adapa to Enoch* (TSAJ; Tübingen: Mohr Siebeck, 2017), 145.

7. John L. Berquist, "Postcolonialism and Imperial Motives for Canonization," *Semeia 75* (1996): 15–35, 29.

8. Jonathan Vroom, *The Authority of Law in the Hebrew Bible and Early Judaism (JSJSup;* Leiden: Brill, 2018), 192–195; Liane Feldman, *The Consuming Fire* (Oakland: University of California Press, 2023), 50.

9. On the relationship between these works, see Mark Leuchter, "Ezra's Mission and the Levites of Casiphia," *Communal Identity in Judean Historiography*, ed. Gary Knoppers and Kenneth R. Ristau (Winona Lake, IN: Eisenbrauns, 2008), 249–253.

10. See similarly Dierdre N. Fulton, "What Do Priests and Kings Have in Common? Priestly and Royal Succession Narratives in the Achaemenid Era," in *Judah and the Judeans in the Achaemenid Period*, ed. Oded Lipschits et al. (Winona Lake: Eisenbrauns, 2011), 238, on the function of the genealogies used in these texts.

11. Leuchter, *The Levites*, 258–259.

12. Boccaccini, *Roots of Rabbinic Judaism*, 181–184.

13. This phenomenological view is already at work in the two-part structure of Nehemiah 8: the exegesis of the Tabernacles festival legislation only takes place following the sapiential exercises accompanying *torah*-reading ceremony in vv. 1–12. The Aaronide Pentateuch is subjected to the imperially derived scribal culture, and the chapter then narrates how its deeper meaning is then put into action. See further Michael Fishbane, *Biblical Interpretation in Ancient Israel* (Oxford: Clarendon, 1985), 109–113. Fishbane views this as an inner-Jewish development, but in light of the cognitive impact of imperialism, this unique intellectual phenomenon, as much as the uniqueness of the *torah*-reading ritual itself (Sara Japhet, "The Ritual of Reading Scripture (Nehemiah 8:1–12)," in *New Perspectives on Old Testament Prophecy and History* (VTSup), fs. Hans M. Barstad, ed. Rannfrid I. Thelle et al. (Leiden: Brill, 2015), 175–190), is a hallmark of Bhabha's Third Space applied to the construction of Jewish identity. In terms of grounding the episode in the context of binding imperial data, Vroom highlights the urgency that the textual interrogation generates (*Authority of Law*, 179–180), which suggests that abiding by the terms of the newly derived stipulations is both a matter of Jewish theological concern and abiding by the "proper place/proper time/proper manner" tropes of Achaemenid mythology. The two, in fact, are a binary pair.

14. See Chapter 1.

15. Jacqueline Vayntrub, "Ecclesiastes and the Problem of Transmission in Biblical Literature," in *Scribes and Scribalism*, ed. Mark Leuchter (London: Bloomsbury, 2021), 82–91.

16. Mark Leuchter, "The Pen of Scribes: Writing, Textuality, and the Book of Jeremiah," in *The Book of Jeremiah: Composition, Reception, and Interpretation*, ed. Jack R. Lundbom et al. (FIOTL; Leiden: Brill, 2018), 3–25.

140 NOTES

17. On Jeremiah's prominence in the final chapters of Chronicles, see Baruch Halpern, "Why Manasseh Is Blamed for the Babylonian Exile: The Evolution of a Biblical Tradition," *VT* 48 (1998): 511–512.
18. Daniel C. Olson, "Jeremiah 4.5–31 and Apocalyptic Myth," *JSOT* 73 (1997): 81–107.
19. Baruch Halpern, "YHWH The Revolutionary: Reflections on the Rhetoric of Redistribution in the Social Context of Dawning Monotheism," in *Jews, Christians, and the Theology of the Hebrew Scriptures*, ed. Alice Ogden Bellis and Joel S. Kaminsky (Atlanta: SBL, 2000), 203–211.
20. For background see Robson, *Knowledge Networks*, 180–194.
21. The imagery of the chapter fits the ubiquity of traditions in both Jewish and Mesopotamian circles that utilized mythic figures to connect scribal groups to the heavens (Sanders, *From Adapa to Enoch*). The hand responsible for the writing on the wall may express YHWH's judgement, but should be viewed within the matrix of scribal mythology and the concept of heavenly scribal patrons connected to terrestrial scribal guilds.
22. Watts, *Ritual and Rhetoric*, 110–113.
23. Annette Yoshiko Reed, *Demons, Angels, and Writing in Ancient Judaism* (Cambridge: Cambridge University Press, 2020).
24. Reed, *Demons,* 216, 228–240.
25. Mark J. Boda, "Redaction in the Book of Nehemiah: A Fresh Proposal," *Unity and Disunity in Ezra-Nehemiah*, 25–54.
26. John W. Wright, "Guarding the Gates: 1 Chronicles 26:1–19 and the Role of Gatekeepers in Chronicles," *JSOT* 48 (1990): 69–81.
27. Mark Leuchter, "The Crisis Episode in 1 Chronicles 21 and the Chronicler's Mythological Agenda," *VT* 73 (2023): 707–735.
28. David L. Petersen, "Genesis and Family Values," *JBL* 124 (2005): 5–23.
29. On Egypt as a locus of chaos and death, see Ronald S. Hendel, "The Exodus as Cultural Memory: Egyptian Bondage and the Song of the Sea," in *Israel's Exodus in Transdisciplinary Perspective*, ed. Thomas E. Levy et al. (Heidelberg: Springer, 2015), 74. The author of the Jacob story hints at this by equating Joseph's descent into Egypt with Jacob's decree that his soul will descend into Sheol (Gen. 37:35–36).
30. Feldman, *Consuming Fire*, 37.
31. On the diminishing royal/imperial patronage of scribal groups, beginning in the Achaemenid era but accelerating thereafter, see Robson, *Knowledge Networks*, 180–194.
32. Rebecca Scharbach Wollenberg, *The Closed Book: How The Rabbis Taught the Jews (Not) to Read the Bible* (Princeton, NJ: Princeton University Press, 2023) 45.
33. Wollenberg, *Closed Book*, 43.
34. T. Sanhedrin 4.7; b. Sanhedrin 21b–22a; b. Bava Bathra 14b.
35. Crucially, Wollenberg notes the connection here to the circumstances surrounding the completion and display of DB (*Closed Book*, 208–209).

Bibliography

Adams, Samuel L.
"Where Is Ezra? Ben Sira's Surprising Omission and the Selective Presentation in the Praise of the Ancestors," in *Sirach and Its Contexts: The Pursuit of Wisdom and Human Flourishing* (JSJSup), ed. Samuel L. Adams et al. (Leiden: Brill, 2021), 151–176.

Adler, Yonatan.
The Origins of Judaism: An Archaeological-Historical Reappraisal (New Haven, CT: Yale University Press, 2021).

Albertz, Rainer (with Bob Becking).
A History of Israelite Religion in the Old Testament Period. 2 vols. (Louisville, KY: Westminster John Knox, 1994).

Albertz, Rainer (with Bob Becking)
(ed.). *Yahwism After the Exile: Perspectives on Israelite Religion in the Persian Era* (Assen: Van Gorcum, 2003).

Almagor, Eran.
"The Political and the Divine in Achaemenid Royal Inscriptions," in *Ancient Historiography on War and Empire*, ed. Timothy Howe et al. (Philadelphia: Oxbow, 2017), 38–41.

Amzallag, Nissim.
"The Authorship of Ezra and Nehemiah in Light of Differences in Their Ideological Background," *JBL* 137 (2018): 271–297.

Amzallag, Nissim.
"Furnace Remelting as the Expression of YHWH's Holiness: Evidence from the Meaning of *qannāʾ* (קנא) in the Divine Context," *JBL* 134 (2015): 233–252.

Anzai, Shin-Ichi.
"Transplantation of the Picturesque: Emma Hamilton, English landscape, and redeeming the Picturesque," in *Gender and Landscape: Renegotiating Morality and Space*, ed. Lorraine Dowler et al. (London: Routledge, 2005), 55–74

Arbib, Michael A.
"Schemas vs. Symbols: A View from the 90s," *Journal of Knowledge Structures and Systems* 2 (2021): 68–74.

Aster, Shawn Zelig.
"The Image of Assyria in Isaiah 2:5–22: The Campaign Motif Reversed," *JAOS* 127 (2007): 249–278.

Athas George (with Mark Leuchter).
"Is Cambyses Also Among the Persians," forthcoming in *HUCA*.

Austin, Michael.
The Hellenistic World from Alexander to the Roman Conquest: A Selection of Ancient Sources in Translation (Cambridge: Cambridge University Press, 2006), no. 271.

Ballentine, Deborah Scoggins.
The Conflict Myth and the Biblical Tradition (New York: Oxford University Press, 2015).

142 BIBLIOGRAPHY

Balogh, Csaba.
"Survival of the Fittest: Habakkuk and the Changing Trail of the Prophetic Tradition," in *Wichtige Wendepunkte: Verändernde und sich ändernde Traditionen in Zeiten des Umbruchs/Pivotal Turns: Transforming Traditions in Times of Transition*, ed. Hodossy-Takács Előd (Leipzig: Evangelische Verlagsanstalt, 2014), 27–43.

Barjamovic, Gojko.
"Propaganda and Practice in Assyrian and Persian Imperial Culture," in *Universal Empire: A Comparative Approach to Imperial Culture and Representation in Eurasian History*, ed. Peter Fibiger Bang and Dariusz Kolodziejczyk (Cambridge: Cambridge University Press, 2012), 43–59.

Barnea, Gad.
"Interpretatio Ivdaica in the Achaemenid Period," forthcoming in *JAJ*.

Barnea, Gad.
"Yahwistic Identity in the Achaemenid Period," forthcoming in *ZAW*.

Barre, Michael L.
"Newly Discovered Literary Devices in the Prayer of Habakkuk," *CBQ* 75 (2013): 446–462.

Bautch, Kelley Coblentz.
"What Becomes of the Angels' Wives? A Text-Critical Study of 1 Enoch 19:2," *JBL* 125 (2006): 766–780.

Beaulieu, Paul-Alain.
"Official and Vernacular Languages: The Shifting Sands of Imperial and Cultural Identities in First-Millenium B.C. Mesopotamia," in *Margins of Writing, Origins of Culture*, ed. Seth L. Sanders (Chicago: Oriental Institution, 2006), 185–215.

Becking, Bob.
Israel's Past as Seen from the Present (BZAW; Berlin: De Gruyter, 2021).

Becking, Bob.
"'We All Returned as One!': Critical Notes on the Myth of the Mass Return," in *Judah and the Judeans in the Persian Period*, ed. Oded Lipschits and Manfred Oeming (Winona Lake, IN: Eisenbrauns, 2006), 3–18.

Bedford, Peter R.
"Homeland: Diaspora Relations in Ezra-Nehemiah," *VT* 52 (2002): 147–165.
Temple Restoration in Early Achaemenid Judah (JSJSup; Leiden: Brill, 2001).

Beim, Aaron.
"The Cognitive Aspects of Collective Memory," *Symbolic Interaction* 30 (2007): 7–26.

Ben Dov, Jonathan.
"A Jewish Parapegma? Reading 1 Enoch 82 in Roman Egypt," in *Time, Astronomy, and Calendars in the Jewish Tradition*, ed. Sacha Stern and Charles Burnett (Leiden: Brill, 2013), 1–25.

Ben Zvi, Ehud.
"Levites of Memory in Chronicles and Some Considerations about Historical Levites in Late-Persian Yehud," in *Chronicles and the Priestly Literature of the Hebrew Bible*, ed. Jeyoung Jeon and Louis C. Jonker (BZAW; Berlin: De Gruyter, 2021), 281–304.

Ben Zvi, Ehud.
Social Memory among the Literati of Yehud (BZAW, 509; Berlin: de Gruyter 2019).

Benson, Melissa.
"Violence in the Behistun Monument: Construction and Cohesion of Achaemenid Imperial Rule under Darius I (522–519 BCE)," PhD Dissertation, University College London, 2020.

BIBLIOGRAPHY 143

Berquist, Jon L.
"Postcolonialism and Imperial Motives for Canonization," *Semeia* 75 (1996): 15–35.

Berthelot, Katell.
Jews and Their Roman Rivals (Princeton, NJ: Princeton University Press, 2021).

Betlyon, John W.
"Egypt and Phoenicia in the Persian Period: Partners in Trade and Rebellion," *Egypt, Israel and the Ancient Mediterranean World*, fs. Donald B. Redford, ed. Gary Knoppers and Antoine Hirsch (Leiden: Brill, 2004).

Bhabha, Homi K.
The Location of Culture (London: New York: Routledge, 1994).

Bhayro, Siam.
The Shemihazah and Asael Narrative in 1 Enoch 6– 11: Introduction, Text Translation and Commentary with Reference to Ancient Near Eastern and Biblical Antecedents (Münster: Ugarit Verlag, 2005).

Blenkinsopp, Joseph P.
"An Assessment of the Alleged Pre-Exilic Date of the Priestly Material in the Pentateuch," ZAW 108 (1996): 495–518.

Blenkinsopp, Joseph P.
The Book of Zechariah (NICOT; Grand Rapids, MI: Eerdmans, 2016).

Blenkinsopp, Joseph P.
A History of Prophecy in Israel (Louisville/London: Westminster John Knox, 1996).

Blenkinsopp, Joseph P.
"A Jewish Sect of the Persian Period," *CBQ* 52 (1990): 5–20.

Blenkinsopp, Joseph P.
Judaism: The First Phase (Grand Rapids, MI: Eerdmans, 2009).

Blenkinsopp, Joseph P.
"The Midianite- Kenite Hypothesis Revisited and the Origins of Judah," *JSOT* 33 (2008): 131–153.

Blenkinsopp, Joseph P.
"The Mission of Udjahorresnet and Those of Ezra and Nehemiah," *JBL* 106 (1987): 409–421.

Boccaccini, Gabriele.
Roots of Rabbinic Judaism: An Intellectual History from Ezekiel to Daniel (Grand Rapids, MI: Eerdmans, 2002).

Boda, Mark J.
"Redaction in the Book of Nehemiah: A Fresh Proposal," in *Unity and Disunity in Ezra-Nehemiah*, ed. Mark J. Boda and Paul L. Redditt (Sheffield: Sheffield Phoenix Press, 2008), 25–54.

Bodner, Keith.
"The Locutions of 1 Kings 22:28: A New Proposal," *JBL* 122 (2003): 533–546.

Boer, Roland.
"Thus I Cleansed Them from Everything Foreign: The Search for Subjectivity in Ezra-Nehemiah," in *Postcolonialism and the Hebrew Bible: The Next Step*, ed. Roland Boer (Atlanta: SBL, 2013), 221–238.

Böhler, Dieter.
Die Heilige Stadt in Esdras und Ezra-Nehemia: Zwei Konzeptionen der Wiederherstellung Israels (OBO; Freiburg: Universitätsverlag; Göttingen: Vandenhoeck & Ruprecht, 1997).

144 BIBLIOGRAPHY

Bonesho, Catherine E.
"Aesthetic of Empire: Material Presentation of Palmyrene Aramaic and Latin Bilingual Inscriptions," *Maarav* 23 (2019): 207–228.

Bos, James M.
Reconsidering the Date and Provenance of the Book of Hosea: The Case for Persian-Period Yehud (LHBOTS; London/New York: Bloomsbury, 2013).

Brettler, Marc Zvi.
How To Read the Jewish Bible (Philadelphia: JPS, 2005).

Brettler, Marc Zvi.
"Judaism in the Hebrew Bible? The Transition from Ancient Israelite Religion to Judaism," *CBQ* 61 (1999): 429–447.

Briant, Pierre.
From Cyrus to Alexander (Winona Lake, IN: Eisenbrauns, 2002).

Carr, David M.
The Formation of Genesis 1–11: Biblical and Other Precursors (Oxford: Oxford University Press, 2020).

Carr, David M.
The Formation of the Hebrew Bible: A New Reconstruction (Oxford: Oxford University Press, 2011).

Carr, David M.
Writing on the Tablet of the Heart (New York: Oxford University Press, 2005).

Carter, Charles E.
The Emergence of Yehud in the Persian Period: A Social and Demographic Study (Sheffield: Sheffield Academic Press, 1999).

Cataldo, Jeremiah W.
A Theocratic Yehud? Issues of Government in a Persian Province (LHBOTS; New York: T & T Clark, 2009).

Cleath, Lisa J.
"Rebuilding Jerusalem: Ezra-Nehemiah as Narrative Resilience," *JSQ* 30 (2023): 1–27.

Clifford, Richard J.
"The Unity of the Book of Isaiah and its Cosmogonic Language," *CBQ* 55 (1993): 1–17.

Collins, John J.
"Cosmology: Time and History," in *Ancient Religions*, ed. Sarah Iles Johnston (Cambridge, MA: Harvard University Press, 2007).

Collins, John J.
"The Development of the Exodus Tradition," in *Religious Identity and the Invention of Tradition*, ed. Jan Willem van Henten and Anton Houtenpen (Assen: Van Gorcum, 2001), 145–155.

Collins, John J.
Daniel (Hermeneia, MN: Fortress Press, 1994).

Collins, John J.
The Apocalyptic Imagination, 3rd ed. (Grand Rapids, MI: Eerdmans, 2016).

Cooper, Alan (with Bernard R. Goldstein).
"The Cult of the Dead and the Theme of Entry into the Land," *BibInt* 1 (1993): 285–303.

Cooper, Alan (with Bernard R. Goldstein).
"At the Entrance to the Tent: More Cultic Resonances in Biblical Narrative," *JBL* 116 (1997): 201–215.

BIBLIOGRAPHY 145

Daniels, Dwight R.
Hosea and Salvation History (BZAW; Berlin: De Gruyter, 1990).

Day, John.
"Cain and the Kenites," in *Homeland and Exile: Biblical and Ancient Near Eastern Studies in Honor of Bustenay Oded* (VTSup), ed. Gershon Galil et al. (Leiden: Brill, 2009), 335–346.

Day, John.
"The Enochs of Genesis 4 and 5 and the Emergence of the Apocalyptic Enoch Tradition," in *Sybils, Scriptures and Scrolls*, fs. John J. Collins (JSJSup 175), ed. Joel Baden et al. (Leiden: Brill, 2017), 293–313.

Demsky, Aaron.
"Who Came First, Ezra or Nehemiah? The Synchronistic Approach," *HUCA* 65 (1994): 1–19.

Dewrell, Heath.
"Textualization and the Transformation of Biblical Prophecy," in *Scribes and Scribalism*, ed. Mark Leuchter (London: T & T Clark, 2021), 95–106.

Douglas, Mary.
"The Abominations of Leviticus," in *Purity and Danger: An Analysis of Pollution and Taboo* (London: Routledge, 1996).

Dozeman, Thomas B.
"Geography and History in Herodotus and Ezra-Nehemiah," *JBL* 122 (2003): 449–466.

Drawnel, Henryk.
"Knowledge Transmission in the Context of the Watchers' Sexual Sin with the Women in 1 Enoch 6–11," *The Biblical Annals* 59 (2012):128–136.

Ego, Beate.
"The Book of Esther: A Hellenistic Book," *JAJ* 1 (2010): 279–302.

Feldman, Liane.
The Consuming Fire (Oakland: University of California Press, 2023).

Feldman, Liane.
The Story of Sacrifice: Ritual and Narrative in the Priestly Source (FAT; Tübingen: Mohr Siebeck, 2020).

Finkelstein, Israel.
"Jerusalem in the Persian (and Early Hellenistic) Period and the Wall of Nehemiah," *JSOT* 32 (2008): 501–520.

Fishbane, Michael.
Biblical Interpretation in Ancient Israel (Oxford: Clarendon, 1985).

Fitzpatrick-McKinley, Anne.
Empire, Power and Indigenous Elites: A Case Study of the Nehemiah Memoir (JSJSup; Leiden: Brill, 2015).

Freedman, David Noel.
The Unity of the Hebrew Bible (Ann Arbor, MI: University of Michigan Press, 1991).

Fried, Lisbeth.
Ezra and the Law in History and Tradition (Columbia: University of South Carolina Press, 2014).

Fried, Lisbeth.
"Ezra's Use of Documents in the Contexts of Hellenistic Rules of Rhetoric," in *New Perspectives on Ezra- Nehemiah: History and Historiography, Text, Literature and Interpretation* (Winona Lake, IN: Eisenbrauns, 2012), 11–26.

Fried, Lisbeth.
"Who Was Nehemiah ben Hacaliah?" *Journal of Hebrew Scriptures* 21 (2021): 6.1–14.

146 BIBLIOGRAPHY

Frisch, Alexandria.
"The Empirical Empire: Perceptions of Empire in Second Temple Literature" (Ph.D. Dissertation, NYU, 2013).

Fulton, Deirdre N.
"What Kind of Governor was Nehemiah? The Titles פחה and תרשתה in MT and LXX Ezra-Nehemiah," *ZAW* 130 (2018): 252–267.

Fulton, Deirdre N.
"What Do Priests and Kings Have in Common? Priestly and Royal Succession Narratives in the Achaemenid Era," in *Judah and the Judeans in the Achaemenid Period*, ed. Oded Lipschits et al. (Winona Lake: Eisenbrauns, 2011), 225–244.

Gardner, Kelli Anne.
"The Figure and Figuration of Women in the Hebrew Bible: Proverbs 1– 9, 31 and Lamentations 1–2" (PhD Dissertation, University of Chicago, 2020).

Garrison, Mark B.
The Ritual Landscape at Persepolis: The Glyptic Imagery from the Persepolis Fortification and Treasury Archives (Chicago: Oriental Institute, University of Chicago, 2017).

Goff, Matthew.
"Monstrous Appetites: Giants, Cannibalism and Insatiable Eating in Enochic Literature," *JAJ* 1 (2010): 19–42.

Goldingay, John.
"Hosea 4 and 11 and the Structure of Hosea," *TynBul* 71 (2020): 181–190.

Grabbe, Lester L.
"The 'Persian Documents' in the Book of Ezra: Are They Authentic?" in *Judah and the Judeans in the Persian Period*, ed. Oded Lipschits and Manfred Oeming (Winona Lake, IN: Eisenbrauns, 2006), 531–570.

Grabbe, Lester L.
Ezra-Nehemiah (OTR; London: Routledge, 1998).

Graf, Fritz.
"Myth," *Religions of the Ancient World: A Guide*, ed. Sarah Iles Johnston (Cambridge: Cambridge University Press, 2004), 45–58.

Granerod, Gard.
"'By the Favour of Ahuramazda I am King': On the Promulgation of a Persian Propaganda Text among Babylonians and Judaeans," *JSJ* 44 (2013): 455–480.

Granerod, Gard.
Dimensions of Yahwism in the Persian Period (BZAW; Berlin: De Gruyter, 2016).

Granerod, Gard.
"YHW the God of Heaven: An interpretatio persica et aegyptiaca of YHW in Elephantine," *JSJ* 52 (2021): 1–26.

Grätz, Sebastian.
Das Edikt des Artaxerxes: Eine Untersuchung zum religionspolitischen und historischen Umfeld von Ezra 7,12–26 (BZAW; Berlin: de Gruyrter, 2004).

Graybill, Rhiannon.
Are We Not Men? Unstable Masculinity in the Hebrew Prophets (Oxford: Oxford University Press, 2016).

Gunneweg, A. H. J.
"Die aramaische und die hebraische Erzahlung tiber die nachexilische Restauration- ein Vergleich," *ZAW* 94 (1982): 299–302.

BIBLIOGRAPHY 147

Haak, Robert D.
Habakkuk (VTSup; Leiden: Brill, 1992).

Hagedorn, Anselm.
"Local Law in an Imperial Context: The Role of Torah in the (Imagined) Persian Period," in *The Pentateuch as Torah*, ed. Gary N. Knoppers and Bernard Levinson (Winona Lake, IN: Eisenbrauns, 2007), 57–76.

Halpern, Baruch.
"Why Manasseh Is Blamed for the Babylonian Exile: The Evolution of a Biblical Tradition," *VT* 48 (1998): 473–514.

Halpern, Baruch.
"YHWH the Revolutionary: Reflections on the Rhetoric of Redistribution in the Social Context of Dawning Monotheism," in *Jews, Christians, and the Theology of the Hebrew Scriptures*, ed. Alice Ogden Bellis and Joel S. Kaminsky (Atlanta: SBL, 2000), 179–212.

Halpern, Baruch.
From Gods to God: The Dynamics of Iron Age Cosmologies (FAT; Tübingen: Mohr Siebeck, 2009).

Hanson, Paul D.
The Dawn of Apocalyptic (Philadelphia: Fortress Press, 1975).

Haran, Menahem.
"Book-Scrolls at the Beginning of the Second Temple Period: The Transition From Papyrus to Skins," *HUCA* 14 (1983): 11–22.

Hasler, Laura Carlson.
"Persia is Everywhere Where Nothing Happens: Imperial Ubiquity and Its Limits in Ezra-Nehemiah," *The Bible and Critical Theory* 16 (2020): 140–154.

Hasler, Laura Carlson.
Archival Historiography in Jewish Antiquity (New York: Oxford University Press, 2020).

Haubold, Johannes.
"The Achaemenid Empire and the Sea," *Mediterranean Historical Review* 27 (2012): 4–23.

Hayes, Nathan.
"Yedaniah's Identity as Priest or Layperson and the Rhetoric of the Letter from the Judean Garrison of Elephantine to Bagavahya," *JBL* 139 (2020): 521–541.

Hendel, Ronald S.
"Of Demigods and the Deluge: Toward an Interpretation of Genesis 6:1–4," *JBL* 106 (1987): 13–26.

Hendel, Ronald S.
"The Exodus as Cultural Memory: Egyptian Bondage and the Song of the Sea," in *Israel's Exodus in Transdisciplinary Perspective*, ed. Thomas E. Levy et al. (Heidelberg: Springer, 2015), 65–77.

Herrenschmidt, Clarisse.
"Les créations d'Ahuramazda," *Studia Iranica* 6 (1977): 17–58.

Hilder, Jennifer.
"Masterful Missives: Form and Authority in Arsama's Letters," in *Aršāma and His World: The Bodleian Letters in Context*, Vol. III, ed. Christopher Tulpin and John Ma (Oxford: Oxford University Press, 2020), 97–109.

Hoffman, Yair.
"A North Israelite Typological Myth and a Judean Historical Tradition: The Exodus in Hosea and Amos," *VT* 39 (1989): 169–182.

148 BIBLIOGRAPHY

Hogue, Timothy.
"The Monumentality of the Sinaitic Decalogue: Reading Exodus 20 in Light of Northwest Semitic Monument-Making Practices," *JBL* 138 (2019): 79–99.

Holm, Tawny.
"Papyrus Amherst 63 and the Arameans of Egypt: A Landscape of Cultural Nostalgia," in *Elephantine in Context*, ed. Reinhard G. Kratz and Bernd U. Schipper (Tübingen: Mohr Siebeck, 2022), 323–351.

Hutter, Manfred.
"Probleme iranischer Literatur und Religion unter den Achämeniden," *ZAW* 127 (2015): 547–564.

Hutton, Jeremy M.
"The Levitical Diaspora (I): A Sociological Comparison with Morocco's Ahansal," in *Exploring the Longue Durée*, fs. Lawrence E. Stager, ed. J. David Schloen (University Park: Pennsylvania State University Press, 2009), 223–234.

Hutton, Jeremy M.
"The Levitical Diaspora (II): Modern Perspectives on the Levitical City Lists (A Review of Opinions)," in *Levites and Priests in History and Tradition*, ed. Jeremy M. Hutton and Mark Leuchter (Atlanta: SBL, 2011), 45–82.

Hutzli, Jurg.
The Origins of P (FAT; Tübingen: Mohr Siebeck, 2023).

Janzen, David.
"The 'Mission' of Ezra and the Persian Period Temple Community," *JBL* 119 (2000): 619–643.

Janzen, David.
"The Cries of Jerusalem: Ethnic, Cultic, Legal and Geographic Boundaries in Ezra-Nehemiah," in *Unity and Disunity in Ezra-Nehemiah*, ed. Mark J. Boda and Paul L. Redditt (Sheffield: Sheffield Phoenix Press, 2008), 117–135.

Janzen, David.
Chronicles and the Politics of Davidic Restoration (London: Bloomsbury, 2017).

Janzen, David.
"Politics, Settlement, and Temple Community in Persian- Period Yehud," *CBQ* 64 (2002): 490–510.

Japhet, Sara.
"Composition and Chronology in the Book of Ezra- Nehemiah," in *From the Rivers of Babylon to the Highlands of Judah* (Winona Lake, IN: Eisenbrauns, 2012), 245–267.

Japhet, Sara.
"Periodization between History and Ideology II: Chronology and Ideology in Ezra-Nehemiah," *From the Rivers of Babylon*, 353–366.

Japhet, Sara.
"The Ritual of Reading Scripture (Nehemiah 8:1- 12)," in *New Perspectives on Old Testament Prophecy and History* (VTSup), fs. Hans M. Barstad, ed. Rannfrid I. Thelle et al. (Leiden: Brill, 2015), 175–190.

Jones, Christopher M.
"Embedded Written Documents as Colonial Mimicry in Ezra- Nehemiah," *BibInt* 26 (2018): 180–181.

Jones, Lloyd Llewellyn.
"The Achaemenid Empire," *King of the Seven Climes: A History of the Ancient Iranian World, 3000 BCE- 651 CE*, ed. Touraj Daryaee (Leiden: Brill/Jordan Center for Persian Studies, 2017), 63–103.

BIBLIOGRAPHY 149

Jonker, Louis C.
"Anything New Under the Sun?! Exploring Further Avenues for Writing Another Commentary on Chronicles," *Acta Theologica* 26 (2018): 325–348.

Jursa, Michael.
"Ein Beamter flucht auf Aramäisch: Alphabetschreiber in der spätbabylonischen Epistolographie und die Rolle des Aramäischen in der babylonischen Verwaltung des sechsten Jahrhunderts v. Chr.," in *Leggo! Studies Presented to Frederick Mario Fales on the Occasion of His 65th Birthday*, ed. Giovanni Lanfranchi et al. (Wiesbaden: Harrasowitz, 2012), 379–397.

Jursa, Michael.
"The Transition of Babylonia from the Neo- Babylonian Empire to Achaemenid Rule," *Proceedings of the British Society* 136 (2007): 73–94.

Kawashima, Robert.
"On the Yahwist's Leviathan," *Near Eastern Archaeology* 78 (2015): 264–271.

Keefe, Alice A.
Woman's Body and the Social Body in Hosea (JSOTSup; Sheffield: Sheffield Academic Press, 2001).

Kiel, Yishai.
"Reinventing Mosaic Torah in Ezra- Nehemiah in the Light of the Law (*data*) of Ahura Mazda and Zarathustra," *JBL* 136 (2017): 323–345.

Killebrew, Ann E.
"Israel during the Iron Age II Period," in *The Oxford Handbook of the Archaeology of the Levant: C. 8000–332 BCE*, ed. Margreet Steiner and Ann E. Killebrew (Oxford: Oxford University Press, 2013), 595–606.

Knoppers, Gary N.
Jews and Samaritans: The Origins and History of Their Early Relations (New York: Oxford University Press, 2013).

Knoppers, Gary N.
"Ethnicity, Genealogy, Geography and Change: The Judean Communities of Babylon and Jerusalem in the Story of Ezra," in *Community Identity in Judean Historiography*, ed. Gary N. Knoppers and Kenneth Ristau (Winona Lake: Eisenbrauns, 2008), 147–172.

Knowles, Melody D.
"Pilgrimage to Jerusalem in the Persian Period," in *Approaching Yehud: New Approaches to the Study of the Persian Period*, ed. Jon L. Berquist (Atlanta: SBL, 2007), 7–24.

Koch, Klaus.
"Ezra and the Origins of Judaism," *JSS* 19 (1974): 173–197.

Kottsieper, Ingo.
"'And They Did Not Care to Speak Yehudit': On Linguistic Change in Judah during the Late Persian Era," *Judah and the Judeans in the Fourth Century B.C.E.*, 95–124.

Kratz, Reinhard G.
"Ezra: Priest and Scribe," in *Scribes, Sages, and Seers: The Sage in the Eastern Mediterranean World* (FRLANT), ed. L. Perdue (Göttingen: Vandenhoeck & Ruprecht, 2008), 163–188.

Kratz, Reinhard G.
"Judean Ambassadors and the Making of Jewish Identity: The Case of Hannaniah, Ezra, and Nehemiah," in *Judah and the Judeans in the Achaemenid Period*, ed. O. Lipschits et al; Winona Lake: Eisenbrauns, 2011), 421–444.

Kugler, Robert R.
From Patriarch to Priest (Atlanta: Scholars Press, 1996).

150 BIBLIOGRAPHY

Kuhrt, Amélie.
"The Achaemenid Persian Empire (c. 550– c. 330 BCE): Continuities, Adaptations, Transformations," in *Empires: Perspectives from Archaeology and History*, ed. Susan E. Alcock et al. (Cambridge: Cambridge University Press, 2009), 93–123.

Kuhrt, Amélie.
"Cyrus the Great of Persia: Images and Realities," in *Representations of Political Power: Case Histories from Times of Change and Dissolving Order in the Ancient Near East*, ed. M. Heinz and M. H. Feldman (Winona Lake, IN: Eisenbrauns, 2007), 169–191.

Kuhrt, Amélie.
"Making History: Sargon of Agade and Cyrus the Great of Persia," in *A Persian Perspective: Essays in Memory of Heleen Sancisi-Weerdenburg*, ed. Wouter Henkelman and Amélie Kuhrt (Leiden: Nederlands Institute voor het Nabije Oosten, 2003), 347–361.

Kuhrt, Amélie.
The Persian Empire: A Corpus of Sources from the Achaemenid Period (London: Routledge, 2010).

Kvanvig, Helge.
Primeval History: Mesopotamian, Biblical, and Enochic: An Intertexual Reading (JSJSup; Leiden: Brill, 2011).
Lakoff, George (with Marc Johnson). *Philosophy in the Flesh: The Embodied Mind and its Challenge to Western Thought* (New York: Basic, 1999).

Lakoff, George.
Don't Think of an Elephant: Know Your Values and Frame the Debate (White River Junction, VT: Chelsea Green, 2004).
Lakoff, George (with Marc Turner). *More Than Cool Reason: A Field Guide to Poetic Metaphor* (Chicago: University of Chicago Press, 1989).

Lambert, David.
"Tôrâ as Mode of Conveyance: The Problem with 'Teaching' and 'Law,'" in *Torah: Function, Meaning and Diverse Manifestations in Early Judaism and Christianity*, ed. William M. Schniedewind et al. (Atlanta: SBL, 2021), 61–80.

Landau, Ayelet (with Lisa Aziz-Zadeh and Richard B. Ivry).
"The Influence of Language on Perception: Listening to Sentences about Faces Affects the Perception of Faces," *Journal of Neuroscience* 30 (2010): 15254–15261.

Langacker, Ronald.
Foundations of Cognitive Grammar: Theoretical Prerequisites (Stanford, CA: Stanford University Press, 1987).

Lebram, Jürgen-Christian.
"Die Traditionsgeschichte der Esragestalt und die Frage nach dem historischen Esra," in *Sources, Structures, Synthesis: Proceedings of the Groningen 1983 Achaemenid History Workshop* (AchH), ed. Heleen Sancisi-Weerdenburg (Leiden: Nederlands Instituut voor het Nabije Oosten, 1987), 126–132.

Leitan Nuwan (with Lucian Chaffey).
"Embodied Cognition and Its Applications: A Brief Review," *Sensoria: A Journal of Mind, Brain and Culture* 10 (2014): 3–10.

Leith, Mary Joan Winn.
"Israel Among the Nations: The Persian Period," in *The Oxford History of the Biblical World*, ed. Michael D. Coogan (New York: Oxford University Press, 1998), 276–316.

Lemaire, Andre.
"Administration in Fourth-Century B.C.E. Judah in Light of Epigraphy and Numismatics," in *Judah and the Judeans in the Fourth Century B.C.E.*, ed. Oded Lipshits et al. (Winona Lake, IN: Eisenbrauns, 2007), 53–74.

BIBLIOGRAPHY 151

Lesses, Rebecca.
"They Revealed Secrets to Their Wives: The Transmission of Magical Knowledge in 1 Enoch," in *With Letters of Light—Otiyot Shel Or: Studies in Early Jewish Apocalypticism and Mysticism in Honour of Rachel Elior*, ed. Dafna Arbel and Andrei Orlov (Berlin: De Gruyter, 2010), 196–222.

Leuchter, Mark.
"Another Look at the Hosea/Malachi Framework in the Twelve," *VT* 64 (2014): 249–265.

Leuchter, Mark.
"The Book of the Twelve and the 'Great Assembly' in History and Tradition," in *Perspectives on the Formation of the Book of the Twelve*, ed. Rainer Albertz et al. (Berlin: De Gruyter, 2012), 337–353.

Leuchter, Mark.
"The Crisis Episode in 1 Chronicles 21 and the Chronicler's Mythological Agenda," *VT* 73 (2023): 707–735.

Leuchter, Mark.
"Ezra's Mission and the Levites of Casiphia," *Communal Identity in Judean Historiography*, ed. Gary Knoppers and Kenneth R. Ristau (Winona Lake, IN: Eisenbrauns, 2008), 173–196.

Leuchter, Mark.
"Genesis 38 in Social and Historical Perspective," *JBL* 132 (2013): 209–227.

Leuchter, Mark.
"Inter-Levitical Polemics in the Late 6th Century BCE: The Evidence from Nehemiah 9," *Biblica* 85 (2014): 269–279.

Leuchter, Mark.
The Levites and the Boundaries of Israelite Identity (New York: Oxford University Press, 2017).

Leuchter, Mark.
"The Levites in Exile: A Response to L.S. Tiemeyer," *VT* 60 (2010): 586–589.

Leuchter, Mark.
"The Medium and the Message, or, What is Deuteronomistic About the Book of Jeremiah?" *ZAW* 126 (2014): 208–227.

Leuchter, Mark.
"Moses Between the Pentateuch and the Book of the Twelve," *HUCA* 90 (2021): 163–183.

Leuchter, Mark.
"The Name 'Berechiah' in Sach 1," *ZAW* 134 (2022): 55–67.

Leuchter, Mark.
"The Pen of Scribes: Writing, Textuality, and the Book of Jeremiah," in *The Book of Jeremiah: Composition, Reception, and Interpretation*, ed. Jack R. Lundbom et al. (FIOTL; Leiden: Brill, 2018), 3–25.

Leuchter, Mark.
The Polemics of Exile in Jeremiah 26–45 (Cambridge: Cambridge University Press, 2008).

Leuchter, Mark.
"The Royal Background of Deut 18,15–18," *ZAW* 130 (2018): 364–383.

Leuenberger, Martin.
"Time and Situational Reference in the Book of Haggai: On Religious- and Theological-Historical Contextualizations of Redactional Processes," in *Perspectives on the Formation of the Book of the Twelve*, ed. Rainer Albert et al. (BZAW; Berlin: De Gruyter, 2012), 157–169.

Levin, Adina.
"Hosea and North Israelite Tradition" (Ph.D. Dissertation, University of Toronto, 2009).

152 BIBLIOGRAPHY

Lewis, Theodore J.
"The Ancestral Estate (נַחֲלַת אֱלֹהִים) in 2 Samuel 14:16," *JBL* 110 (1991): 597–612.

Lipschits, Oded.
"Demographic Changes in Judah between the Seventh and the Fifth Centuries B.C.E.," in *Judah and the Judeans in the Neo-Babylonian Period*, ed. Oded Lipschits and Joseph Blenkinsopp (Winona Lake, IN: Eisenbrauns, 2003), 323–376.

Lipschits, Oded.
The Fall and Rise of Jerusalem (Winona Lake, IN: Eisenbrauns, 2005).

Lipschits, Oded (with Manfred Oeming), ed.
Judah and the Judeans in the Persian Period (Winona Lake, IN: Eisenbrauns, 2006).

Lipschits, Oded.
"Persian Period Finds from Jerusalem: Facts and Interpretations," *Journal of Hebrew Studies* 9.20 (2010): 1–30.

Lipschits, Oded (with Yuval Gadot, and D. Langgut).
"The Riddle of Ramat Raḥel: The Archaeology of a Royal Persian Period Edifice," *Transeuphrates* 41 (2012): 57–79.

Lipschits, Oded (with Oren Tal).
"The Settlement Archaeology of the Province of Judah: A Case Study," in *Judah and the Judeans in the Fourth Century B.C.E.*, ed. Oded Lipschits et al. (Winona Lake, IN: Eisenbrauns, 2007), 33–52.

Lundbom, Jack R.
"Baruch, Seraiah, and Expanded Colophons in the Book of Jeremiah," *JSOT* 36 (1986): 89–114.

Lundbom, Jack R.
Deuteronomy: A Commentary (Grand Rapids, MI: Eerdmans, 2013).

Ma, John.
"Aršama the Vampire," in *Aršama and His World: The Bodleian Letters in Context* (Vol. 3), ed. Christopher Tulpin and John Ma (Oxford: Oxford University Press, 2020), 190–208.

Malinowski, Branislaw.
Magic, Science, Religion and Other Essays (Glencoe: Free Press, 1948).

Mandell, Alice.
"Writing as a Source of Ritual Authority: The High Priest's Body as a Priestly Text in the Tabernacle-Building Story," *JBL* (2022) 141: 43–64.

McClellan, Daniel O.
YHWH'S Divine Images: A Cognitive Approach (Atlanta: SBL, 2022)

Mildenberg, Leo.
"Artaxerxes III Ochus (358–338 B.C.): A Note on the Maligned King," *ZDPV* 115 (1999): 201–227.

Milik, Jozef T.
The Books of Enoch: Aramaic Fragments from Qumran Cave 4 (Oxford: Clarendon, 1976).

Miller II, Robert D.
Yahweh: Origin of a Desert God (Göttingen: Vandehoeck & Ruprecht, 2021).

Miller II, Robert D.
"When Pharaohs Ruled: On the Translation of Judges 5:2," *Journal of Theological Studies* 59 (2008): 650–654.

Milstein, Sara.
Tracking the Master Scribe: Revision Through Introduction in Biblical and Mesopotamian Literature (Oxford: Oxford University Press, 2016).

BIBLIOGRAPHY 153

Mitchell, Christine.
"Achaemenid Persian Concepts Pertaining to Covenant and Haggai, Zechariah and Malachi," in *Covenant in the Persian Period: From Genesis to Chronicles*, ed. Richard J. Bautch and Gary N. Knoppers (Winona Lake, IN: Eisenbrauns, 2015), 295–301.

Mitchell, Christine.
"Berlin Papyrus P. 13447 and the Library of the Yehudite Colony at Elephantine," *JNES* 76 (2017): 139–147.

Mitchell, Christine.
"The Politics of Judahite Creation Theologies in the Persian Period," in *Political Theologies in the Hebrew Bible* (JAJSup), ed. Mark G. Brett and Rachelle Gilmour (Paderborn: Brill Schöning, 2023), 23–41.

Mitchell, Stephen.
"In Search of the Pontic Community in Antiquity," in *Representations of Empire: Rome and the Mediterranean World*, ed. A. K. Bowman et al. (Oxford: Oxford University Press, 2002), 35–64.

Monroe, Lauren A. S.
Josiah's Reform and the Dynamics of Defilement (New York: Oxford University Press, 2011).

Moore, James D.
"Who Gave You a Decree? Anonymity as a Narrative Technique in Ezra 5:3, 9 in Light of Persian-Period Decrees and Administrative Sources," *JBL* 140 (2021): 69–89.

Mroczek, Eva.
The Literary Imagination in Jewish Antiquity (New York: Oxford University Press, 2016).

Nichols, Andrew.
"The Iranian Concept AŠA and Greek Views of the Persians," *Studi classici e orientali: LXII, 2016* (Pisa: Pisa University Press, 2016), 61–86.

Nickelsberg, George.
1 *Enoch* (Hermeneia; MN: Fortress Press, 2001).

Niehr, Herbert.
"Religio- Historical Aspects of the 'Early Post- Exilic' Period," in *The Crisis of Israelite Religion: Transformation of Religious Tradition in Exilic & Post- Exilic Times*, ed. Bob Becking and Marjo C.A. Korpel (Leiden: Brill, 1999), 228–244.

Nihan, Christophe.
From Priestly Torah to Pentateuch (FAT; Tübingen: Mohr Siebeck, 2007).

Nihan, Christophe.
"Moses and the Prophets': Deuteronomy 18 and the Emergence of the Pentateuch as Torah," *SEA* 75 (2010): 21–55.

Nihan, Christophe.
"The Torah Between Samaria and Judah: Shechem and Gerizim in Deuteronomy and Joshua," *The Pentateuch as Torah*, 187–223.

Nissinen, Martti.
Prophetie, Redaktion, und Fortschreibung im Hoseabuch (AOAT; Neukirchen- Vluyn: Neukirchener, 1991).

Nogalski, James D.
"One Book of Twelve Books? The Nature of the Redaction Work and Implications of the Cultic Source Material in the Book of the Twelve," in *Two Sides of a Coin*, ed. Thomas C. Römer (Piscataway, NJ: Gorgias Press, 2010), 11–46.

Oblath, Michael.
"Of Pharaohs and Kings: Whence the Exodus?" *JSOT* 87 (2000): 23–42.

154 BIBLIOGRAPHY

Olson, Daniel C.
"Jeremiah 4.5–31 and Apocalyptic Myth," *JSOT* 73 (1997): 81–107.

Olyan, Saul M.
"Purity Ideology in Ezra–Nehemiah as a Tool to Reconstitute the Community," *JSJ* 35 (2004): 1–16.

Otto, Eckart.
Deuteronomium im Pentateuch und Hexateuch: Studien zur Literaturgeschichte von Pentateuch und Hexateuch im Lichte des Deuteronomiumsrahmen (FAT; Tübingen: Mohr Siebeck, 2000).

Overholt, Thomas J.
The Threat of Falsehood: A Study in the Theology of the Book of Jeremiah (London: SCM Press, 1970).

Pajunen Mika S. (with Hanne von Weissenberg).
"The Book of Malachi, Manuscript 4Q76 (4QXIIa), and the Formation of the 'Book of the Twelve,'" *JBL* 134 (2015): 731–751.

Pakkala, Juha.
Ezra the Scribe (BZAW; Berlin: De Gruyter, 2004).

Pearce Laurie E. (with Cornelia Wunsch).
Documents of Judean Exiles and West Semites in Babylonia in the Collection of David Sofer (Cornell University Studies in Assyriology and Sumerology; Bethesda, MD: CDL Press, 2014).

Pearce Laurie E.
"'Judean': A Special Status in Neo-Babylonian and Achemenid Babylonia?" in *Judah and the Judeans in the Achaemenid Period*, ed. Oded Lipschits et al. (Winona Lake, IN: Eisenbrauns, 2011), 267–278.

Peckham, Brian.
"The Composition of Hosea," *HAR* 11 (1987): 331–353.

Peckham, Brian.
"History and Time," *Ki Baruch Hu: Ancient Near Eastern, Biblical, and Judaic Studies in Honor of Baruch A. Levine*, ed. Robert Chazan et al. (Winona Lake, IN: Eisenbrauns, 1999), 330–349.

Peckham, Brian.
"Writing and Editing," in *Fortunate the Eyes that See*, fs. D.N. Freedman, ed. Astrid Beck et al. (Grand Rapids, MI: Eerdmans, 1995), 364–383.

Petersen, David L.
"Genesis and Family Values," *JBL* 124 (2005): 5–23.
Zechariah 9–14 and Malachi (OTL; Louisville, KY: Westminster John Knox, 1995).

Pioske, Daniel.
"The Scribe of David: A Portrait of a Life," *Maarav* 20 (2013): 163–188.

Polak, Frank.
"Style Is More than the Person: Sociolinguistics, Literary Culture and the Distinction between Written and Oral Narrative," in *Biblical Hebrew: Studies in Chronology and Typology*, ed. Ian Young (JSOTSup; London: T & T Clark, 2003), 38–103.

Polaski, Donald C.
"What Mean These Stones? Inscriptions, Textuality and Power in Persia and Yehud," in *Approaching Yehud: New Approaches to the Study of the Persian Period*, ed. John L. Berquist (Atlanta: SBL, 2007), 37–48.

BIBLIOGRAPHY   155

Portier-Young, Anathea.
"Constructing Imperial and National Identities: Monstrous and Human Bodies in Book of Watchers, Daniel, and 2 Maccabees," *Interpretation* 74 (2020): 159–170.

Portier-Young, Anathea.
"Symbolic Resistance in the Book of the Watchers," in *The Watchers in Jewish and Christian Tradition*, ed. Angela Harkins et al. (Minneapolis: Augsberg Fortress Press, 2014), 39–49.

Potts, Daniel L.
"Cyrus the Great and the Kingdom of Anshan," in *The Idea of Iran: Birth of the Persian Empire*, ed. V. S. Curtis and S. Stewart (London: Tauris, 2005), 7–28.

Rainey, Brian.
Religion, Ethnicity, and Xnophobia in the Bible: A Theoretical, Exegetical and Theological Survey (London: Routledge, 2018).

Rappaport, Roy A.
Ritual and Religion in the Making of Humanity (Cambridge: Cambridge University Press, 1999).

Rausche, Benedikt.
"The Relevance of Purity in Second Temple Judaism According to Ezra- Nehemiah," in *Purity and the Forming of Religious Traditions in the Ancient Mediterranean World and Ancient Judaism*, ed. Christian Frevel and Christophe Nihan (Leiden: Brill, 2013), 457–475.

Redditt, Paul L.
"The Census List in Ezra 2 and Nehemiah 7: A Suggestion," in *New Perspectives on Ezra-Nehemiah* (Winona Lake, IN: Eisenbrauns, 2012), 224–240.

Reed, Annette Yoshiko.
Fallen Angels and the History of Judaism and Christianity: The Reception of Enochic Literature (Cambridge: Cambridge University Press, 2005).

Reed, Annette Yoshiko.
"Heavenly Ascent, Angelic Descent, and the Transmission of Knowledge in 1 Enoch 6-16," in *Heavenly Realms and Earthly Realities in Late Antique Religions*, ed. Annette Yoshiko Reed and Ra'anan Boustan (Cambridge: Cambridge University Press, 2004), 47–66.

Rendtorff, Rolf.
"Esra und das 'Gesetz,'" *ZAW* 96 (1984): 165–184.

Rendsburg, Gary A.
"Merneptah in Canaan," *Journal of the Society for the Study of Egyptian Antiquities* 11 (1981): 171–172.

Richelle, Matthieu.
"Elusive Scrolls: Could any Hebrew Literature Have Been Written Prior to the Eighth Century BCE?" *VT* 66 (2016): 556–594.

Ristau, Kenneth.
Reconstructing Jerusalem: Persian Period Prophetic Perspectives (Winona Lake, IN: Eisenbrauns, 2016).

Robson, Eleanor.
Ancient Knowledge Networks: A Social Geography of Cuneiform Scholarship in First-Millennium Assyria and Babylonia (London: UCL Press, 2020).

Rollinger, Robert.
"Thinking and Writing about History in Teispid and Achaemenid Persia," in *Thinking, Recording, and Writing History in the Ancient World*, ed. Kurt Raaflaub (Malden: Wiley Blackwell, 2014), 187–212.

156 BIBLIOGRAPHY

Romer Thomas C. (with Marc Z. Brettler)
"Deuteronomy 34 and the Case for a Persian Hexateuch," *JBL* 119 (2000): 401–419.

Rom-Shiloni, Dalit.
"'How Can You Say, "I Am Not Defiled..."?' (Jeremiah 2:20–25): Allusions to Priestly Legal Traditions in the Poetry of Jeremiah," *JBL* 133 (2014): 757–775.

Rom-Shiloni, Dalit.
"From Ezekiel to Ezra- Nehemiah: Shifts of Group Identities within Babylonian Exilic Ideology," in *Judah and the Judeans in the Achaemenid Period*, ed. Oded Lipschits et al. (Winona Lake: Eisenbrauns, 2011), 127–151.

Rom-Shiloni, Dalit.
"Ezekiel as the Voice of the Exiles and Constructor of Exilic Ideology," *HUCA* 76 (2005): 1–45.

Rom-Shiloni, Dalit.
Exclusive Inclusivity: Identity Conflicts between the Exiles and the People Who Remained (6th–5th Centuries BCE) (London: Bloomsbury, 2013).

Root, Margaret Cool.
"Defining the Divine in Achaemenid Persian Kingship: The View from Bisitun," in *Every Inch a King: Comparative Studies on Kings and Kingship in the Ancient and Medieval Worlds*, ed. Lynette Mitchell and Charles Melville (Leiden: Brill, 2013), 23–65.

Root, Margaret Cool.
The King and Kingship in Achaemenid Art (Leiden: Brill, 1979).

Rosel, M.
"Israels Psalmen in Agypten? Papyrus Amherst 63 und die Psalmen xx und lxxv," *VT* 50 (2000): 81–99.

Rung, Eduard.
"The End of the Lydian Kingdom and the Lydians After Croesus," in *Political Memory in and after the Persian Empire*, ed. Jason M. Silverman and Caroline Waerzeggers (Atlanta: SBL, 2015), 7–22.

Sanders, Seth L.
From Adapa to Enoch (TSAJ; Tübingen: Mohr Siebeck, 2017).

Sanders, Seth L.
"Enoch's Imaginary Ancestor: From Ancient Babylonian Scholarship to Modern Academic Folklore," *JAJ* 9 (2019): 155–177.

Schaper, Joachim.
"The Temple Treasury Committee in the Time of Nehemiah and Ezra," *VT* 47 (1997): 200–206.

Schaper, Joachim.
"Torah and Identity in the Persian Period," in *Judah and the Judeans in the Achaemenid Period*, ed. Oded Lipscits et al. (Winona Lake, IN: Eisenbrauns, 2011), 27–36.

Schaper, Joachim.
Priester und Leviten im Achaemenidischen Juda: Studien zur Kult- und Sozialgeschichte Israels in Persischer Zeit (FAT; Tübingen: Mohr Siebeck, 2000).

Schart, Aaron.
"The First Section of the Book of the Twelve Prophets: Hosea—Joel—Amos," *Interpretation* 61 (2007): 138–152.

Schart, Aaron.
Die Entstehung des Zwolfprophetenbuchs (BZAW; Berlin: De Gruyter, 1998).

BIBLIOGRAPHY 157

Schloen, J. David.
"Caravans, Kenites, and Casus Belli: Enmity and Alliance in the Song of Deborah," *CBQ* 55 (1993): 18–38.

Schmid, Konrad.
"Exodus in the Pentateuch," in *The Book of Exodus: Composition, Redaction, and Interpretation* (FIOTL), ed. Thomas Dozeman et al. (Leiden: Brill, 2014), 27–60.

Schmid, Konrad.
The Scribes of the Torah (Atlanta: SBL, 2023).

Schniedewind, William M.
How the Bible Became a Book: The Textualization of Ancient Israel (New York: Cambridge University Press, 2004).

Schniedewind, William M.
Who Really Wrote the Bible? The Story of Scribal Communities (Princeton, NJ: Princeton University Press, forthcoming).

Schor, Fran.
Weaponized Whiteness: The Constructions and Deconstructions of White Identity Politics (Leiden: Brill, 2020).

Seitz, Christopher R.
"The Prophet Moses and the Canonical Shape of Jeremiah," *ZAW* 101 (1989): 3–27.

Signorile, Vito.
"Acculturation and Myth," *Anthropological Quarterly* 46 (1973): 117–134.

Silverman, Jason M.
"Imperialism, Identity, and Language Choice in Persian Yehud: Towards Understanding the Socio-Political Implications in the Achaemenid Empire," *AABNER* 1 (2021): 145–192.

Silverman, Jason M.
"Achaemenid Sources and the Problem of Genre," in *Conceptualizing Past, Present, and Future*, ed. S. Fink and R. Rollinger. Melammu Symposia (Münster: Ugarit-Verlag, 2018), 261–278.

Silverman, Jason M.
"From Remembering to Expecting the 'Messiah': Achaemenid Kingship as (Re)Formulating Apocalyptic Expectations of David," in *Political Memory in and After the Persian Empire*, ed. Jason M. Silverman and Caroline Waerzeggers (Atlanta: SBL, 2015), 419–446.

Silverman, Jason M.
"Iranian Details in the Book of Heavenly Luminaries (1 Enoch 72– 82)," *JNES* 72 (2013): 195–208.

Silverman, Jason M.
Persian Royal-Judaean Elite Engagements in the Early Teispid and Achaemenid Empire: The King's Acolytes (LHBOTS; London: T & T Clark, 2021).

Silverman, Jason M.
"Sheshbazzar, a Judean or a Babylonian? A Note on His Identity," in *Exile and Return: The Babylonian Context* (BZAW), ed. Jonathan Stokl and Caroline Waerzeggers (Berlin: De Gruyter, 2015), 308–321.

Silverman, Jason M.
"Was There an Achaemenid Theology of Kingship? The Intersections of Mythology, Religion, and Imperial Religious Policy," in *Religion in the Achaemenid Persian Empire: Emerging Judaisms and Trends*, ed. Diana Edelman et al. (Tubingen: Mohr Siebeck, 2016), 172–196.

158 BIBLIOGRAPHY

Smith, Mark S.
"The Baal Cycle," in *Ugaritic Narrative Poetry*, ed. S. B. Parker (Atlanta: Scholars Press, 1997) 81–180.

Smith, Mark S.
The Genesis of Good and Evil (Louisville: Westminster John Knox, 2019).

Smith, Mark S.
The Origins of Biblical Monotheism (New York: Oxford University Press, 2002).

Soheil, Mehr Azar.
The Concept of Monument in Achaemenid Empire (New York: Routledge, 2019).

Sommer, Benajmin D.
"Dating Pentateuchal Texts and the Perils of Pseudo- Historicism," in *The Pentateuch: International Perspectives on Current Research* (FAT), ed. Thomas B. Dozeman et al. (Tübingen: Mohr Siebeck, 2011), 86–108.

Sonia, Kerry.
Caring for the Dead in Ancient Israel (Atlanta: SBL, 2020).

Sperling, S. David.
"Pants, Persians and the Priestly Source," in *Ve- Eileh Divrei David* (Leiden: Brill, 2017), 196–209.

Spiegel, Shalom.
"A Prophetic Attestation of the Decalogue: Hosea 6:5 with some Observations on Psalm 15 and 24," *HTR* 27 (1934): 105–144.

Stackert, Jeffrey R.
"Political Allegory in the Priestly Source: The Destruction of Jerusalem, the Exile, and Their Alternatives," in *The Fall of Jerusalem and the Rise of the Torah* (FAT), ed. Peter Dubovský et al. (Tübingen: Mohr Siebeck, 2016), 211–223.

Steiner, Richard C.
"Bishlam's Archival Search Report in Nehemiah's Archive: Multiple Introductions and Reverse Chronological Order as Clues to the Origin of the Aramaic Letters in Ezra 4–6," *JBL* 125 (2006): 641–685.

Steinhorn, Leonard.
"The Fundamental Flaw in 'Make America Great Again,'" *The Washington Post*, July 26, 2022.

Stern, Elsie.
"Royal Letters and Torah Scrolls: The Place of Ezra- Nehemiah in Scholarly Narratives of Scripturalization," in *Contextualizing Israel's Sacred Writings: Ancient Literacy, Orality and Literary Production*, ed. Brian B. Schmidt (Atlanta: SBL, 2015), 239–262.

Strine C. A. (with C.L. Crouch)
"YHWH's Battle Against Chaos in Ezekiel: The Transformation of Judahite Mythology for a New Situation," *JBL* 132 (2013): 883–903.

Sugirtharajah, R. S.
Postcolonial Criticism and Biblical Interpretation (Oxford: Oxford University Press, 2002).

Sweeney Marvin A.
"A Form Critical Re-Reading of Hosea," *Journal of Hebrew Scriptures* 2 (1998): 1–16.

Tropper, Amram.
Wisdom, Politics, and Historiography: Tractate Avot in the Context of the Graeco- Roman Near East (Oxford: Oxford University Press, 2004).

BIBLIOGRAPHY 159

Tuggy, David.
"Schematicity," in *The Oxford Handbook of Cognitive Linguistics*, ed. Dirk Geeraerts and Hubert Cuyckens (Oxford: Oxford University Press, 2007), 82–116.

Turner, Victor.
The Forest of Symbols: Aspects of Ndembu Ritual (Ithaca, NY: Cornell University Press, 1967).

Turner, Victor.
Ritual Process: Structure and Anti-Structure (Chicago: Aldine, 1969).

Tversky, Barbara. (with Birdgette Martin Hard).
"Embodied and Disembodied Cognition: Spatial Perspective- taking," *Cognition* 110 (2009): 124–129.

Tversky, Barbara. (with Birdgette Martin Hard).
"Biased Retellings of Events Yield Biased Memories," *Cognitive Psychology* 40 (2000): 1–38.

van der Toorn, Karel.
Becoming Diaspora Jews: Behind the Story of Elephantine (New Haven, CT: Yale University Press, 2019).

van der Toorn, Karel.
"Ezra In Egypt? The Significance of Hananyah's Mission," *VT* 67 (2017): 602–610.

van der Toorn, Karel.
Family Religion in Babylonia, Syria and Israel (Leiden: Brill, 1996).

Vanderhooft, David S.
"'El- mĕdînâ ûmĕdînâ kiktābāh: Scribes and Scripts in Yehud and in Achaemenid Transeuphratene," in *Judah and the Judeans in the Achaemenid Period*, ed. Oded Lipschits et al. (Winona Lake, IN: Eisenbrauns, 2011), 529–544.

Vanderhooft, David S.
"Habakkuk," in *The Oxford Encyclopedia of the Books of the Bible*, ed. Michael D. Coogan (Oxford: Oxford University Press, 2011).

Vayntrub, Jacqueline.
"Before Authorship: Solomon and Prov. 1:1," *BibInt* 26 (2018): 182–206.

Vayntrub, Jacqueline.
"Ecclesiastes and the Problem of Transmission in Biblical Literature," in *Scribes and Scribalism*, ed. Mark Leuchter (London: Bloomsbury, 2021), 82–92.

Vielhauer, Roman.
Das Werden des Buches Hosea: Eine redaktionsgeschichtliche Untersuchung (BZAW; Berlin: de Gruyter, 2007).

von Rad, Gerhard.
"The Beginning of History Writing in Ancient Israel," in *The Problem of the Hexateuch and Other Essays* (London: SCM, 1984), 166–204.

Vroom, Jonathan.
The Authority of Law in the Hebrew Bible and Early Judaism (JSJSup; Leiden: Brill, 2018).

Waerzeggers Caroline.
"Very Cordially Hated in Babylonia? Zēria and Rēmūt in the Verse Account," *Altorientalische Forschungen* 39 (2012): 316–320.
"The Babylonian Revolts Against Xerxes and the 'End of Archives'," *AfO* 50 (2003/2004): 150–73.

160 BIBLIOGRAPHY

Waetzoldt, Hartmut.
"Keilschrift und Schulen in Mesoptoamien und Ebla," in *Erziehungs und Unterrichtsmethoden im historischen Wandel*, ed. Lenz Kriss-Rettenbeck and Max Liedtke (Bad Heilbrunn: Linkhardt, 1986), 36–50.

Waters, Matt.
Ancient Persia: A Concise History of the Achaemenid Empire 550– 330 BCE (Cambridge: Cambridge University Press, 2014).

Weinfeld, Moshe.
Deuteronomy and the Deuteronomic School (Oxford: Clarendon, 1972).

Whitters, Mark.
"The Persianized Liturgy of Nehemiah 8:1–8," *JBL* 136 (2017): 63–84.

Wiesehöfer, Josef.
Die 'dunklen Jahrhunderte' der Persis: Untersuchungen zu Geschichte und Kultur von Fars in frühhellenistischer Zeit (330–140 v. Chr.) (Munich: Beck, 1994).

Williamson, H.G.M.
"The Composition of Ezra i–vi," *JTS* 34 (1983): 1–30.

Williamson, H.G.M.
"The Aramaic Documents in Ezra Reconsidered," *JTS* 59 (2008): 54–62.

Williamson, H.G.M.
Ezra, Nehemiah (WBC; Waco, TX: Word, 1985).

Wills, Lawrence M.
"Jewish Novellas in a Greek and Roman Age: Fiction and Identity," *JSJ* 42 (2011): 141–165.

Wills, Lawrence M.
"Jew, Judean, Judaism in the Ancient Period: An Alternative Argument," *JAJ* 7 (2016): 169–193.

Wilson Wright, Aren.
"From Persepolis to Jerusalem: A Reevaluation of Old Persian- Hebrew Contact in the Achaemenid Period," *VT* 65 (2015): 152–167.

Wilson, Ian Douglas.
"Yahweh's Anointed: Cyrus, Deuteronomy's Law of the King, and Yehudite Identity," *Political Memory in and After the Persian Empire*, 325–361.

Wöhrle, Jakob.
"Frieden durch Trennung: Die priesterliche Darstellung des Exodus und die persische Reichsideologie," in *Wege der Freiheit: Zur Entstehung und Theologie des Exodusbuches*, fs. Rainer Albertz, ed. Reinhard Achenbach et al. (Zürich: Theologischer Verlag Zürich, 2014), 87–111.

Wöhrle, Jakob.
Der Abschluss des Zwölfprophetenbuches: Buchübergreifende Redaktionsprozesse in den späten Sammlungen (BZAW; Berlin: de Gruyter, 2008).

Wolff, Hans Walter.
"Hoseas Geisteige Heimat," *TLZ* 81 (1956): 243–250.

Wolff, Hans Walter.
Dodekapropheten: Micha (BKAT; Neukirchen-Vluyn: Neukirchener Verlag, 1982).

Wollenberg, Rebecca Scharbach.
The Closed Book: How the Rabbis Taught the Jews (Not) to Read the Bible (Princeton, NJ: Princeton University Press, 2023).

Wright, John W.
"Guarding the Gates: 1 Chronicles 26.1- 19 and the Role of Gatekeepers in Chronicles," *JSOT* 48 (1990): 69–81.

Yang, Inchol.
"Nehemiah as a Mimic Man under the Achaemenid Empire: A Postcolonial Reading of Nehemiah 5," *The Expository Times* 133 (2022): 409–420.

Yoder, Christine Roy.
"The Woman of Substance (אשת־חיל): A Socioeconomic Reading of Proverbs 31:10–31," *JBL* 122 (2003): 427–47.

Yoo, Philip.
"'After These Things' and Its Composition in Genesis," *VT* 68 (2018): 660–672.

Yoo, Philip.
Ezra and the Second Wilderness (Oxford: Oxford University Press, 2017).

Zapff, Burkhard M.
Redaktionsgeschichtliche Studien zum Micahbuch im Kontext des Dodekapropheten (BZAW; Berlin: De Gruyter, 1997).

Author Index

For the benefit of digital users, indexed terms that span two pages (e.g., 52–53) may, on occasion, appear on only one of those pages.

Adams, Samuel L., 128n.17
Adler, Yonatan, 4, 118n.13, 125n.47
Albertz, Rainer, 117n.9, 133n.18
Almagor, Eran, 138n.75
Amzallag, Nissim, 95, 128n.16, 136n.33
Anzai, Shin-Ichi, 138n.68
Arbib, Michael A., 118n.35
Aster, Sawn Zelig, 134n.42
Austin, Michael, 128n.23
Aziz-Zadeh, Lisa, 118n.29

Ballentine, Debra Scoggins, 9–10, 118–19nn.37–39
Barjamovic, Gojko, 121n.53
Barnea, Gad, 32, 122n.58, 131n.67
Barre, Michael L., 134n.52
Bautch, Kelley Coblentz, 137n.58
Beaulieu, Paul-Alain, 121n.39
Becking, Bob, 55, 117n.9, 123n.2, 127n.2
Bedford, Peter R., 131n.62, 131n.73
Beim, Aaron, 118n.36
Ben Dov, Jonathan, 135n.3
Ben Zvi, Ehud, 11, 71, 119n.43, 132n.3
Benson, Melissa, 120n.13
Berquist, Jon L., 117n.8, 125n.46, 139n.7
Berthelot, Katell, 117n.8, 119n.6
Betlyon, John W., 119n.45
Bhabha, Homi K., 5–6, 8–9, 48, 118nn.20–21, 139n.13
Bhayro, Siam, 96–97, 134n.1, 137n.38, 137nn.40–41, 137n.45
Blenkinsopp, Joseph P., 69, 119n.9, 129n.38, 130n.48, 130n.58, 131n.72, 131n.77, 132n.16, 133n.21, 133n.24, 137n.46
Boccaccini, Gabriele, 122n.66, 135n.3, 135n.4, 138n.76, 139n.3, 139n.12
Boda, Mark J., 134n.57, 140n.25
Bodner, Keith, 133n.24
Boer, Roland, 5, 118n.17, 131n.78
Böhler, Dieter, 128n.17
Bonesho, Catherine E., 125n.39

Bos, James M., 132n.15
Brettler, Marc, Z., 118n.12, 124n.34, 135–36n.15
Briant, Pierre, 119n.1, 119n.3, 119n.4, 119n.8, 119nn.11–12, 130n.57, 131n.75, 137n.50

Carr, David M., 91, 124n.22, 127n.4, 133n.28, 135n.6, 135nn.10–11, 136n.21, 136n.24, 136n.30, 136n.34
Carter, Charles E., 117n.7, 117n.9
Cataldo, Jeremy W., 124n.24, 126n.71
Chaffey, Lucian, 118n.29
Cleath, Lisa J., 126–27n.1
Clifford, Richard J., 130n.51
Collins, John J., 120n.15, 133n.18, 137n.42, 137n.49
Cook, Stephen, L., 74, 75–76, 132n.16, 133n.26
Cooper, Alan, 135n.12, 136n.32
Crouch, C. L., 118n.27
Cuyckens, Hubert, 118n.35

Day, John, 135n.8, 136n.21
Demsky, Aaron, 59, 129n.26
De Pury, Albert, 50–51, 52–53, 126n.52
Dewrell, Heath, 123n.7
Douglas, Mary, 138n.65
Dozeman, Thomas B., 138n.69
Drawnel, Henryk, 137n.39

Ego, Beate, 128n.24

Feldman, Liane, 124n.37, 126nn.59–60, 126n.61, 126n.69, 139n.8, 140n.30
Finkelstein, Israel, 127n.14
Fischbane, Michael, 139n.13
Fitzpatrick-McKinley, Anne, 121n.32, 122n.64
Floyd, Michael H., 134n.53
Freedman, David Noel, 133n.38
Fried, Lisbeth, 127n.9, 127n.13, 129n.38, 131n.74
Frisch, Alexandria, 96, 98, 137n.37, 137n.53
Fulton, Deirdre N., 129n.38, 139n.10

164 AUTHOR INDEX

Gadot, Yuval, 122n.63
Gardner, Kelli Anne, 101, 138nn.60–61, 138nn.62–63, 138n.66, 138n.68
Garrison, Mark B., 121n.51
Geeraerts, Dirk, 118n.35
Goff, Matthew, 138n.77
Goldingay, John, 133n.38
Goldstein, Bernard R., 135n.12, 136n.32
Grabbe, Lester L., 127–28n.15
Graf, Fritz, 118n.37
Granerod, Gard, 41, 42, 123n.17, 124n.19, 124n.20, 124n.21
Grätz, Sebastian, 127n.13
Graybill, Rhiannon, 138n.67
Gunneweg, A. H. J., 130–31n.61

Haak, Robert D., 84, 134n.46, 134n.50
Hagedorn, Anselm, 124n.24, 129n.28
Halpern, Baruch, 134n.58, 135n.13, 135n.14, 140n.17, 140n.19
Hanson, Paul D., 139n.3
Haran, Menahem, 46, 124n.38, 137n.55
Hard, Bridgette Martin, 118n.29
Hasler, Laura Carlson, 55, 58, 60, 69, 126–27n.1, 128n.21, 128n.24, 129n.29, 130–31n.61, 131n.76
Haubold, Johannes, 121n.49
Hayes, Nathan, 124n.23
Hendel, Roland S., 94, 136n.25, 136n.30, 136–37nn.34–35, 140n.29
Hilder, Jennifer, 121n.46
Hoffman, Yair, 133n.20
Hogue, Timothy, 133n.39
Holm, Tawny, 123n.17
Hutter, Manfred, 120n.27
Hutton, Jeremy M., 122n.66, 126n.63
Hutzli, Jurg, 126n.67

Ivry, Richard B., 118n.29

Janzen, David, 122n.67, 127nn.11–12, 127–28n.15, 129n.26, 129n.31, 131n.67
Japhet, Sara, 61, 129n.27, 129n.37, 130n.56, 139n.13
Johnson, Marc, 7, 118n.31
Jones, Christopher M., 129n.34
Jones, Lloyd Llewellyn, 119n.45
Jonker, Louis C., 121n.36
Jursa, Michael, 121n.38, 122n.69

Kawashima, Robert, 136n.22, 136n.23
Keefe, Alice A., 138n.67
Kent, Roland G., 15

Kiel, Yishai, 124n.36, 127n.7
Killebrew, Ann E., 136n.19
Knoppers, Gary, 117n.2, 130nn.54–55
Knowles, Melody D., 127n.5
Koch, Klaus, 122n.72, 130n.51
Kottsieper, Ingo, 127n.3
Kratz, Reinhard G., 130n.59, 131n.74
Kugler, Robert R., 134n.54
Kuhrt, Amélie, 17, 119n.2, 119n.5, 119n.7, 128n.21
Kvanvig, Helge, 135n.2, 136n.16, 137n.38, 137n.43

Lakoff, George, 7, 38, 118n.29, 118n.31, 118n.32, 123n.13
Lambert, David, 44, 77, 124n.26, 133n.30, 133n.33
Landau, Ayelet, 118n.29, 123n.12
Langacker, Ronald, 7, 118n.30
Langut, D., 122n.63
Lebram, Jürgen-Christian, 128n.17
Leitan, Nuwan, 118n.29
Leith, Mary Joan Winn, 117n.9
Lemaire, Andre, 126n.64
Lesses, Rebecca, 137–38nn.58–59
Leuchter, Mark, 117n.4, 122n.65, 122n.73, 123n.8, 124nn.29–30, 124n.33, 126n.54, 126n.58, 126n.63, 128n.25, 129n.32, 130n.47, 130n.50, 130n.55, 131nn.1–2, 132nn.4–5, 132n.9, 132n.11, 132n.14, 133n.22, 133n.25, 133n.34, 134n.48, 134n.55, 134n.60, 136n.28, 136n.34, 137n.57, 139n.4, 139n.9, 139n.11, 139n.16, 140n.27
Leuenberger, Martin, 132n.6
Levin, Adina, 132n.17
Lewis, Theodore J., 136n.31
Lipschits, Oded, 61, 117n.9, 119n.46, 122n.61, 122n.63, 122n.67, 129n.35, 138–39n.1
Lundbom, Jack R., 123n.5, 133n.24

Ma, John, 117n.8
Malinowski, Branislaw, 18–19, 120n.14
Mandell, Alice, 126n.69
Marsh, Elizabeth J., 8, 118n.34
McClellan, Daniel, 8, 118n.33
Mildenberg, Leo, 119n.44, 119nn.47–48
Milik, Jozef T., 134n.1
Miller, Robert D. II, 126n.54, 136n.17, 136n.21, 137n.46
Milstein, Sara, 125n.42
Mitchell, Christine, 39, 40–41, 44–45, 120n.14, 120n.23, 120n.30, 121n.43, 121n.47,

AUTHOR INDEX   165

121n.50, 121n.54, 121n.55, 122n.57, 124n.18, 126n.70, 132n.4, 133n.36, 138n.70
Mitchell, Stephen, 128n.23
Moore, James D., 68, 127–28n.15, 131nn.68–70
Mroczek, Eva, 128n.25

Nichols, Andrew, 120n.19, 120nn.21–22, 120n.24
Nickelsburg, George, 135n.3
Niehr,Herbert, 117n.3
Nihan, Christophe, 50, 51–52, 126n.62, 133n.21
Nissinen, Martti, 132n.15
Nogalski, James, 72, 132n.12

Oblath, Michael, 133n.18
Oerning, Manfred, 117n.9
Olson, Daniel C., 140n.18
Olyan, Saul M., 127n.9
Otto, Eckart, 124n.35
Overholt, Thomas J., 134n.56

Pajunen, Mika, S., 132n.8
Pakkala, Juha, 129n.27, 129n.33, 130n.60, 131n.75
Pearce, Laurie E., 119n.10, 122n.60
Peckham, Brian, 47, 125n.41, 131n.66, 133n.38
Petersen, David L., 113, 133n.31, 135n.7, 140n.28
Pioske, Daniel, 36–37, 123nn.2–3
Polak, Frank R., 134n.45
Polaski, Donald, 25, 121n.35, 128n.20, 129n.31
Portier-Young, Anathea, 135n.3, 138n.72
Potts, Daniel L., 120n.26

Rainey, Brian, 52, 126n.66
Rappaport, Roy A., 119n.42
Rausche, Benedikt, 139n.3
Redditt, Paul L., 131n.75
Reed, Annette Yoshiko, 112, 113–14, 137n.36, 137n.48, 140n.23, 140n.24
Rendsburg, Gary A., 126n.54
Rendtorff, Rolf, 127n.7
Richelle, Matthieu, 36–37, 123n.2
Ristau, Kenneth, 123n.10
Robson, Eleanor, 122n.69, 140n.20, 140n.31
Rollinger, Robert, 29, 121n.48
Rom-Shiloni, Dalit, 63–64, 122n.68, 126n.57, 126n.69, 130n.48
Romer, Thomas, 124n.34
Root, Margaret Cool, 26–27, 32, 103, 119n.5, 120n.27, 121n.45, 121n.56, 134n.59, 138n.73

Rosel, M., 123n.17
Rung, Eduard, 120n.18

Sanders, Seth, 3–4, 26, 34, 98, 99, 117n.11, 121n.31, 121n.33, 121n.34, 121n.41, 122n.59, 122n.71, 124n.25, 125nn.44–45, 128n.20, 129n.30, 135n.6, 135n.8, 137n.42, 137n.51, 137n.54, 137n.56, 139n.6, 140n.21
Schaper, Joachim, 4–5, 117n.4, 118n.16, 119n.49, 127n.9
Schart, Aaron, 133n.27, 133n.32
Schloen, David, 92–93, 136n.18
Schmid, Konrad, 50–51, 52–53, 126nn.52–53, 126n.65, 126n.68, 130n.53
Schmitt, Rüdiger, 15
Schniedewind, William, 36–37, 122n.62, 123n.4, 133n.23, 134n.43, 136n.20
Schor, Fran, 119n.41
Seitz, Christopher M., 132n.13
Signorile, Vito, 120n.14
Silverman, Jason, 61, 68, 120n.16, 120n.27, 120n.30, 121n.37, 123n.15, 125n.40, 129n.36, 131n.71, 131n.73, 135n.3
Smith, Mark S., 118n.26, 136n.28, 136n.29
Soheil, Meh Azar, 121nn.52–53
Sommer, Benjamin, 57–58, 128n.18
Sonia, Kerry, 135n.12
Spiegel, Shalom, 81, 134n.40
Stackert, Jeffrey, 130n.49
Steiner, Richard C., 130–31n.61
Steinhorn, Leonard, 119n.40
Stern, Elsie, 48, 125n.49
Strine, C., 118n.27
Sugirtharajah, R. S., 6, 118n.23
Sweeney, Marvin, 132n.15

Tal, Oren, 119n.46, 138–39n.1
Tropper, Amram, 2, 117n.5, 117n.6
Tuggy, David, 118n.35
Turner, Mark, 118n.29
Turner, Victor, 6, 118n.25
Tversky, Barbara, 8, 118n.29, 118n.34

van der Toorn, Karel, 4–5, 77, 118nn.14–15, 123n.6, 123n.17, 124n.31, 126n.58, 130n.59, 132n.16, 133n.18, 133n.29, 134n.44, 135n.12
Vanderhooft, David S., 124n.38, 134n.46, 134n.51
Vayntrub, Jacqueline, 98–99, 109, 128n.25, 137n.52, 139n.15
Vielhauer, Roman, 132n.15

166 AUTHOR INDEX

von Rad, Gerhard, 36–37, 123n.1
von Weissenberg, Hanne, 132n.8
Vroom, Jonathan, 125n.48, 127n.6, 139n.8, 139n.13

Waerzeggers, Caroline, 34, 122nn.69–70, 130n.57
Waetzoldt, Hartmut, 122n.69
Waters, Matt, 119n.47
Watts, James W., 111, 137n.47, 139n.5, 140n.22
Weinfeld, Moshe, 134n.47
Whitters, Mark, 128n.22, 131n.67
Wiesehöfer, Josef, 128n.23
Williamson, H. G. M., 57–58, 127n.4, 127n.9, 128n.19, 129n.27, 130–31n.61
Wills, Lawrence M., 5, 118nn.18–19, 128n.24

Wilson, Ian Douglas, 122n.62
Wöhrle, Jakob, 132n.7
Wolff, Hans Walter, 74, 132n.16, 133n.21, 133n.27
Wollenberg, Rebecca, Scharbach, 114, 127n.8, 140nn.32–33, 140n.35
Wright, Aren Wilson, 119n.47
Wright, John W., 140n.26
Wunsch, Cornelia, 119n.10

Yadin-Israel, Azzan, 117n.2
Yang, Inchol, 118n.22
Yoder, Christine Roy, 138n.64
Yoo, Philip Y., 66–67, 127n.10, 129n.27, 130n.52, 131n.65

Zapff, Burkhard M., 133n.27

Scripture Index

For the benefit of digital users, indexed terms that span two pages (e.g., 52–53) may, on occasion, appear on only one of those pages.

BIBLICAL

Gen. 1: 91
Gen. 1–11: 90
Gen. 2:4a: 90, 113
Gen. 2–3: 94, 100
Gen. 2–4: 95
Gen. 3:5: 92, 135–36n.15
Gen. 4: 90, 92–94, 95, 100, 113
Gen. 4:18: 92
Gen. 4:20–22: 92
Gen. 4:24: 92
Gen. 5: 90, 91, 94, 96–97, 113
Gen. 5:5: 91
Gen. 5:8: 91
Gen. 5:11: 91
Gen. 5:14: 91
Gen. 5:17: 91
Gen. 5:20: 91
Gen. 5:20–21: 91
Gen. 5:22: 90, 91
Gen. 5:23: 91
Gen. 5:24: 90, 91
Gen. 6:1–4: 94, 95, 96–97, 100, 102–3, 113, 135–36n.15, 136n.34
Gen. 6:4: 94, 103–4
Gen. 6:9: 90, 91
Gen. 7:22: 94
Gen. 12:3: 90
Gen. 22–24: 91
Gen. 25:4: 93–94
Gen. 37:35–36: 140n.29
Gen. 38: 102

Exod. 1:1–7: 113
Exod. 15:18 (1–12): 50–51
Exod. 40:3–11: 64
Exod. 41:17–20: 64
Exod. 42:14–17: 64
Exod. 43:1–7: 64

Num. 5:11–31: 45

Deut. 5:1: 45
Deut. 5:6, 14: 130n.53
Deut. 18:15–18: 72–73, 87–88, 133n.21
Deut. 28: 130n.53
Deut. 32: 52
Deut. 33:10: 83
Deut. 34:10–12: 44–45, 73, 77

Judg. 11:37: 102
Judg. 19: 102

1 Sam. 28: 95
1 Sam. 28:13: 136n.28
1 Sam. 30:29: 92–93

2 Kgs. 11: 135n.14
2 Kgs. 15: 135n.14
2 Kgs. 16:15: 135n.14
2 Kgs. 18: 135n.14
2 Kgs. 18:19: 103
2 Kgs. 19:21: 102
2 Kgs. 21:24: 135n.14
2 Kgs. 23:30: 135n.14

Isa. 1:8: 102
Isa. 1:21: 136n.20
Isa. 10–11, etc.: 50–51
Isa. 26:5: 136n.20
Isa. 28:1: 136n.20
Isa. 37:22: 102
Isa. 44:28–45:3: 16, 65
Isa. 65–66: 69

Jer. 1:9: 72–73
Jer. 1:13–14: 97
Jer. 4:23–26: 135n.9
Jer. 6:2: 102
Jer. 6:22–25: 97
Jer. 9:11–12: 84
Jer. 25:8: 97
Jer. 26:17–19: 75
Jer. 26–45: 63–64

168 SCRIPTURE INDEX

Jer. 31:14: 102
Jer. 36: 37
Jer. 46–51: 72–73
Jer. 50:3: 97

Hos. 1–3: 102
Hos. 2:2: 136n.28
Hos. 4:1–2: 80
Hos. 4:2: 80
Hos. 4:3: 135n.9
Hos. 5:13: 82, 136n.20
Hos. 5:14: 136n.20
Hos. 6:5: 80–81, 82
Hos. 7:10: 136n.20
Hos. 7:11: 82, 136n.20
Hos. 7–9: 50–51
Hos. 8:1: 79, 80, 82
Hos. 8:1–6: 74
Hos. 9:8–7: 81
Hos. 10:7: 136n.20
Hos. 11:1–5: 50–51
Hos. 11:5: 82
Hos. 12:13–14: 74
Hos. 12:14: 81
Hos. 12–14: 74
Hos. 14:10: 86

Amos 3–5: 136n.20

Mic. 1–3: 136n.20
Mic. 3:9–12: 75–76
Mic. 4:13: 102
Mic. 6:1–4: 75–76
Mic. 6:4: 50–51, 76–77

Hab. 1:3: 84
Hab. 1:4: 83, 84
Hab. 1:7–9: 83–84
Hab. 1:5–11: 83
Hab. 1:7: 84
Hab. 1–4: 83
Hab. 2: 84–85
Hab. 2:2: 85
Hab. 3: 84, 85

Zech. 1:4: 73–74
Zech. 1–8: 37–38
Zech. 2:10: 102
Zech. 3:14: 102

Mal. 2:4, 8: 85–86
Mal. 2:6–8: 85, 86
Mal. 2:7: 86
Mal. 3:16–18: 85–86

Mal. 3:22: 77–78, 87–88
Mal. 3:22–24: 77

Ps. 9:14: 102

Prov. 9: 101
Prov. 9:13–18: 100–1
Prov. 31:10–31: 101

Song. 1:5: 102
Song. 2:7: 102
Song. 1:5: 102
Song. 8:4: 102

Lam. 2:1: 102
Lam. 4:22: 102

Esther 3:8: 53–54

Dan. 2: 111
Dan. 5: 111
Dan. 9: 108, 109
Dan. 9:2: 108
Dan. 10–12: 108
Dan. 11: 137n.49

Ezra 1: 66–67
Ezra 1–3: 67
Ezra 1–6: 66–67
Ezra 1:1–4: 66, 109, 134n.57, 139n.6
Ezra 2: 56–57, 61, 112
Ezra 2–3: 66
Ezra 4:2, 10; 6:22: 17
Ezra 4:4: 123n.9
Ezra 4–6: 57, 66, 67, 127n.6
Ezra 4:6–8: 67–68
Ezra 4:23: 67–68
Ezra 5: 68
Ezra 5:1–2: 66
Ezra 6:14: 66, 67–68
Ezra 7: 13–14, 44, 57, 58, 60, 61, 67–69, 127n.6
Ezra 7:1a: 59, 66–67
Ezra 7:1b-2: 64
Ezra 7:1b-6: 61, 63, 64, 65, 66–68
Ezra 7:1b-10: 59, 60, 61
Ezra 7:5: 59
Ezra 7:6: 59, 65, 67–68
Ezra 7:6b: 65
Ezra 7:6,10: 44, 122n.72
Ezra 7:7–9: 68
Ezra 7:11: 60
Ezra 7[11]12–26: 59
Ezra 7–10: 56–57
Ezra 7:12–26: 57

SCRIPTURE INDEX 169

Ezra 7:14–17: 67–68
Ezra 8: 61
Ezra 8:1: 60–61
Ezra 8:15–19: 34, 60–61, 67–68
Ezra 8:16, 18: 34–35
Ezra 8:22, 25, 36: 60–61
Ezra 9–10: 61, 69, 101
Ezra 9:4: 67–68
Ezra 10:3: 67–68

Neh. 1–6, 12–13: 56
Neh. 2:8–9: 60
Neh. 7: 56–57, 61, 112
Neh. 8: 1–2, 44, 58, 61, 67, 112, 139n.13
Neh. 8:1–8: 128n.22
Neh. 8:1–12: 67–68, 139n.13
Neh. 8:2: 44
Neh. 8–10: 56–57
Neh. 9:17: 72
Neh. 10: 112
Neh. 11–12: 112
Neh. 13:30: 112, 131n.78

1 Chr. 1:3: 93–94
1 Chr. 1:33: 93–94
2 Chr. 21: 112–13
1 Chr. 21:1: 112–13
1 Chr. 25:4: 112–13
2 Chr. 36:22–23: 139n.6
2 Chr. 30:27: 112–13

LXX
Gen. 6:3: 136n.27

RABBINIC

MISHNA
Avot 1:1: 1, 114–15
Avot 1:2: 1–2

JER. TALMUD
y. Berakhot 1:2: 110
y. Kiddushin 1:1: 110
y. Avodah Zarah 3:1: 114
y. Avodah Zarah 42c: 114

BAB. TALMUD
b. Eruvin 13b: 110
b. Bava Metziah 59b: 114
b. Bava Bathra 14b: 140n.34
b. Moed Qatan 25b: 114
b. Sanhedrin 21b-22a: 140n.34

TOSEFTA
t. Sanhedrin 4:7: 140n.34

OTHER

I ENOCH
1 En. 1–36: 89
1 En. 6–7: 100
1 En. 6:5: 102
1 En. 6:6: 96–97
1 En. 6–11: 89, 96–97, 137n.38, 137n.49
1 En. 7:6: 102
1 En. 8:1–4: 99–100
1 En. 8:4: 102
1 En. 9:2: 102
1 En. 10: 102
1 En. 10:9: 138n.76
1 En. 10:12: 104
1 En. 12–18: 137n.38
1 En. 15:8–9: 104, 112
1 En. 25–27: 137n.38

ELEPHANTINE
TAD A4.7: 42
TAD 4.7–4.8 (Jedaniah's Letter): 123n.9
A4.7–4.8 (Jedaniah's Letter): 41

PERSIAN:
A1Pa (Inscription from Persepolis): 29–30
A1Pb (Akkadian inscription in the "Hall of
    Hundred Columns"): 30

Daiva Inscription: 27

DB 4, 8: 66
DB 17–18, 53, 54: 22–23
DB 27–35: 66
DB 43–44: 131n.63
DB 52, 54: 21–22
DB 63: 21
DB 70: 24, 27, 32, 42, 45–46, 48

DNb 50–60: 45

XPh (Xerxes at Persepolis): 31, 103–4
XP1: 39, 40

GREEK
Herodotus, *Hist.* 3.27–29: 119n.9

UGARIT
KTU 1.6 V 11–12, 24–25: 136n.26

The manufacturer's authorised representative in the EU for product safety is Oxford
University Press España S.A. of El Parque Empresarial San Fernando de Henares,
Avenida de Castilla, 2 – 28830 Madrid (www.oup.es/en or product.safety@oup.com).
OUP España S.A. also acts as importer into Spain of products made by the manufacturer.

Printed in the USA/Agawam, MA
August 8, 2025

891696.011